Society's Child

Society's Child

Identity, Clothing, and Style

Ruth P. Rubinstein

State University of New York
Fashion Institute of Technology

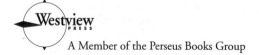

Westview
PRESS
A Member of the Perseus Books Group

Copyright © 2000 by Westview Press, A Member of the Perseus Books Group

Published in 2000 in the United States of America by Westview Press, 5500 Central Avenue, Boulder, Colorado 80301-877, and in the United Kingdom by Westview Press, 12 Hid's Copse Road, Cumnor Hill, Oxford OX2 9JJ

Find us on the World Wide Web at www.westviewpress.com

Rubinstein, Ruth P.
  Society's child : identity, clothing, and style / Ruth P. Rubinstein.
    p. cm.
  Includes bibliographical references and index.
  ISBN 0-8133-6671-2
  1. Children—Costume—Social aspects. I. Title.
GT1730.R82   1999
391'.3—dc21
99-40346
CIP

The paper used in this publication meets the requirements of the American National Standard for Permanence of Paper for Printed Library Materials Z39.48-984.

10   9   8   7   6   5   4   3   2   1

For Jonathan, Jay, Sari, Kate,
David, and Joanne with all my heart.

Contents

Conclusion: Children's Clothes and Depiction of
Children as Socio-Cultural Constructs

Illustrations

Preface

Society's Child is a study of children's clothes from the Renaissance through the 1990s. It proceeds from Phillipe Ariès's contention that childhood is as much a cultural construction as a biological one and that children's clothes identify the role children are expected to play in a society during a particular period. The book provides a reader interested in children, culture, family, communication, psychology, history, and fashion with an analysis of the connection between the meaning of childhood, the style of children's clothes, and the role children are expected to play in a society. The book should be of interest to intelligent general readers and should find a place on reading lists of numerous undergraduate courses, such as Cultural Studies, Socialization and Human Behavior, Family and Sex Roles, American Studies, Art History, Communications, Critical Theory, Fashion Theory, and History of Costume and Sociology.

Society's Child examines the role of children's clothes in creating networks of social ties, networks constituted by blood relationship, privilege, friendship, marriage, and acquaintance. Moreover, the book demonstrates how the style of children's clothes is related to the transformation of society and the social class structure.

Society's Child suggests that in the contemporary world, the world of advanced capitalist democracy, children's clothes are a complex composite of discourses related to person, identity, culture, and society.

Ruth P. Rubinstein

Acknowledgments

I wish to express my appreciation to the many individuals who helped make this book a reality. My research and writing would have been impossible without the archival materials made available to me by the publisher of the trade magazine *Earnshaw's*. Thomas Hudson and his executive assistant, Evelyn Legasapi, offered me the assistance I needed, enabling me to work in their library unimpeded. They also enabled me to illustrate the points I was making by allowing me to use their pictures.

A brief internship at the New York showroom of the manufacturing company Hartstrings gave me invaluable insight into the business of making and selling children's clothes.

The traditional way to get peer criticism is to ask colleagues and former mentors to review one's work. I used a nontraditional way. I sought peer review by presenting each chapter as a paper at meetings of professional organizations. I thus thank the American Sociological Association (ASA), the Eastern Sociological Society, the Society for the Study of Social Problems, and the Columbia Faculty Seminars, all of whom made it possible for me to present research activity in its early stages. I am particularly grateful to William Sewell Jr. for supporting the notion of the dynastic child. As the discussant of my paper at the ASA 1997 Annual Meeting in Toronto, his comments were crucial to my continuing with this project. My heartfelt thanks.

Members of the Seminar on Content and Method in the Social Sciences, organized by the Faculty Seminars of Columbia University, also earned my gratitude. Under the directorship of Professor Joseph A. Maier, my work enjoyed the careful scrutiny of both European and American scholars who attended the seminar regularly.

The use of art as historical data has many potential dangers. The following members of the Fashion Institute of Technology Art History faculty aided me, each in his or her own way. Generous with their knowledge and time were the following: Celia Bergoffen, Robert Cahn, David Dearinger, Zehava Goldberg, Laurence Homolka, Katherine Michaelsen, Justin O'-Connor, Marcia Wallace, Andrew Weinstein, and Laurel Weintraub.

I also benefited from the information and experience of the F.I.T. Children's Wear Design faculty: Joanne Arbuckle, Hildi Jaffe, and Rose Rosa.

Members of other disciplines who came to my aid were Roger Melera, Helen Xanakis, and Treva Giambrone.

To Naomi Bricker, Andrew Diamond, Mary Direnzo, Beryl Rentof, Steven Rosenberger, Joshua Waller, Lorraine Weberg, Marian Weston, Paul Stotler, Michael McAuliffe, Tabitha Hanslick, John Corins, and Maris Heller, librarians in F.I.T.'s Reference Department, Interlibrary Loan, and Special Collections, I owe many thanks. Without the special books and pictures they made available to me, this book would have continued to be merely a dream.

Embedded in the realm of motherhood and children, Barabara Katz-Rothman from Baruch College in New York City and Dana King were the first to suggest that I explore the subject of children's clothes with respect to meaning.

Finally, I am indebted to the Fashion Institute of Technology, its students, faculty, and administration, who encourage creative endeavor in many areas, including the study of culture. I also must thank Ernest Poole and Hope Fisher, who became my friends in the course of completing this enterprise.

At Westview Press I would like to thank Leo A. W. Wiegman, executive editor, Kay Mariea, Silvine Marbury Farnell, and Andrew Day for helping me put all the pages and pictures together, turning the manuscript into a real book. I made every effort to get permission for all the illustrations used; if inadvertently some have slipped through, I hope the owners will forgive me.

R. P. R.
New York

1

Introduction:
Is Childhood Disappearing?

As the end of the twentieth century approaches, liveliness and energy imbue children's clothing. A variety of new fabrics make it possible to produce comfortable good-looking washable clothes that can be used for sports and play or as everyday attire by infants and boys and girls. The portrayal of children wearing these clothes in the media suggests that childhood is a time of wonder, openness, spontaneity, creativity, and fun. Characters from children's story books, movies, and comic books ornament the clothes of both sexes. Adult fashion and basic adult styles have been translated into children's sizes. Children's dress is vibrant and characterized by style, as designer Norma Kamali observed in discussing her own line.[1] More than ever, personal choice determines consumption, even for children under two. Unlike any other material objects in children's lives, clothes offer a firm base from which to develop competencies, solutions, and feelings of intimacy, femininity, masculinity, and prowess.[2]

Nevertheless, social critics are concerned about the future of childhood in American society. The character of children is a source of uneasiness. What is the meaning of contemporary children's dress? Is it one more indication that children are in some way in trouble? Certainly these questions are valid ones. Children's clothes offer an important index to attitudes toward and treatment of children, as Philippe Ariès suggested in *Centuries of Childhood*.[3] Medieval children, for example, were often neither welcome nor obviously liked. Many of those who were born departed quickly. Others never acquired a voice that might have recorded or preserved their impressions of themselves, their parents, or their world.[4] Childhood was a period of transition that passed quickly and was just as quickly forgotten, suggested David Herlihy.[5] In art, children were depicted as miniature adults; their bodies and style of dress made them look like small-scale adults.

"Nothing in medieval dress distinguished the child from the adult," Ariès observed. As soon as children's swaddling clothes were abandoned they were dressed like the others of their social class, in a tunic or a robe. This lack of differentiation in dress was reflected in language, too. The term <u>child</u> was used to designate a preadult category, and words like infant, adolescent, and youth were used interchangeably.[6] Children were expected to take an active part in everyday life, in the work and in the play. They were expected to contribute to the household in every way they could.

The variety and style of children's clothes in the United States in the 1980s and 1990s have been treated with suspicion. Social observers argue that children—that is, girls prior to age twelve, and boys prior to age fourteen—are being rushed into adult-like appearance and behavior. "Little girls' dresses," like the ones Shirley Temple wore in the 1930s, or clothes similar to those seen in the *Dick and Jane Readers* have mostly disappeared, Neil Postman argued.[7] Children's games, too, have become increasingly official, mock-professional, and extremely serious. "There is no fooling around, no peculiar rules invented to suit the moment, no protection from the judgment of spectators," when playing Little League baseball and Pee Wee football.[8] Observing that children are taking on adult-like appearance and behavior, Postman and others like him ask, "Is childhood disappearing?"

A whole rationale has been developed for attributing the changes taking place in children's lives and clothes to female participation in the labor force. Women were no longer willing to sacrifice their own well-being and take on an unfair share of the burdens of childcare, argued Marie Winn.[9] As both parents abandoned the home for the workplace, children became something of a burden, suggested Postman.[10] Children were expelled from a world in which adults take care of children whereas children are children, dependent upon and unequal to adults. The absence of the mother from home leaves children to their own devices.[11]

Some social observers suggest dire consequences. The family is where biological characteristics form the basis for the learning of social roles.[12] It is where human beings are "engendered," where children's clothes structure the gender role. Ungendered children's clothes allow children to play nontraditional social roles, affecting the stratification of society by gender.

Historian of the family Carl N. Degler, for example, argued that the new egalitarian sentiments in American society have upset the institution of the family, which depended for its existence and character on female subordination.[13] Interaction within the family had been based on hierarchy: father, mother, and children.[14] Children's misbehavior is the fault of the women's movement in the late 1970s, which led to tensions within the family and was reflected in the maladaptation of children to society, Degler explained.[15]

Children wear adult-style clothing because children are the last remaining subjects that men can control, argued Letty Pogrebin.[16] The contemporary male has no animals to tame, no frontiers to conquer; women are rebellious and machines are outthinking and displacing men. They, thus, insist that their sons dress in their own image.

In the 1990s children are being raised to enter the world of maturity long before they are mature, and the clothes children wear reflect it, argued author Lucinda Franks.[17] Parents treat their children with respect as if they are little adults. Children are encouraged to make their own decisions. Children's rights have been emphasized and children have become the center of family life. Child-rearing practices were changed by the generation of parents that came of age in the Vietnam War years; they were determined not to be blind subjects of those in authority.[18] Examples of the new ethos have to do with clothes. Franks tells of a father arguing with his six-year-old daughter about going to school with a rip in the knee of her jeans. He asked her to change. She asked him for a good reason why she shouldn't wear them. "'Because my father would have never let me,' her father answered. 'Just because your father made a mistake,' she replied, 'why should you?'"[19]

A second example of the new ethos is perhaps related to the symbolic meaning of dress. A fourth-grade child invited kids to his home for a dating party at a time when his parents were out of the house. The girls wore halter tops and tiny bicycle shorts. "It's hard to know whether the girls wanted to look like Julia Roberts in *Pretty Woman,* or they knew what they were up to," one of the mothers observed.[20] "Today's crop of under–12's, particularly in the middle- and upper-middle income families and particularly in urban America, seems to have reinvented—or even bypassed—childhood as we knew it," Franks concluded.[21]

Since the publication in 1983 of "A Nation at Risk," a report that rated American education "woefully inadequate," kindergartners have begun taking home as much as a half hour of homework every day, though some parents complain that this is too soon.[22] Jansport, the company whose sturdy backpacks dominate high school hallways, has introduced a mini-sized pack emblazoned with cartoon characters for kindergarten students. The kindergartners don't have to "borrow" the bag of an older sibling; they have their own bags to carry their books to school.

Research findings published on November 11, 1998, reported that American children have become more responsible. They spend more time in school, more time doing household chores, and less time eating and watching television than children did 16 years ago. In comparison to 1981, children study longer, play less, and are more often held responsible for their actions.[23] Less than a month later, on December 1, 1998, in an article on the Op-Ed page in the *New York Times* cultural observer Eugenie Allen complained, "Can't a kid just veg out anymore?"[24]

The suspicion that childhood is changing has continued to grow. It has been supported by widely circulated news about children who have killed. A twelve-year-old girl in Texas was found guilty of injury to a child in the death of a two-and-a-half-year-old child who was left to the care of the older girl's grandparents, who ran an unlicensed day-care center. The defendant was eleven at the time. The prosecutors said that she was angry about being left to baby-sit, so the eleven-year-old girl kicked and beat the child. She was sentenced to up to twenty-five years in custody.[25]

Since 1994, the laws in forty-three states have been changed to make it easier to prosecute juveniles as adults.[26] This attempt to retreat from the definition of childhood that guided most of the twentieth century calls into question the belief that children are inherently less culpable than adults and that they have a greater capacity to learn. The notion of children as innocent beings, free from responsibility, is being increasingly disregarded; the public demand that children who commit major crimes be disciplined as adults is growing. Psychological research that claims that children are different from adults has also been faulted.[27]

Together, these phenomena have been seen as constituting a revision of the concept of childhood that came together after 1918, which dictated that children should reside in a world regulated by "affection and education not work or profit."[28]. The enactment of child labor laws, mandatory school attendance policies, and a juvenile justice system in which children and adults exist in separate and distinct realms freed children from contributing to the family's economic resources.[29] At that time, schools and parents determined what clothes the children would wear.

If childhood is a cultural construct as Ariès suggested,[30] then children's clothes offer a base from which to examine the role of children and the meaning of childhood today. Childhood is structured by a set of ideas supported by dress. In the course of western history particular concepts of childhood have been reflected in the clothes that children have worn. In western society childhood has been characterized by two distinct visions: (1) As developmentally complete, children like adults are persons born of sin and helped by punishment. (2) As developmentally immature, children need a childhood that helps prepare them for adult life; they are innocent and need to be taught. Style reflects expectations for children's behavior.[31]

Clothes became a means of communication long before people could read or write.[32] To convey a message to an uneducated public a visual form was required.[33] Images were produced and transmitted and treated as messages from which meaning was inferred, suggested Sol Worth in his *Studying Visual Communication.*[34]

Throughout much of history, official taste, the values of the state, and the ideologies of the dominant groups were presented as visual images, and these acted as conduits for broader communal discourse. Cultural values were reflected in the paintings, sculpture, decorative arts, monumental architecture, as well as in the clothing of a period. They served to encourage or discourage action and interaction.[35] Rulers used visual imagery in this way because they recognized that visual imagery may be the most effective means of conveying information.

Clothes, moreover, were constructs that also directly structured and controlled behavior. Infants were swaddled, young children were dressed in long dresses and in miniature adult attire that displayed rank. This limited and controlled children's behavior in the same way that military uniforms and church vestments make clear the parameters of interaction.

In addition to informing of a presence, announcing an upcoming event, impressing, influencing, or inspiring, style indicates societal expectations for behavior. Repetitive exposure to a particular style can encourage the belief that people share similar ideas and sentiments and behavior expectations.[36] A change in style is built on ideas already in existence.[37] The Gothic cathedral developed in response to the need for bringing greater crowds around the pulpit or the altar, sociologist Gabriel Tarde suggested.[38] The elements involved in Gothic architecture are characterized by the forceful expression of certain exaltations, or impulses of the Christian soul, reflective of hopes and fears. Everything in Gothic architecture concurs in the goal of creating this expression.[39] The messages created by a producer must come out of the audience's perceptual sphere, they must be familiar in some way for innovation to take place, argued Everett M. Rogers and F. Floyd Shoemaker.[40]

Visual images are statements articulated by particular artists and sometimes are designed according to a patron's requirements. Such articulation may be personal and idiosyncratic, but at times it may reflect a new sensibility. Right up to the thirteenth century the portrayal of children followed the formulaic tradition of representing children as little adults. As spirituality lost its hold and social life became oriented towards reality in the 15th and 16th centuries, children were included in crowd scenes.[41] In the seventeenth century, after James I of Great Britain lost his two daughters, one three days old and the other two years of age, the likeness of their clothing and accessories was faithfully reproduced in sculpture to create the illusion of reality.[42]

As visual images clothes are also constructs that have physical and tactile dimensions. Clothes that are cumbersome or too closed and tight, are likely to discourage interaction. So does attire that doesn't fit, is uncomfortable, or difficult to put on and take off. On the other hand, clothes that are soft or silky encourage touch. It is like petting a kitten. Clothes whose texture is coarse or rough discourage contact, which would be like touching an alligator. Style, texture, and fit are elements that tell something about the quality of interaction to expect.

The clothes children are expected to wear, the portrayal of children in art, and society's view of childhood reveal the group's plans and hopes and fears. Has childhood in contemporary society ceased to be a preparatory phase for adult life? Are children being integrated into adult society, as in the medieval period? In order to understand the meaning of contemporary children's clothes and what they reveal about society's hopes for the future, this study searched for patterns. It examined changes in the style of children's clothes and in portrayals of children in art in Renaissance Italy, seventeenth-century Holland, England and France between 1500 and 1800, nineteenth-century England, Colonial America, and the United States.

Notes

1. Fashion designer Norma Kamali explained that in creating her children's line collection she took into account what adult women were wearing, in particular what mothers, sisters, and friends were wearing, and the colors children prefer. Personal communication, March 17, 1997.

2. John Gilbert, (1986) *Another Chance, Post-War America 1945-1985*. Chicago, Ill.: Dorsey Press, p. 283.

3. Philippe Ariès, (1962) *Centuries of Childhood: A Social History of Family Life*. Trans. Robert Baldock. New York: Vintage Books, pp. 33–34.

4. David Herlihy, (1978) "Medieval Children," in *Essays on Medieval Civilization: The Walter Prescott Webb Memorial Lectures*. Austin: University of Texas Press, pp. 109, 120–121.

5. Herlihy, op. cit, pp. 109–131.

6. Ariès, op. cit., p. 50.

7. Neil Postman, (1982) *The Disappearance of Childhood*. New York: Laurel Books, p. 123.

8. Postman, op. cit., p. 129.

9. Marie Winn, (1983) *Children Without Childhood*. New York: Pantheon, pp. 5, 96.

10. Postman, op. cit., p. 129.

11. Almost 56 percent of married women with children under the age of fourteen were employed in the early 1980s and their numbers have kept growing, affecting more and younger children.

12. Gayle Rubin, (1975) "The Traffic in Women: Notes on the Political Economy of Sex," in Rayna R. Reiter, ed., *Toward An Anthropology of Women*. New York: Monthly Review Press.

13. Carl N. Degler, (1980) *At Odds: Women and Families in America from the Revolution to the Present.* New York: Oxford University Press, p. vi.

14. Degler, op. cit., p. 471.

15. Ibid.

16. Letty Cottin Pogrebin, (1983) *Family Politics, Love and Power on an Intimate Frontier.* New York: McGraw-Hill p. 42

17. Lucinda Franks, (1993) "Little Big People," *New York Times Magazine,* Oct. 10, pp. 28–34.

18. In Franks, op. cit., and Sarane Spence Boocock, (1976) "Children in Contemporary Society," in A. Skolnick, ed., *Rethinking Childhood.* Boston: Little Brown.

19. Franks, op. cit., p. 34.

20. Ibid.

21. Franks, op. cit., p. 31.

22. Mary B. W. Tabor, (1996) "Homework is Keeping Grade-Schoolers Busy; Families Are Finding it a Mixed Blessing," *New York Times.* April 6.

23. A study conducted by the University of Michigan Institute for Social Research and reported in the *New York Times,* Nov. 11, 1998.

24. Eugenie Allen, (1998) "Totally Homework," *New York Times,* Dec. 1.

25. Ibid.

26. William Glaberson, (1998) "Rising Tide of Anger At Teen Age Killers," *New York Times,* May 24.

27. Postman, op. cit., p. 63.

28. Viviana A. Zelizer, (1985) *Pricing the Priceless Child: The Changing Social Value of Children.* New York: Basic Books, p. 209.

29. In some states children were expected to assist in the support of ailing parents.. Zelizer, op. cit., pp. 56–72.

30. Ariès, op. cit., pp. 108–115.

31. Ariès, op. cit., pp. 50–51.

32. Priests' clothes in ancient Mesopotamia and the Pharaohs' attire in ancient Egypt identified power and authority.

33. E. H. Gombrich, (1972) "Action and Expression in Western Art," in Robert A. Hinde, ed., *Non-Verbal Communication.* New York: Cambridge University Press, pp. 373–393.

34. Sol Worth, (1981) *Studying Visual Communication.* Philadelphia: University of Pennsylvania Press, p.16. Leo Steinberg, (1996) *The Sexuality of Christ in Renaissance Art and in Modern Oblivion.* Chicago: University of Chicago Press, pp. 6–15.

35. Maurice Halbwachs, (1980) *The Collective Memory,* trans. F. I. Ditter Jr. and V. Y. Ditter. New York: Harper and Row,

36. Worth, op. cit., p. 137.

37. Worth, op. cit., p. 153.

38. Gabriel Tarde, (1969) *On Communication and Social Influence.* Selected Papers, edited by Terry N. Clark, p. 153.

39. Clement Greenberg, (1961) *Art and Culture: Critical Essays* Boston: Beacon Press, pp. 3–21.Clement Greenberg, in an essay in his book, "Avant-Garde and Kitsch," argues that high art exists under constant threat of co-optation by popu-

lar culture. Kitsch is a tool of the power elite in maintaining social control of the masses.

40. Everett M. Rogers and F. Floyd Shoemaker, (1971) *Communication of Innovation*. New York: Free Press.

41. Ariès, op. cit., p. 105.

42. Ariès, op. cit., p. 42.

2

The Dynastic Child

In medieval times childhood was a period of transition that passed quickly and was quickly forgotten, Ariès observed.[1] The ravages of war, epidemics, and the plague resulted in a high mortality rate for infants, children, and adults, constantly upsetting existing social arrangements. Children mingled with adults, performing whatever tasks they could.[2] They wore long robes in the style of the adults.

As commercial exchange intensified and urban life was reborn children became important. They could be trained for the new occupations that emerged, trained as, for example, notaries, accountants, clerks, and artisans.[3] Foundling hospitals and orphanages were established to improve children's chances of survival.

Battles for political control characterized the social life of the city-states of Renaissance Italy. Ambition, competition, and violence were rife. Even "the sons of the Popes were founding dynasties," observed Jacob Burckhardt.[4] City-states such as Florence, Milan, Urbino, Mantua, and Ferrara emerged. Ultimately, each city-state came under the domination of a single family, developing its own foreign policy, alliances, and ability to declare war and institute taxes.[5] Each of the states functioned within the resources available to the ruler and each acquired its own distinct character.[6]

Monarchs and popes had often used a magnificent display in the form of art, architecture, and clothing to support their claim to a status.[7] These visual images were intended to inspire reverence and awe.[8]

In Renaissance Italy (spanning the fourteenth, fifteenth, and sixteenth centuries) men who had no noble ancestry[9] used visual imagery, among other things, to establish dynasties, lines of succession based on one's progeny. Unlike the more complex feudal lineages of the Middle Ages, these Renaissance dynasties might derive their legitimacy from a solitary married couple.[10] Through sumptuous clothing for their children, new art and architecture, and private quarters, warriors and wealthy merchants sought to create lines of succession. Family advancement, in terms of access to power and wealth, is a concern of every parent beyond the working class, observed historian Lawrence Stone.[11] Marrying their daughters into the wealthy families and the nobility was the another way ruling elites sought to increase their wealth and power.

Child-Rearing Theories

Humanist, architect, writer, and adviser on various artistic and intellectual matters, Leon Battista Alberti (1404–1472), an illegitimate son of a great Florentine family in exile, wrote at length on the importance of fathers to the formation of a child's personality.[12] It is the father's duty to help his son become virtuous and high-principled, to strive for honor and fame. He has to help his son develop competence and power, the sacred attributes that constitute virtue.[13]

A mother is significant only in terms of the nourishment she can give the baby.[14]The quality of the milk should be the primary attribute that determines who will nurse the infant, the mother or a maid.[15] The nurse or maid should be, "neither sickly nor immoral and . . . free from those vices and diseases which corrupt milk or blood. . . . We must make sure that she will bring neither scandal nor shame into the house."[16]

Children's Clothes

Children's clothes made out of silk and brocade and embroidered with gems were designed to convey wealth and beauty. Children were betrothed when they were quite young, even as infants. Their betrothal affected the marital desirability and the continuity of the family line.

In the fresco in the Medici chapel, *The Procession of the Magi*, 1459 (see Fig. 2.1), Benozzo Gozzoli portrays Lorenzo de Medici at the age of ten. He is on a horse; both horse and rider are dressed in adult ceremonial costumes studded with gold, and blazing with red, blue, and yellow against the green foliage. Lorenzo is wearing an Italian style houppelande, a voluminous cloak that ends at mid-calf with evenly spaced organ-pipe pleats. The sleeves are slit. The garment is made out of patterned silk or brocade and trimmed with a brocaded band at the neckline and edges. The belt is below the natural waistline (according to the fashion in Italy) and may have been embroidered or otherwise ornamented. He is wearing an adult costume and his demeanor conveys haughtiness.

A portrait of the daughter of Cosimo I, *Marie de Medici*, by Bronzino, 1540 (see Fig. 2.2), seems to present her as seven years old. She is portrayed in adult-style dangling gold earrings with white pearls, a necklace

FIGURE 2.1 *The Procession of the Magi.* The "coronation" of Lorenzo de Medici. Benozzo Gozzoli, 1459. Medici/Riccardi Palace, Florence. Alinari/Art Resouces, N.Y.

FIGURE 2.2 *Marie de Medici.* She wears a sumptuous silk dress, a pearl necklace, earrings, a medal dangling on a chain on her chest, and a loose-fitting chain around her waist. A. Bronzino, 1540. Uffizi, Florence. Alinari/Art Resouces, N.Y.

FIGURE 2.3 *Infant Prince Federigo d'Urbino.* The ornamented bassinet as a prelude to the throne. Federico Barocci, 1605. Pitti Palace, Florence. Alinari/Art Resouces, N.Y.

above the neckline, a medallion on a heavy chain, and a dress in white shimmering cloth with puffed sleeves.[17] The dress, the medallion, and the other jewelry identify her family's wealth and power.

A painting by Federico Barocci (1605) of the infant prince Federigo d'Urbino (see Fig. 2.3) portrays him in a bejeweled crib-like stand. On the bedding the artist has depicted a playful display of embroidered flowers and leaves. The coverlet, folded over, reveals a shimmering white satin with gold.[18] A portrait of a young Florentine princess of about four by Fr. Porbus (sixteenth century) depicts her in puffed sleeves and black lace, with a small bouquet of flowers in her hair.[19] She is dressed and ornamented to enhance her desirability.

Boys and youths destined for succession were dressed in velvet silk in a style the height of the contemporary fashion.[20]

Clothing regulations allowed the young to dress in a fashionable, sumptuous manner for three years after a wedding. Festive occasions brought the young to the street parading, dancing, and demonstrating their family's wealth.[21]

FIGURE 2.4 *Beatrice d'Este,* 1475-1497. The daughter of Ercole I, duke of Ferrara, was betrothed to Ludovico Sforza when she was five years old and married him at sixteen. In her portrait, she is wearing the latest fashionable attire: a surcoat in black velvet that opens from the shoulder over a red dress, which has a square neckline. Her hair is arranged in a most distinctive manner. It is formed as a netting of double gold cords bordered with pearls. Ambrosio di Predi, 1491. Milan, Pinacoteca. Scala/Art Resources, N.Y.

Development of the jeweler's art had coincided with improvements in the dying of silk and in the weaving of brocades and velvets.[22] Fashionable appearance focused on an affinity between the style, textile, and ornament. Gold and jeweled belts were used to complete an ensemble.[23] Pieces of jewelry were composite arrangements of stones to meet the color and style needs of the outfit.[24] Sleeves were embellished, evoking imaginary forms of bells, trumpets, birds' wings, and crops, or left open to reveal the underlying color and texture.[25]

Daughters of the leading families, such as Beatrice and Isabella d'Este (see Fig. 2.4), wore extreme forms of fashion and were often a source of style.[26]

Portraits of parents, their children, and their court also identified the line of succession. Urbino had been a small hill town with no significant cultural history, little local industry, and few natural resources. Federigo da Montefeltro was recognized as the duke of Urbino in 1447. He was a condottiere, a mercenary soldier who was hired to lead and carry out military combat, and his talents were employed by many major city states, including Rome. In fact, his mercenary contracts became the state of Urbino's major source of income. Under his rule the city-state acquired stability and wealth, and his court "glittered like a diadem."[27]

Federigo built beautiful palaces throughout his territory. The ducal palace in Urbino was built into a steep hillside, but it also opened onto the city's central square. The space in the palace was organized around Federigo's desires. Among these was the separation of private quarters, his residence, from the area where he met the public and held audience. Special quarters were also earmarked for household help.[28] The duke was known for his interest in scholarship. The palace included a library where learned visitors, among them Castiglione, recorded that he had "a large number of the most beautiful and rarest manuscripts".[29]

A father and son portrait from 1476–1477 by Pedro Berruguete demonstrates the duke's concern for succession (see Fig. 2.5). In the painting the duke is portrayed seated, concentrating on the book he is reading. He is dressed in armor with ceremonial robes over it. His sword is strapped to his side. His son, Guidobaldo, a fragile-looking child, is standing to his right. Guidobaldo's left arm is leaning against his father's solid knee and in his right hand he is holding a scepter. The scepter is engraved with the word *Pontifex*, which refers to the pope's granting the child the right of succession. (It was granted in 1464.)[30] Guidobaldo's mother was Battista Sforza (1446–1472), a princess in the court of Milan (see Fig. 2.6). She gave birth to eight girls in succession; her ninth attempt resulted in a son, the heir.[31]

In the father-son portrait the boy is wearing a long dress made of satin-like heavy fabric. A string of pearls frames the neckline of his dress and his belt sparkles. The sleeves are long and embroidered with pearls and a delicate jeweled diadem (a crown) sits on his head. The diadem, the jeweled attire, the scepter, and the physical link to the father proclaim the child's succession. The painting can be easily understood as a paternal declaration of family continuity.

Mantua was another city-state that had originally been small and poor. Its location on a lake in the midst of swamps (with malaria outbreaks frequent) meant that it did not have much to recommend it physically. The town was flat, damp, and humid. The streets were muddy, with a constant croaking of frogs heard in the background. Ludovico, the marquis of Gonzaga, though the son of men of arms, was considered neither a

FIGURE 2.5 *Portrait of Federigo da Montefeltro and His Son.* Designating the heir. The duke is shown dressed in armor, with his sword strapped to his side. His son Guidobaldo, a fragile-looking child, is leaning against his father's knee. He is holding onto a scepter engraved with the word Pontifex, an allusion to the pope having granted him the right of succession. Pedro Berruguete, 1476–1477. Galleria National delle Marche, Urbino. Photo, Greg Kitchen.

brilliant soldier nor fearless. He owned large amounts of land in both city and country. His wife, Barbara of Brandenburg, was granddaughter of the imperial elector, Frederick I of Hohenzollern, a German noble. His thirteen-year-old son was at the papal court. Ludovico was handed a seductive opportunity when the pope, Pius II, decided to hold the Church Congress of 1459–1460 in Mantua. To prepare for the papal congress he engaged artists, engineers, and craftsmen to convert the old fortified Gonzaga Castle into a "luxurious princely residence."[32] Ludovico transformed Mantua and also created a dynasty.

The Palazzo del Podesta was restored according to Leon Battista Alberti's plans; and the monastery and church of Sant'Andrea, located in

FIGURE 2.6 *Battista Sforza*. Daughter of a dynastic family
of Milan, she was married to the duke of Urbino, Federigo
da Montefeltro. Part of a double portrait the duke had
commissioned. Piero della Francesca, 1472. Uffizi, Florence.
Alinari/Art Resouces, N.Y.

FIGURE 2.7 *Court Scene.* The fresco presents Ludovico Gonzaga, his wife
Barbara of Brandenburg (the family's link to royal blood), their children, a
nurse, a female dwarf, secretaries, advisers, leading officials, and courtiers. It
celebrates an event full of significance for the family's dynastic future. Andrea
Mantegna, Camera degli Sposi (north wall), 1465–1474. Ducal Palace, Mantua.
Photo, Greg Kitchen.

the center of the city, was rebuilt to house the vessel containing a pre-
cious relic, a drop of the blood of St. Andrew. Alberti argued that his
monumental church design was spacious, *more* eternal, and *more* cheerful
and cost much less than a competing design by the Florentine architect
Manetti.[33] A larger number of pilgrims would thus be attracted.

The painter Andrea Mantegna decorated the main private room of the
Gonzaga family between 1465 and 1474 (after the papal congress), a
room called the *Camera degli Sposi* (room of the bride and groom). It was
used as the marquis's bedroom and as an audience room, where the marquis received important visitors, lords, ambassadors, and diplomats. The
room has several frescoes which were intended to impress these visitors.
The largest and most important fresco (see Fig. 2.7), a "family portrait,"
is over the fireplace. Ludovico is portrayed with his wife Barbara of Brandenburg, and their children, courtiers, and advisers, including the court
dwarf and the family dog. The adults and children are portrayed in cos-

tumes of rich silk and brocade, showing off the attractive and marriageable Gonzaga daughters.[34]

At the far left of the fresco Ludovico is shown conversing with a messenger. The messenger has just brought the marquis a letter, dated December 30, 1461, a summons from the duchess of Milan. It informs him
that Duke Francesco Sforza is gravely ill. In the event of his death, the
Sforza rule would be challenged and Ludovico's military services would
be called upon.[35]

The smaller fresco on an adjoining wall is called the *Meeting Scene* (see
Fig. 2.8). It represents the family gathered to meet one of their members
who had just been elevated to cardinal (December 22, 1461). Ludovico's
hand is raised in greeting, as two children, Sigismondo and Francesco
(who in fact had not yet been born at the time) and other members of the
family come forward with him to greet the young cardinal, the son of Ludovico and Barbara. The young cardinal is wearing a floor-length light
blue tunic and a red capelet. The meeting is witnessed by Barbara of Brandenburg's brother-in-law, King Christian I of Denmark, and Emperor Frederick III (Mantua's overlord), neither of whom were actually present.[36]

Barabara, Ludovico's wife and Francesco's mother, is standing at
Francesco's side, her right hand in his left. She is facing her husband and
is attentive to the greeting. A small child is standing in front of her holding on to several fingers of her left hand. An older child is standing between him and his father. This child is close enough to attach himself to
his father's left hand. Dressed in fashionable attire like their father, the
boys are wearing tabards (jackets with the sides left open), pinafores over
doublets, and sleeves with slits through which decorative elements show.
The boys are also wearing parti-color hose, white on the right leg and red
on the left, the style in fashion during this period. Around their longish
hair they wear twisted silk wreaths.[37]

Considered splendorous by guests and critics, the art that Ludovico
commissioned increased his prestige. Marriages were arranged, enhancing his ability to create a dynasty.[38] His son Federico (1441–1484) married
Margaret of Bavaria and governed Mantua between 1478 and 1484. His
grandson Francesco II was the marquis between 1484 and 1519,and married Isabella d'Este, the daughter of Ercole I, duke of Ferrara. His great-
grandson Federico was the marquis between 1519 and 1530, and was
then elevated to become the duke of Mantua until his death in 1540. He
married into the house of Monferratto.

Perhaps the most obvious attempt to create a dynasty took place in
Florence, a city whose population strongly rejected the kind of control exercised by a sovereign. The early Medici ancestors were farmers in the
Val d'Arno who worked the fields with their own hands.[39] Nevertheless,
they came to control the political and commercial life of fifteenth-century

FIGURE 2.8 *The Meeting Scene.* The fresco celebrates Gonzaga prestige, flaunting their papal and imperial connections. The meeting between father and cardinal-son is witnessed by Barbara of Brandenburg's brother-in-law, King Christian I of Denmark, and Emperor Frederick III (Mantua's overlord). It includes the children Sigismondo and Francesco, who had not yet been born. Andrea Mantegna, Camera degli Sposi (west wall), 1465–1474. Ducal Palace, Mantua. Photo, Greg Kitchen.

Florence. The Medici dynasty began with Giovanni de Alverardo (1360–1429), who founded the Medici bank. He realized that by using a promissory note one could win a war, secure a throne, or bribe one's way into a useful dynastic connection.[40] Since Florence was a cloth-making center, moneyed interests (not land, monarchical, or church interests) governed its life. Its major products were wool, silk, and later alum, used for cleaning wool and fixing dyes.[41]

His son Cosimo de Medici (1389–1464), his grandson Piero (1416–1469), and his great-grandson Lorenzo (1449–1492) continued the Medici bank and its international network in Bruges, Geneva, Lyon, and Antwerp. Cosimo and later each son in his turn controlled the politics of the city of Florence. Only names of persons approved by the Medici family went into a leather purse from which the names of those who were to fill public office were drawn.[42] Cosimo Medici's desire to establish a dynasty is reflected in the art he commissioned, the chapels, houses, and villas he built and decorated, and the wife he married—Contessina de' Bardi, daughter of an established Florentine family. Cosimo left the house in which he was born and moved to live in the Bardi palace.

Botticelli painted The *Adoration of the Magi* (early 1470) after Cosimo's death (1464). The children who were alive at the time of Cosimo's death are included in the painting. Cosimo is identifiable as the first and oldest Magus, kneeling in awe before the Christ Child.[43] Below the first Magus two other Magi kneel in intense conversation; they are probably Cosimo's sons, Giovanni and Piero the Gouty. The youth at the extreme left is Lorenzo. At the left, a dark-haired youth gazing downwards resembles the portraits of Giuliano, Lorenzo's brother.[44]

After Cosimo's exile in 1433–1434, to prevent such an event in the future, at about 1440 he built the Medici Palace, a fortress-like structure. Originally an entire corner was a loggia, an open air arcade, where the Medici bank business was conducted. The palace was set around a central courtyard where much of the family life, as well as commercial and political activities took place. The house was luxuriously fitted. The principal bedroom was decorated with battle scenes by Paolo Uccello.[45]

The Medici Palace became a model for the homes of other wealthy families. Together with the Medici, the Albizzi, the Bardi, the Strozzi, and the Pitti attracted architects, sculptors, painters, and artisans, who were kept busy designing, building, and decorating.[46]

Cosimo's son Piero the Gouty took over after his father died. He married Lucrezia Tornabuoni, who was from the nobility. Her family had abandoned its noble status to enter politics. Her grandfather had attached himself to the Medici family and the two families had been close.[47] She was Lorenzo's mother. Lorenzo's sisters married sons of other prominent families, such as Rossi, Pazzi, and Rucellai. Lorenzo's

FIGURE 2.9 *Adoration of the Magi.* Cosimo de' Medici is the first and oldest magus, kneeling before the Christ Child holding his feet. (Cosimo had died earlier in 1464.) Two of Cosimo's sons, Giovanni and Piero, are kneeling behind. Other members of the family, including his son Lorenzo, as well as the artist, Botticelli himself, are in attendance. Sandro Botticelli, early 1470. Uffizi Gallery, Florence. Alinari/Art Resources.

mother chose a princess from the ancient Roman dynasty of the Orsini, Clarice Orsini, to be Lorenzo's wife. Clarise's relatives included cardinals, archbishops, and military generals. The family also held high offices in Naples and owned a long line of fortresses along the high road leading out of Florence.[48]

Domestic Renaissance Architecture

Domestic Renaissance architecture was about money and showing off. During the medieval period, public and private worlds lacked clear demarcation. The building facades were often unadorned and they lacked aesthetic identity. They were almost anonymous.[49] Although family residential areas were constructed so that they could be sealed off in times of public unrest, commercial activity required public access to the building and there was a constant penetration of street life. Within a palace, moreover, ownership was frequently divided, and shops, apartments, even single rooms could be held by a number of different parties not necessarily members of the same family, as art historian Richard A. Goldthwaite pointed out.[50] In the Italian city-states of the fourteenth and fifteenth centuries a degree of separation between public and private life took place.[51] New palaces were erected or housing already in existence was transformed and redesigned to serve as the dwelling places for the nuclear family. These palaces were important in conferring prestige on the family.[52]

In the mid-fifteenth-century, Palla di Palla Strozzi cleared out a busy urban commercial space, an area full of shops of all kinds, and erected a private home. Over half-a-dozen modest and undistinguished buildings were demolished to build the private residence called the Strozzino. The new architecture focused on creating a facade and a private internal space to shelter and support the conjugal family.[53]

The living space of the nuclear family became a unit apart and distinct from the network of kin. At the center of this unit was the conjugal couple (a husband and wife) and the offspring of their union.[54] Alberti (1404–1472), in his treatise on architecture, associated domestic palaces with familial affections.[55]

The Renaissance palace acquired a monumental facade which symbolized a new individualistic morality, a basic transformation of Florentine society, Goldthwaite argued.[56] The palace conferred prestige upon its builder and amplified his potential for establishing a dynasty.[57] It protected the family from the outside world by high windows and walls and awe-inspiring gates. Specific spaces were designated for private and public discourse. Members of the larger family or clan could visit, play, and party, but were allocated to a particular part of the house. As Alessandra Strozzi put it, the palace was a refuge, not only for her sons but for all her "descendants in the male line."[58]

In a plan for a Renaissance palace from the second half of the fifteenth century by Giovanni Bellini there are provisions for two centers of sociability: a covered upper porch and a large lower loggia (a covered gallery or arcade) where groups of relatives, friends, and neighbors could gather and public ceremonies could be held.[59] Later, even the loggias were incorporated into the private space.[60]

Cassoni: Illustrated Marriage Chests

An illustrated marriage chest, the cassone, was a visual construct that announced an upcoming marriage and the establishment of a new family.[61]

FIGURE 2.10   *Tournament.* The trials and tribulations of marriage? Cassoni Masters, nd. Tours, France. Scala/Art Resources, N.Y.

It was filled with the bride's trousseau and carried through the city streets from her house to that of her future husband in the days before the marriage. Everyone would thus be aware of the upcoming event. There were many marriage alliances among the ruling families of Italy, and artists were engaged to decorate the cassoni created for the occasions. Ercole de Roberti (c. 1450–1496) and other painters and sculptors worked on gilding and painting marriage chests. Between mid-1489 and 1490, for example, artists and craftsmen were busy with the marriage of the Duke of Ferrara's eldest daughter, Isabella, to Francesco Gonzaga of Mantua.[62]

Some cassoni were illustrated with pictures of classical battles, such as the *Invasion of Greece* (1463), *The Triumph of the Greeks Over the Persians* (1463), scenes from Virgil's *Aeneid*, and tournaments, such as the *Tournament on the Piazza di S. Croce* (see Fig 2.10), all of which portray violence.[63] This choice of subject matter was popular because Altieri, the Roman humanist, located the origins of marriage in an act of violence, the rape (in the sense of carrying off by force) of the Sabine women. The story of the rape of the Sabine women proposes that collective submission to enforced carnal knowledge is essential for the survival of the race, the stability of society, and the continuity of the process of civilization. The brutal threatening images also suggested awareness of the larger social violence the marriage had a potential to create or relieve, observed art historian Hughes.[64] Tournaments and battles were popular themes on wedding chests. They contained admonitory messages, hopes and fears about what marriage could be for society as well as the individual couple. On a chest designed in 1465 for a marriage that united the Davanzatti and Redditi families, amid the arms of the two marrying families a celebratory feast follows a collective rape.[65]

Florentine Renaissance wedding chests were usually bought by the groom's family.[66] They were used to furnish the bridal chamber. On one hand, the cassoni served to remind the bride of her conjugal duties and the personal costs that the new relationship would entail. Visual narratives retold the stories of Penelope and Griselda and their extraordinary devotion to distant and unreasonable husbands, and "might simply be read as a recommendation of cheerful, wifely submission to the conjugal ideal," Hughes observed.[67] On the other hand, the illustrations alerted the men to the lineal strength that stood behind their brides and the conflicts that they might experience.[68] Illustrations depicting the rape of Helen and the Trojan War had a different message. They were designed to warn men of the upper class that if they were to fulfill their political and historical destiny they must rise above and leave behind the claims of female desire. The content of these illustrations served to warn husbands of the strength of female provocation and the catastrophes that might ensue, Hughes suggested.[69]

Through the illustrations the couple was informed of the variety of duties they were taking on and feelings they might experience in the marriage. The illustrations were expected to reinforce ideas about the trials and tribulations and potential pitfalls of married life. Naturally not all the artists and patrons shared a single point of view towards love, towards marriage, and especially towards the relation between love and marriage.[70]

Wives suffered a loss in power when they married, concludes Hughes.[71] In the new domestic household, the wife had to forgo participation in public life for the sake of intimacy within the household. She was expected to submit to the demands of domestic life and the designs of her husband. With the arrival of an offspring the husband's authority was temporarily suspended, as members of the wife's family took over her care. The goal of the marriage, to produce an heir, had been fulfilled. The wife was now more tightly bound to *his* lineage. The fulfillment of the marriage through children made the wife more personally involved with her husband, and so more vulnerable to the various experiences of marriage, whether harmony and joy or conflict and grief.[72]

Latin Christendom, having undergone legal and ideological unification, insisted on familial exogamy—that is, that people marry outside their own family group—and on marriage as a contract and sacrament effective through the will of both parties. This new insistence provided support for the emergence of the nuclear family, as historian of the family Henry Bresc has pointed out.[73]

Mother-Child Images

Along with private quarters, a new model for mother-child interaction involving an obvious display of feelings emerged during the Renaissance. It was based on the established genre of Christian devotional imagery.[74] In the thirteenth century, Jesus is often portrayed as a somber figure seated on Mary's lap. For example, in Cimabue's *Madonna Enthroned* (c. 1280) (see Fig. 2.11), he wears a long tunic and the philosopher's pallium (a cloak), and the mother is presenting her son to the faithful.[75]

By the fourteenth century the stately robes are often replaced by a diaphanous veil or transparent chemise. The child may also be portrayed entirely naked; Christ is presented as a frolicking infant in Vital da Bologna's *Madonna and Child* (c. 1345).[76] In *Madonna and Child* by Alesso Baldovinetti (1460) (see Fig. 2.12), the child is naked and asking his mother to continue swaddling him while she assumes the posture of adoring him. In the fourteenth century the medieval preference for the ethereal and awe-inspiring Mother was replaced by the nursing Madonna, noted art historian Frederick Hartt.[77] The new paintings, moreover, show Jesus receiving from Mary tenderness, care, protection, and compassion.[78] Mother and child are shown encountering one another with knowing eye-contact exchanges, according to art historian Leo Steinberg.[79] The new mother-child orientation represented in art offers a new ideal for mother-child interaction.[80] It revolved around reciprocal affection. Autonomy from lineal obligations, living in private quarters, and establishing ties of affection with one's children—all these factors together created a framework in which progeny could carry on a father's accomplishments. Sumptuous attire, like extravagant depictions of children in art, was designed to signify this new pattern of inheritance, which had led to the emergence of the dynastic child.

Notes

1. Philippe Ariès, (1962) *Centuries of Childhood: A Social History of Family Life.* Trans. Robert Baldock. New York: Vintage Books, p. 34.

2. Ariès, op. cit., p. 37.

3. David Herlihy, (1978) "Medieval Children," in *The Walter Prescott Webb Memorial Lectures.* Austin: University of Texas Press, pp. 109, 120–121.

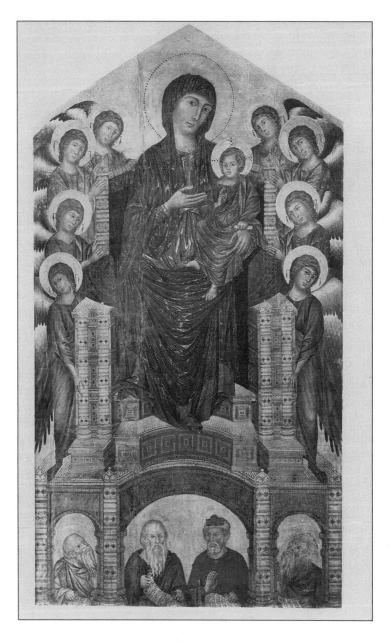

FIGURE 2.11 *Enthroned Madonna.* Mary, the mother, presents the
Christ Child to the faithful. He is dressed in philosopher's robes
and represented as a miniature adult. Cimabue, c. 1280. Uffizi
Gallery, Florence. Alinari/Art Resouces, N.Y.

FIGURE 2.12 *Madonna and Child.* The child is trying to engage his mother. He is appealing to her to finish swaddling his soft little body. Mary's hands are folded in pious adoration. Alesso Baldovinetti, 1460. Louvre, Paris. Photo, Greg Kitchen.

    4. Jacob Burckhardt, (1860/1950) *The Civilization of the Renaissance in Italy.* New York: Phaidon Publishers, pp. 4–13.
    5. Sidney Alexander, (1974) *Lions and Foxes: Men and Ideas of the Italian Renaissance.* New York: Macmillan, Chap. 1.
    6. Burckhardt, op. cit., p. 83.

7. Thorstein Veblen (1899), in *The Theory of the Leisure Class,* discusses this phenomenon. Also, priests and kings in the ancient world, Mesopotamia, and Egypt, for example, as well as those in European society used attire to convey the message.

8. Consider, for example, the magnificent attire of the pharaohs and the avenue of the sphinxes in Karnak.

9. Marcel Brion, (1969) *The Medici: A Great Florentine Family.* New York: Crown Publishers, p. 11.

10. Martin Von Alfred, (1963) *Sociology of the Renaissance.* New York: Harper Torchbooks, pp. xviii–xix.

11. Lawrence Stone observed this concern in relation to education. He notes that a father above the working class has always wished to give his male children a schooling as least good as and if possible better than his own as a means of social mobility. Lawrence Stone (1968) "Literacy and Education in England 1640–1900," *Past and Present* 42, pp. 69–139.

12. Guido A. Guarino, (1971) *The Albertis of Florence: Leon Battista Alberti's* Della Famiglia. Lewisburg, Pa.: Bucknell University Press, pp. 61–64.

13. Guarino, op. cit., p. 53.

14. Ibid.

15. Guarino, op. cit., pp. 56, 58.

16. Guarino, op. cit., p. 56.

17. E. Rodocanachi, (1922) *La Femme Italienne Avant, Pendant, Après, La Renaissance.* Paris: Librairie Hachette, p. 16.

18. Ibid.

19. Ibid.

20. Brion, op. cit. 150.

21. Jacqueline Herald, (1981) *Renaissance Dress in Italy 1400–1500.* London: Bell & Hyman, p. 109.

22. Herald, op. cit., pp. 90-92.

23. Herald, op. cit., p. 180.

24. Herald, op. cit., p. 107.

25. Herald, op. cit., p. 167.

26. Herald, op. cit., p. 142.

27. Alexander, op. cit., pp. 129–130.

28. Frederick Hartt, (1969) *History of Italian Renaissance Art, Painting, Sculpture, and Architecture.* Englewood Cliffs, N.J.: Prentice Hall, and New York: Harry N. Abrams, pp. 243–246.

29. Alison Cole (1995) *Virtue and Magnificence: Art of the Italian Renaissance Courts.* Englewood, N.J.: Prentice Hall, pp. 70–73.

30. Cole, op. cit., pp. 89–90.

31. Ibid. Hartt claims that it was five girls.

32. Cole, op. cit., pp. 143–144.

33. Cole, op. cit., p. 147.

34. Cole, op. cit., pp. 154–155.

35. Cole, op. cit., p. 154.

Hartt suggested that the letter had a different message (op. cit., p. 356). But according to Cole (op. cit., p. 154), recently discovered documents suggest that the letter informs Ludovico of the upcoming visit by his son, who had just been promoted to the princely rank of Cardinal (Dec. 22, 1461).

36. Cole, op. cit., p. 155.

37. Jacqueline Herald (op. cit.) noted that portrayals of fifteenth-century dress appear extremely fanciful and unlikely to be worn. Yet contemporary descriptions of Pisanello's designs, for example, point to the general accuracy of such portrayals (p. 127). Textiles with heraldic significance were woven in Florence (p. 86). Parti-color hose, if worn in the colors of the particular household, played an heraldic role (p. 110). Also, see Cole, op. cit., p. 156.

38. Ludovico was successful at creating a Gonzaga dynasty. His son Federico (1441–1484) married Margaret of Bavaria, and his grandson Francesco (1466–1519) married Isabella d'Este, the eldest daughter of Ercole d'Este, the duke of Ferrara, and Eleonora of Aragon. Moreover, in 1530 the rank of Federico II was elevated from a marquis to that of a duke. Cole, op. cit., Appendix "Genealogies."

39. Brion, op. cit., p. 12.

40. Maurice Rowdon, (1974) *Lorenzo the Magnificent*. Chicago: Henry Regnery, p. 30.

41. Brion, op. cit., pp. 23–24.

42. Hartt, op. cit., 250.

43. Hartt, op. cit., p. 282.

44. Hartt, op. cit., p. 285.

45. Hartt, op. cit., pp. 124–126.

46. Hartt, op. cit., p. 250.

47. Rowdon, op. cit., p. 50.

48. Rowdon, op. cit., p. 74.

49. Richard A. Goldthwaite, (1972) "The Florentine Palace," in *American Historical Review* 77, p. 983.

50. Ibid., pp. 980–981.

51. Gromort, Georges (1922) *Italian Renaissance Architecture*, trans. George F. Waters. Paris: A. Vincent, pp. 33–43.

52. Goldthwaite, op. cit., p. 978.

53. Goldthwaite, op. cit., pp. 984–985.

54. Goldthwaite, op. cit., pp. 977–1012.

55. Quoted in Goldthwaite, op. cit., p. 1004.

56. Goldthwaite, op. cit., p. 996.

57. Goldthwaite, op. cit., p. 991.

58. Goldthwaite, op. cit., pp. 991–992.

59. Georges Duby,(1988) *A History of Private Life: Revelations of the Medieval World*. Trans. Arthur Goldhammer. Cambridge, Massachusetts: The Belknap Press of Harvard University Press, pp. 238–239.

60. This new privacy was in contrast to the half private and half public living arrangements among aristocratic households of the eleventh and twelfth centuries on the Continent and in England. The great houses were frequented by three different types of guests: 1. official residents of the house, 2. friends who came and went, and 3. outsiders, those who had no special emotional bonds with the master of the house. The household could be quite numerous. In thirteenth-

century England Thomas of Berkeley's household comprised more than two hundred people, and the bishop of Bristol needed a hundred horses to carry his household whenever he traveled. Sire de Gouberville in his journal for the years 1549–1562 reports that adults, children, and animals often spent the night under the same roof of his manor house. Bedrooms and even beds were shared with family, friends and strangers. In Katherine Fedden, (1933) *Manor Life in Old France From the Journal of the Sire de Gouberville for the Years 1549–1562.* New York: Columbia University Press, pp. 42–69.

61. The cassone had been in use for some time, but it achieved new prominence in the fifteenth century. Ellen Callman, (1979) "The Growing Threat to Marital Bliss as Seen in Fifteenth-Century Florentine Paintings." *Studies in Iconography* 9, p. 73.

62. Cole, op. cit., p. 134.

63. E. H. Gombrich, (1955) "Appolonio Di Giovanni: Florentine Cassone Workshop Seen through the Eyes of a Humanist Poet." *Journal of Warburg and Courtauld Institutes* 18, pp. 16–34.

64. Diane Owen Hughes, (1986) "Representing the Family: Portraits and Purposes in Early Modern Italy," in Robert I. Rotberg and Theodore K. Rabb, eds., *Art and History Images and their Meaning.* New York: Cambridge University Press, pp. 11–12.

65. Hughes, op. cit., p. 12.

66. Brucia Witthoft, (1982) "Marriage Rituals and Marriage Chests," in *Artibus et historiae.* IRSA; Firenze: distribuzione LICOSA, 1 980, pp. 43–59.

67. Hughes, op. cit., p. 13.

68. Hughes, op. cit., p. 11.

69. Hughes, op. cit., p. 15

70. Callman, op. cit., pp. 73–92.

71. Hughes, op. cit., p. 8. Also, one way to read the three portraits that Van Dyck painted of Paola Adorno, the marchesa of Brignole-Sale, is that they describe her own lineal death, her ceasing to be part of the family she was born into. In the first portrait he shows her in a white dress spun with a gold thread—a cloth that the sumptuary laws throughout nothern Italy allowed only young brides and nubile daughters. In the second she is shown in a dress of red and gold brocade, the costume of a married woman. In the third portrait she appears in a black dress and her young son is present. The black costume, which custom and sumptuary law required her to don within three years of a marriage, signifies and records her lineal death. Hughes, op. cit., pp. 30–31.

72. Hughes, op. cit., p. 18.

73. Henry Bresc, (1996) "Europe: Town and Country," in Andre Burguiere et al., eds., *A History of the Family,* trans. Sarah Hanbury Tenison et al. Cambridge, Mass.: Belknap Press, pp. 433–434.

74. After Gombrich's view of a brief narrative; the protagonist is the subject, the action the verb. The child is the object. "Action and Expression in Western Art," in Robert A. Hinde, ed., (1972) *Non-Verbal Communication.* Cambridge: Cambridge University Press, p. 382.

75. Paintings such as Cimabue's are sober ceremonial images of the Virgin as Queen of Heaven. In contrast to Cimabue's fantastic throne, which needs steady-

ing hands from the attending angels, Giotto's structure is firmly placed above a marble step which can be climbed and the Madonna sits firmly on the throne. "It is as if they recognized that attunement to others demands a modicum of calm in oneself." F. Hartt (1993) *Art: A History of Painting, Sculpture, Architecture.* New York: Abrams, pp. 566–568.

76. Attributed to Emile Male in Leo Steinberg, (1983) *The Sexuality of Christ in Renaissance Art and in Modern Oblivion.* New York: Pantheon, p. 34.

Leo Steinberg traces the change in devotional images to the spread of Franciscan piety, with its stress on Christ's human nature. Genital exhibition is a symbolic mode of aggression, or fertility worship. Both of these motives are appropriate to a time of sexual swagger. See Michelangelo's *David*, 1501–1504, for example.

77. F. Hartt, (1993) op. cit. pp. 566–568.

78. Steinberg, op. cit., p. 28.

79. Steinberg, op. cit., p. 141.

80. When depicting secular stories not previously illustrated, artists and patrons alike felt more at ease with familiar visual models and familiar modes of thought, pointed out art historian Ellen Callman in "The Growing Threat to Marital Bliss as Seen in Fifteenth-Century Florentine Paintings," op. cit., pp. 73–92.

3

Marital Portraits and Paintings of Children in Seventeenth-Century Dutch Art

There was no monarchy or traditional aristocracy in republican and predominantly Calvinist Holland. Traditional patrons of art were absent. Nevertheless, even though Calvinists opposed images in church buildings, they had no objections to their placement in private homes. The Dutch took great pride in their homes, their upkeep, care, and decoration. Not only did commercial families want pictures, so did almost everyone else, observed art historian Frederick Hartt.[1] Peter Mundy, a British visitor to Amsterdam in 1640, at the height of Dutch artistic activity, observed that he could think of no other people having the affection for the art of painting that the Dutch did, "all in general striving to adorn their houses especially the outer, or street room, with costly pieces, Butchers and bakers not much inferior in their shoppes . . . yea many tymes blacksmithes, Coblers, etts, will have some picture or other by their Forge and in their stalle."[2]

A wave of skilled refugees had fled religious persecution in the southern Netherlands, and they helped to stimulate new economic activity in the seventeenth-century Dutch republic. The new wealth made the creation and consumption of art possible.

Unlike the peoples of other European countries, the seventeenth-century Dutch did not turn over the infant to a servant or a hired maid for feeding. Mothers nursed their babies themselves. The expression of tender feelings characterized interaction between parents and children. Physical punishment of children and the beating of a spouse were discouraged; a mate who beat his or her partner had to pay a fine. Cases of children disobedient enough to require thrashing were rare. The moral education of children was central to the culture.[3]

Travelers to the Dutch Republic repeatedly complained that parents were too lenient. They were reluctant to enforce discipline. Children's misbehavior, these travelers contended, was the result of parental tenderness, which blinded them to their children's shortcomings. At the time it was thought that a strict upbringing results in obedience. Leniency results in misbehavior, explained Bentham in 1698.[4]

Two doctrines, humanism and Calvinism, conjointly informed child-rearing practices, as well as the relationship between the marital couple.[5] The Calvinist notion of the male's lordship over his wife was altered by an understanding that a strong household required a strong manager and that the male attempt to enforce his rule would not be best for anyone.[6] The relationship between the marital couple also revolved around feelings. Companionship was one of the major reasons for getting married. Warm, tender feelings between a husband and his wife were expected.[7]

Children's Clothes

Infant wear helped initiate newborns into their new society almost at birth. Rather than swaddling, as was customary through much of Europe, the Dutch dressed infants in a short shift and a coat. The outfit made kicking and moving about possible. Infants began their life as objects of maternal intimacy.[8] An infant sucking at its mother's breast buried itself deeply in her bosom, and with the milk, the infant imbibed cultural values.[9] Even in a well-disciplined household, the danger of moral weakness existed, observed art historian Mary Frances Durantini.[10] Clothes helped socialize older children to their society.

A family portrait from 1635 by Dirck Santvoort, *The Amsterdam Burgomaster Dirck Jacobsz. Bas and His Family,* (see Fig. 3.1) portrays some of the basic ideas regarding the family and its use of clothes. The parents are portrayed in the costume of the regents, the cumbersome, sober, conservative attire worn by the men and women who ruled the municipality, province, and state. The wife wears a black voluminous dress with a white, wide, stiff, millstone ruff with close pleats; the husband a black jacket, full breeches, and a millstone white collar full enough that it almost touches his mustache.[11] Their unmarried offspring are dressed in the international fashion, outfits that hug the body, revealing its shape, made of fabrics that are intricate in design, thus creating interest. The attire is ornamented, but the colors are subdued; the ruff is replaced by the requisite lace collar, which was flat and white. There is a young child in the foreground, a boy wearing a long elaborate dress with flat, white lace collar and leading strings. What identifies him as a boy is the male-style collar and a cap with a feather.[12]

FIGURE 3.1   *The Amsterdam Burgomaster Dirck Jocobsz. Bas and His Family.*
Rather than displaying parental rank, the children are wearing fashionable
attire. Dirck Santvoort, 1635. Rijksmuseum, Amsterdam.

On other solemn occasions, such as the Sabbath dinner, age and sex are
clearly identified and the children's attire displays familial wealth. A 1609
copper engraving, *Saying Grace* by Claes Jansz Visscher, portrays a family
having its Sabbath meal. Order, sobriety, and neatness characterize the
scene. The husband is facing his wife and the older children are seated
across from each other. As was customary for younger children, the two
younger boys, five and seven, are standing at the end of the table where
the parents are seated across from each other. The five-year-old boy is
standing near his mother. He is wearing a skirt, a male ruff, and a set of
leading strings, the shoulder-strings that were used to teach young children how to walk. They were kept on later as a way of preventing children from falling.[13] The seven-year-old child is wearing below-the-knee
breeches and a jerkin (a sleeveless, often padded, jacket). He has already
graduated to adult-style male dress.[14] The table is loaded with food,
promising that hunger will be abolished. Serenity and decorum prevail.

A child's sex was signified even in the appearance of the very young.
The Leyden Municipal Architect Willem van der Helm with his Wife and Son
(1655), a painting by Barent Fabritius (See Fig. 3.2), shows a small boy,
barely out of infancy, wearing a dress with ornamental sleeves and a
small, flat, square, male-style collar. A valuable triple chain with a medallion, his godfather's gift, decorates his outfit. It bears a baptismal in-
scription identifying him as fourteen months old; it also contain the family's coat-of-arms, and a monogram.[15]

FIGURE 3.2 *The Leyden Municipal Architect Willem van der Helm with His Wife and Son.* A portrait of a nuclear family, similar to a modern snapshot. The infant is wearing a dress, but the male-style collar identifies his sex. Barent Fabritius, 1655. Rijksmuseum, Amsterdam.

To protect the young child from assault by demonic forces, the Dutch had young children wear coral.[16] A pretzel worn on the arm as a bracelet was an amulet against evil and dark powers. Schama traced the origin of the pretzel as an amulet to the dough that remained after monastic bakers had trimmed and decorated a loaf. The dough ends were looped and connected to form hands in prayer.[17] A black dress, long and full with white cuffs, a full-length white apron, and black cap with white trim made a young girl a miniaturized version of a God-fearing Calvinist mother (see Fig. 3.3). Conveying modesty, the costume offered "a safe haven for girls' sexual destiny," Schama suggested.[18]

Paintings of children often portray moral dilemmas parents and children faced. In the painting by Dirk Hals, *Two Children Playing Cards*, the boy is wearing adult-style attire. It consists of an ornamented, hip-length

FIGURE 3.3 *Portrait of a Child.* The painting represents parental consideration of the child's gender and her well-being, and reflects the culture's view of life. The girl wears an apron, which alludes to her proper domain in the future, the kitchen. She is also wearing a protective coral necklace and holding a pretzel. Jacob Gerritszoon Cuyp, n.d. Collection of Sir John Plumb, Cambridge University. By permission.

flared coat, close-fitting sleeves, matching wide breeches and a broad-rim hat. He is sitting on the floor. The girl is wearing a floor-length jumper over a white shirt with sleeves that are long and cuffs that fall freely, alluding to the potential for loosening of the rules.[19] On the one hand, playing cards improved learning; at the same time, the activity could lead to gambling, an adult folly.[20] Blowing bubbles was also a popular theme. The moralist Jacob Cats in *Houwelyck* (Marriage) argued that paintings that portray children playing with an inflated bladder or balloon were often intended as criticism of the futility of being concerned with worldly pursuits. Children ignore the better, useful part of the animal, the meat and the fat. They are only interested in the bladder because it can be blown up like a balloon. A tiny puncture, however, will cause the balloon to shrivel up and "die," rendering the toy useless.[21] With their "iridescent prettiness and airy evanescence" bubbles signify the illusory and fleeting. They invite fascination with their beauty, and at the same time they heighten the awareness that beauty "endures but so brief a phase." Bubbles were symbolic of childhood itself, which lasts only a short period, then dies.[22]

When gracing the dinner table, children were portrayed as gentle and obedient. On less solemn occasions children were loved, cared for, and criticized; they laughed and they cried.[23] Jan Steen's version of the *Feast of St. Nicholas*, from about 1650 (see Fig 3.4), portrays such an informal gathering, consisting of seven children and three adults. The mother, sitting on a chair, extends her arms towards the little girl who seems to have received the most presents. The girl carries some in a pail she holds on her arm, she has some wrapped in her apron, and one she holds tightly (a little figure of St. Nicholas). She seems happy but is unwilling to share the treats with anyone, not even her mother.[24] By comparison to her sisters and brothers, the girl is sumptuously dressed. Her attire consists of a yellow silk dress, a gathered-up white overskirt, sleeves and overdress of pink-orange silk, and a white collar and bonnet with a narrow pink-orange ribbon.

One of her older siblings, a boy, is rubbing his eyes and crying. Santa has given him a branch from the birch tree rather than treats. In Germany and other places in Europe a branch from a birch tree was often used to punish children who misbehaved. He is dressed in a doublet, petit-coat breeches, a flat, white, droopy collar and no lace.[25] His hat has neither a ribbon nor a feather. The other children look unkempt. They are dressed in ill-fitting bits and pieces of clothes. The girl's attire, rich and extravagant, would suggest that she was the favored child.

Aping adult transgressions and performing gestures that undermined solemn moralizing [26] were two types of behavior for which children were considered naughty. Parents should instruct their children on behavior considered "good" and that considered "evil." Roemer Visscher, in a painting called *Sinnepoppen* (1614), meaning "Don't teach it to your children," depicts a crab with cards and dice. Gambling is obviously a bad habit. The text explains that the crab is a creature that can move easily in all directions. To steady their children's behavior parents must lead their children along the path of virtue.[27]

FIGURE 3.4 *Feast of St. Nicholas.* The little girl seems to be the
favorite, because her clothes are finer than those of the older
boy. He is mocked when St. Nicholas fails to leave good things
in his shoe—good girl, bad boy at Christmas. Jan Steen, 1650.
Rijksmuseum, Amsterdam.

Parents are often ignorant of the role they play in the sinful behavior of
their children, suggested Jan Steen (1626) in his paintings. In *The World
Upside Down* (1663), Steen, a Catholic and a tavern keeper, points out that
by drinking parents make themselves unable to take notice of what their
children are doing and thus less able to control their behavior.[28] Children
may run wild, steal, and make mischief.[29] In foolishness, time is forgotten. Parents thus create an improper household.

In his writings, the critic-poet Jacob Cats, whose books were popular
and ranked close to the Bible, advised parents to be models of virtue, at
least in front of their children. "When youth are nearby, let nothing friv-

olous be professed."[30] When the adults are absorbed in their own world of drinking, as in Steen's *The Effects of Intemperance* (1663), the fashionably and sumptuously dressed adults are slumped over unconscious.[31] The children in everyday practical clothing are sober and completely alert to the "possibilities" of getting into their own kind of mischief. They ignore the injunction against feeding the kitten pie, encourage the parrot to drink wine, and pilfer from an adult's pocket. By their laxity the adults have given the children an opportunity "to get into trouble."[32]

Socio-Cultural Context: Marital Portraits

The family was the center of interaction, activity, and celebration. While the father was the master of the family, the mother was dominant within the home. The home was where most Dutch women spent nearly their entire lives. Marriage portraits were a characteristic artifact among the middle class. Marriage portraits were so popular that artists complained that their commissions constrained their creativity and their independence.[33]

A tradition of marriage portraiture emerged in Flanders in the fifteenth century. Robert Campin's pendant portraits of a man and his wife and Jan van Eyck's *Giovani Arnolfini and His Bride* (c. 1434) stimulated a rich tradition in Flanders of commemorating a marriage or a betrothal. The Dutch painter Anthonis Mor, under the influence of Titian (c. 1490–1576), is credited with introducing marriage portraiture to Holland. In the seventeenth century marriage portraits evolved into a genre and often included iconographic symbols.[34] Domestic interiors were now furnished with marriage portraits, both marriage and domesticity acquiring new significance.[35] A marriage portrait was costly. The possession of one announced economic success.[36]

In his study of Holland's seventeenth-century culture, Johan Huizinga pointed out that the Dutch were endowed with visual perception and pictorial talent.[37] The best qualities of Dutch art lie in its unpretentious and sincere rendering of reality.[38] Portraiture flourished in the seventeenth century.[39] Prior to the seventeenth century, marriage portraits are straightforward depictions of the married couple,[40] but they are less numerous and the married couple is portrayed rooted in domestic life.[41] They are busy, each in his or her own sphere, performing traditional tasks. A 1529 marriage portrait by Maarten van Heemskerk, *Portrait of a Woman* and *Portrait of a Man*, for example, is "a carefully described domestic interior." A cornice running along the wall emphasizes the unity of the setting. The man in Heemskerk's portrait projects the image of a practical businessman. He is behind a table settling accounts and glancing at the viewer. The woman has her own space and is absorbed in her spinning. Their relationship is seen as based on each inhabiting a different sphere.[42] Money-counting and spinning, prosaic activities, are identified as domestic virtues.[43] An emotional connection between the couple is absent.

Seventeenth-century Dutch marriage portraits are distinguished for clearly conveying a sense of connectedness between a married couple.[44] This sense is there for couples portrayed together, in a double portrait, or apart, in a pair of portraits. The portraits are also distinguished for being representations of formality and decorum, Smith noted.[45] Husbands and wives were portrayed with a formal demeanor; patrons cared about being represented in a particular way. A portrait was to a degree a cooperative project between the artist and the patron. Together they made choices. In the early part of the century, they tended to choose attire that was formal; the garb was that worn by the regents. It was a shield-like, full-bodied attire, mostly black, with a wide, stiff and impractical millstone ruff.[46]

Marital connectedness was conveyed through physical closeness, gestures conveying support, and involvement in an interaction. It was also communicated through the couple's attire. Their clothing was complementary. It was in the same vein or mood. It could be sober, elegant, ostentatious, romantic, or playful.

In a 1631 pair of portraits by Nicholas Eliasz, *Portrait of Reiner Hinlopen* and *Portrait of Trijntje van Nooy*, for example (see Figs. 3.5 and 3.6), the couple presents a common front; they are a "team." Their poses mirror each other. There is a black background behind them and they share a common source of illumination. The two portraits subtly come together in the eye of the viewer to form a common balanced composition.[47]

Visual representations of the conjugal couple portrayed them as having achieved a meeting of the minds. These portrayals suggested a consciousness of identity and reflected the couple's understanding of the image they would like to portray, Smith pointed out.[48] There was often a preference for a portrait that reflected a desired stereotype or identity. The attire is intrinsically symbolic.[49] It could be sober, even austere, or elegant, ostentatious, flamboyant. Merchants were often portrayed in a flamboyant style, for example. They were less anchored in the social hierarchy.[50] Rembrandt's portraits of *Johanes Elison* (1634) and *Maria Bockenole* (1634) and those of *Maerten Soolmans* (1634) and *Oopjen Coppit* (1634) illustrate such distinctions. The clothing and appearance of the first couple, an elderly minister and his wife, is restrained. That of Soolmans and his wife is theatrical and showy, mimicking the attire of the aristocracy.[51]

FIGURE 3.5   *Portrait of Reiner Hinlopen.*

Jointly sanctioned by the couple, the marital portrait documented their union, making the expenditure justifiable and morally unblemished, since the home was the citadel of middle-class Dutch culture, the primary unit of society, the source of all harmony and grace. The home was expected to hold at bay the mass battalions of encroaching worldliness, schism, tyranny, and vanity.[52] Though it was a picture of themselves, the marital portrait exonerated the couple from the suspicion of avarice.[53]

FIGURE 3.6   *Portrait of Trijntie van Noy.* This portrait is a companion piece to the preceding one. In Dutch marital portraits the couple presents a shared image. The similar attire of this married couple, for example, makes them mirror images of one another. Rijksmuseum, Amsterdam.

Notes

1. Frederick Hartt, (1993) *A History of Painting Sculpture Architecture.* Fourth Edition. Englewood Cliffs, N.J.: Prentice Hall and Harry N. Abrams, p. 816.
2. Quoted in Hartt (1993), op. cit., p. 816.
3. Simon Schama, (1988) *The Embarrassment of Riches: An Interpretation of Culture in the Golden Age.* Berkeley: University of California Press, p. 420.

4. Mary Francis Durantini (1979) *Studies in the Role and Function of the Child in Seventeenth Century Dutch Painting.* Ann Arbor, Mich.: University Microfilms International, pp. 15, 34, 82 139.

5. Schama, op. cit., p. 512.

6. Schama, op. cit., pp. 420–421.

7. Durantini, op. cit., p. 88.

8. The painting by Gerard Dou, *Young Mother* (1655–1660), illustrates this intimacy.

9. Schama, op. cit., p. 483.

10. Durantini, op. cit., p. 16, Plate 8.

11. Frithjof van Thienen, (1951) *The Great Age of Holland: 1600–60.* London: George Harrap and Co., p. 82.

12. Thienen, op. cit., p. 23.

13. Thienen, op. cit., p. 7.

14. Thienen, op. cit., pp. 6–7, 22.

15. Thienen, op. cit., pp. 25–26.

16. Schama, op. cit., p. 547.

17. Schama, op. cit., p. 550.

18. Schama, op. cit., p. 547.

19. Schama, op. cit., p. 546.

20. Schama, op. cit., p. 506.

21. Jacob Cats, *Houwelijck*, in *Al de Werken*, Rotterdam 1870, p. 142; quoted in Durantini, op. cit., p. 242.

22. From Cats, quoted in Schama, op. cit., p. 513.

23. David R. Smith, (1982) *Masks of Wedlock, Seventeenth Century Dutch Marriage Portraiture.* Ann Arbor, Mich.: University of Michigan Research Press, p. 139.

24. Durantini, op. cit., p. 93.

25. Percy Macquoid, *(1923) Four Hundred Years of Children's Costumes, From the Great Masters 1400–1800.* London: The Medici Society, p. 91.

26. Schama, op. cit., p. 554.

27. Ibid., pp. 86–87.

28. Ibid., pp. 77–78.

29. This kind of household had already been warned against in the sixteenth century, in Pieter Balten's print *The Dissolute Household*. On the left the mother ignores her spinning and rests her head on her hand in an image of sloth or melancholy. On the right the father plays a bagpipe, a common symbol of lust. The number and intensity of such warning is greater in the seventeenth century. Durantini, op. cit., pp. 77–78.

30. Quoted in Durantini, op. cit., p. 87.

31. Schama, op. cit., p. 496.

32. Cats, quoted in Durantini, op. cit., p. 85.

33. Smith, op. cit., pp. 1–2.

34. Smith, op. cit., pp. 17–18.

35. Smith, op. cit., pp. 17, 25.

36. Hartt, (1993) op. cit., pp. 816–817.

37. Quoted in Jakob Rosenberg, (1969) "Rembrandt in His Century," in Harold Spencer, ed., *Readings in Art History*, vol. 2. New York: Charles Scribner and Sons, p. 191.

38. Rosenberg, op. cit., p. 194.

39. Smith, op. cit., p. 1.

40. Smith, op. cit., p. 16.

41. Ibid.

42. Smith, op. cit., p. 14.

43. Smith, op. cit., p. 62.

44. Smith, op. cit., pp. 1–3, 17, 25.

45. Smith, op. cit., p. 14.

46. Before 1600 the male ruff was loose and irregularly pleated. Thienen, op. cit., pp. 5–8.

47. Smith, op. cit., pp. 14–15, 44.

48. Smith, op. cit., p. 3.

49. Smith, op. cit., pp. 34–36

50. Smith, op. cit., p. 6.

51. Elison's somber clothing, his dignity, and the hand he lays on his heart in a conventional gesture of avowal are common attributes of a clergyman. This personal aura blends easily with the social norms appropriate to his age and profession, Smith pointed out. Soolman's manner and appearance, his aristocratic image with its shades of van Dyck, is a form of self-dramatization, heightening a flamboyant sense of self. Smith, op. cit. p. 6.

52. Simon Schama (1980) "Wives and Wantons: Versions of Womanhood in 17th-Century Dutch Art." *Oxford Art Journal*. April, pp. 5–13.

53. Schama, (1988) op. cit., p. 334.

4

The Public Child: Portraying Parental Power and Wealth

In much of Europe between 1500 and 1800 children were treated as little adults, as young persons requiring no special empathy. When they appeared in public, children were dressed in costumes that represented the family's social rank. The costumes of children of the higher classes were expected to uphold the family's claim to status and rank.

Upper-Class Children

A boy born to an aristocratic family initially wore dresses. Sometime between about six and seven years of age middle-and upper-middle class boys passed through a critically important *rite de passage* when the petticoats were shed and they were "breeched"—began to wear adult-style breeches.[1] "Boys were shifted from the long frocks of their childhood into the breeches and sword-carrying attire of the adult world."[2] The term "being undressed" meant not wearing the sword.[3] Boys who began wearing breeches and swords were shifted from the domain of their mothers to that of their fathers.

Children's attire mimicked the latest fashion. In their silk stockings, satin breeches, and embroidered coats, boys were turned into "exact replicas of their fathers," observed costume historian James Laver.[4] The attire was expensive, burdensome, and restrictive of movement.

The costume's ornament and trim were determined by the boy's parents. The sumptuousness of the fabric, the quality and detail of the attire, and the general lines of the period's desired appearance, the fashion, indicated the family's rank. During this period children were reared with utmost severity and discipline.[5]

Infants born to the royal family wore ostentatious costumes; the family used pomp and pageantry to display their divine association. From the

FIGURE 4.1   *The Birth of Louis XIII.* The queen has just given birth to a dauphin, heir to the throne. Peter Paul Rubens, 1621–1625. Louvre, Paris. Giraudon/Art Resource, N.Y. By permission.

moment Louis XIV was born (1638), everything he did he did in public, that is, surrounded by his court. Even the most trivial of events was celebrated: "He ate in public, went to bed in public, woke up and was groomed, urinated and defecated in public."[6] (See Fig. 4.1). Members of the royal court were almost always in attendance; it was an honor.

Princes and other noble personages displayed their rank vicariously. They were enabled to award their insignia and colors to their subjects.[7] Children of status and rank would remove parts of their clothing when they wanted to play.[8] Playing tennis, however, was not a leisure activity, as the formal dress in the accompanying picture of a young English prince reveals (see Fig. 4.2). It was considered training for skills a gentleman would need to move fast and think quickly. The prince was dressed in formal dress for tennis to get accustomed to the experience.

Dressing the child in miniature adult attire symbolized the continuity of the family's prerogatives, rights, and privileges. The belief in family continuity was basic to a culture where agriculture was the basic mode of subsistence. Mother Earth was viewed as the origin of all life; and humans, like other beings, were seen as springing from the earth and returning to it after death. Like the seasons, the generations followed each other.[9] Sterility was more than a serious affliction. It broke the cycle of na-

FIGURE 4.2 *Prince James Duke of Yorke.* Born Oct. 13, 1633. At the age of five he is playing tennis. Except for boots, he is wearing adult attire. Engraver, M. Merian, c. 1638. British Museum, Catalogue of Engraved British Portraits. By permission.

ture and disrupted the continuity of the family line. A baby's first steps were interpreted as a sign that the family would endure.

Accordingly, each person was tied by blood to the family. Though each person possessed a body of his or her own, the body was not totally one's own; it also belonged to the family. It was the family that was important, not the person. The individual was master of his or her body only to the extent that his or her desires did not contradict family interests.[10] As a result there was a conflict between what the family wanted and the right of the individual "to live his own life." In a sense, humans perpetuated life without being allowed to live it, contended French historian Jacques Giles. The principal duty of humans was to pass life on to the next generation.[11] The go-cart and leading strings in Figure 4.3 seem to symbolize the control the family exercised.

In England the emphasis was on the continuity of the male line. Given the uncertainty of survival, the procreation of a large number of children was desirable.[12] The hope was that at least one male child would live to

FIGURE 4.3   A Child in a Go-Cart Learning to Walk. He is wearing a frock, an apron with pointed bib, and leading strings. Artist unknown, 1650-1660. Norwich Castle Museum. By permission.

a marriageable age.[13] The rule of primogeniture, however, excluded younger sons and daughters from the bulk of the inheritance and the family title.[14] Younger sons hung around the estate or near it as a kind of walking sperm-bank, in case the eldest son died childless and had to be replaced.[15]

With the centralization of authority in England, France, and Spain, the societies were organized around a public display of rank. Rules of conduct were handed down by the king. The traditional personal tie between lord and vassal was replaced by a judiciary. Special persons were recruited by the king as judges to represent his authority. The role these dignitaries were expected to play and their rank were identified in their clothing—the wig, the gown, and perhaps a scepter. The royal court became the center of activity and, its offices, instead of those in the house of the feudal lord, became the focus of ambitious hopes. Members of the traditional aristocracy who inherited their titles, however, continued to wear the appropriate emblems (crests) and colors (russet, blue or green).[16]

At times children were awarded their own rank. In such a case they wore the costume that displayed their own social standing, rather than that of the family's. Louis XIV, for example, appointed some children as

FIGURE 4.4   *The Family of Charles I of England.* The children of Charles I are dressed in lavish fashions. They wear silk, lace, pearls, and threads of silver and gold, all alluding to parental rank. The infant is mostly naked, well formed, and healthy. He is reaching towards the dog, trying to pet him. The boy wears shoes decorated with roses like an adult's. Van Dyck. Alinari/Art Resources, N.Y. By permission.

colonels and cardinals—Monsieur de Fronsac was made colonel at age of seven, and the duc de Lauzan entered the French Guards at the age of twelve.[17]

These children, however, enjoyed no special benefits. They participated in festivals and public events. Speaking of his boyhood, the duc de Lauzan wrote that he was brought up like all other children. Like them he was helpless on his own and often needed servants to help him dress. His fine clothes were reserved for public appearance. At home, he was half-clothed and always hungry.[18]

Girls, it seems, were absent from public festivals. They were sent to a convent, often at a very early age. They remained there until they married.[19]

FIGURE 4.5   A Peasant Family's Clothing. In contrast to royalty, a peasant family's clothing has no superficial dazzle. Their clothes are simple and torn in some places. The children's feet are bare. Louis le Nain, 1593–1648, *Family of Peasants*, n.d. Louvre, Paris. Alinari/Art Resources, N.Y. By permission.

In the first half of the eighteenth century, some members of the English aristocracy clothed their children in a style more suitable for children, as seen in Joshua Reynolds's portrait of Viscount Althorp, for example. In silk, satin, and velvet, the clothes indicated access to wealth. Portraits of such boys show them at ease in their clothing. [20] In a painting from 1750 portraying a boy from an aristocratic family, the boy is depicted in a silk velvet suit with a matching satin waistcoat, both trimmed with decorative buttons. He is also wearing a shirt and stockings. The waistcoat has been left unbuttoned to display the shirt's ruffle. Attire expected of a son of wealthy parents was a silk coat, a linen shirt trimmed with lace, waistcoat, breeches, silk stockings, and high-heeled shoes. Boys could carry a sword or a cane and wear a powdered wig.[21]

Children of Working-Class Parents

Children of working-class parents were simply attired. They wore a tunic or coat, breeches or trousers of wool or leather, a coarse wool or linen shirt, wool stockings, and strong leather shoes. Peasants were often poor (see Fig. 4.5). They lived in rickety houses and smoke-filled

FIGURE 4.6 *The Wash Woman.* A working-class household, where the
expression of feeling is restrained. The child blows a bubble, suggesting
transience, while the mother looks sideways, as if waiting for someone to come
in. Chardin, 1740s. Louvre, Paris. Alinari/Art Resources, N.Y.

rooms. They were dressed mostly in rags. The clothes were ill-fitting,
torn, or full of gaping holes. Some children of the poor had even less
(See Fig. 4.6). Children who were orphans were dressed in uniforms
that charity schools provided. Their design was based on the style worn
by ordinary children. The object of these uniforms was to remind their
wearers of their servile state "and that they were objects of charity."[22]
For example, the uniform at the Blue Coat School in London, which was
founded in 1552, was based on the Tudor style.[23] Blue dye was the
cheapest, and blue was the color traditionally worn by servants, apprentices, and other humble groups. The students received a livery of
russet cotton, and at Easter they were issued one in blue.[24] The outfit
consisted of a coat long enough to reach the ankles, a leather belt,
yellow stockings (introduced in 1638), and linen neck band (substitut-
ing for the original Tudor ruff). The style was based on the ecclesiastical
cassock.[25]

In the early part of the sixteenth century a larger proportion of children began attending school. School uniforms, which often consisted of a black robe over one's clothing, were common. Flogging was the standard method of punishment for academic lapses. Martin Luther told of the "monotonous drumming of canes in his home and in school." He was moreover faced with a father "who had at his disposal techniques of making others feel morally inferior."[26] He was sent to school at the age of seven where the teachers drummed facts and habits into the growing minds by mechanical repetition and "on the behind," other parts being exempt.[27] Neither a schoolboy nor a university student was permitted to appear in public in anything but a uniform. The threat of physical punishment accompanied the rule. Wearing the uniform marked Luther as one of a particular class, the literate one. While wearing his uniform, he abstained from throwing snowballs and other frivolous activities, even ice-skating. Instead he used his musical gifts, his lute-playing and singing, to remain a "welcome goodfellow" among his circle of friends.[28]

In contrast, school uniforms for members of the upper class seem to appear about two hundred years later, in the eighteenth century. The uniforms are those of secondary school students, highly picturesque and elegant, J. T. Smith recalled in his *Book for a Rainy Day*.[29] He told of the uniforms worn by boys attending Mr. Founteyne's boarding school: "My youthful eyes were dazzled with the various colors of the dresses of the youth, who walked two by two, some in pea green, others in sky blue and several in the brightest scarlets; some of them wore gold laced hats, while the flowing locks of others, allowed to remain uncut in schools, fell over their shoulders."[30]

Infant Attire

Infant attire supported physical and emotional suppression. During the first four months after birth strips of fabric were tightly wound around the body to hold the head, body, and limbs together. Later the arms were freed but the legs and body remained bound. This practice of "swaddling" (see Fig. 4.7) immobilized infants and physically isolated them from the hectic immediate surroundings. The medical reason behind the practice, historian Lawrence Stone observed, was the fear that because of their tenderness the limbs would "bow, bend and take diverse shapes."[31] There was also the widespread fear that unless restrained the infant might tear off its ears, scratch out its eyes, or break its legs.[32]

Swaddling slows down the infant's heartbeat and induces longer sleep and less crying. Swaddling converted a wriggling, squirming baby into a neat manageable bundle that could be transported like a parcel. It could also be left unattended in odd corners, or hung on a peg on the wall with-

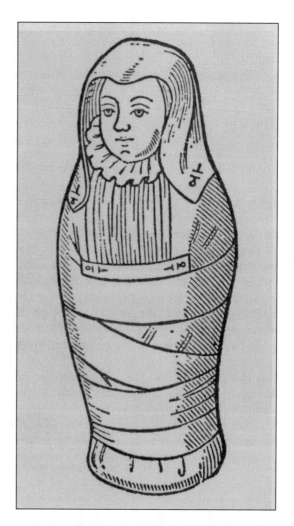

FIGURE 4.7
Swaddled Infant.
Richard Best, d. 1587.
Merstham Church,
Surrey.

out danger of being trampled on by the stream of people and animals coming in and going out of the household.[33] The practice of swaddling also meant that unless the nurse or mother was willing to unwind and wind up the bands, which was a very tedious process, the infant child would be left for hours to lie in its own excrement.[34] By the early eighteenth century swaddling was falling into disfavor, and infants wore diapers (called clouts) and long dresses.[35]

Towards the end of their first year, when children began to learn to walk, they wore ankle-length dresses and no diapers underneath.[36] In England, little boys were kept in skirts and frilly underwear (an undergarment enclosing the lower trunk and having an independent sheath for all or part of each leg) until about the age of five. Since white was prevalent, it was difficult for them to move about and play without dirtying their clothing. Thus their fear of punishment prevented young children from taking part in games and hampered initiative and the taking of risk.

Girls

To return to the earlier period, once removed from the swaddling bandages the boys were left relatively free, but beginning in the sixteenth century and through much of the nineteenth century, in England and France, girls were encased in bodices and corsets reinforced with iron and whalebone to ensure that their bodies were molded to the prevailing adult fashion. Girls of all social classes wore simplified versions of their mothers' attire. The separation of bodice and skirt became fashionable at the beginning of the sixteenth century, and it was now possible to make the bodice straighter and tighter and the skirt fuller. In order to keep the bodice straight and tight a heavy under-bodice was used.[37] Dressed in miniature adult clothes, girls were expected to conform to the ideal adult feminine shape and carriage. In particular, they were expected to maintain an upright posture and to walk slowly and gracefully.[38]

The practice of putting young girls in corsets often led to the distortion or displacement of the organs sometimes even death, concluded historian Lawrence Stone. He told about the death in 1665 of Elizabeth, George Evelyn's two-year-old daughter. The physician attributed the death to the iron bodice that thwarted the development of her lungs and so pressed on the breastbone that two of her ribs were broken. The bodice hampered her ability to breathe, bringing about death.[39]

Discipline

Except for children of royal birth, there was a strict demand for a child's total obedience. Despite Luther's criticism of physical punishment, it continued to be popular at home and at school. Caning and whipping was a common practice for children who violated paternal injunctions. Physical punishment was based on the traditional Christian view that the child is born in sin and the only hope of holding it in check is by the ruthless repression of its will.[40] Much of the children's literature in England before the nineteenth century was filled with stories threatening divine vengeance for sin.[41]

Children were expected to submit to parental authority. Through much of this period, childrearing practices consisted of adults attempting to exact obedience from children. Children, recipients of adults' "wisdom,"

FIGURE 4.8   *The Father's Illness, or, The Punished Child.* Feelings of sorrow and guilt were the family's vocabulary of interaction. Members of the family are visibly upset at the father's condition. An alienated son returns and is overcome with guilt. Greuze, 1778. Louvre, Paris. Giraudon/Art Resource, N.Y. By permission.

were treated with utmost severity and discipline. To get children home on time, for example, adults frightened them with a variety of tales about spirits and devils or threatened them with the bogeyman.[42] Isabella de Moerloose wrote that she was severely beaten by her mother, who believed she was possessed by an evil spirit. Her mother tried to drive the evil spirits away by administering "a rain of blows." These made a deep impression on her. Years later she was still frightened by her mother and would burst into tears if her mother was unfriendly to her.[43]

Breaking the child's will was the prime aim of early education. From the stress on domestic discipline and the utter subordination of the child it naturally followed that children were expected to demonstrate deference to adults. It was customary for children to kneel before their parents every morning to ask for their blessing. Even when grown up, sons were expected to keep their hats off in their parents' presence, while daughters were expected to kneel or stand in their mothers' presence. The child's total submission to clergy, parents, schoolmaster, and others in authority was typical.[44] Through harsh discipline children were encouraged to follow the path set by their parents. Those who rebelled were expected to experience bitter repentance eventually (see Fig. 4.8).

Self and Feelings

Philosophers and artists such as Locke, Rousseau, and Greuze, rejected this narrow and gloomy understanding of childhood. In their writings and in their art they offered more joyful and life-giving alternatives.

John Locke (1632–1704) rejected the goal of absolute paternal authority as desirable for children and society. His views initiated public discourse, a discourse that encouraged a new view of children, their education, and their clothing. In an essay called *False Principles* (1690) Locke argued that the authority for bringing children up belongs to both parents, not just the father. He explained that the contention that authority over a child belongs to the father is based the biblical idea that Adam was the creator of humankind, the claim that "Adam's title to sovereignty gives control over children only to fathers."[45] People who use this claim, Locke argued, do not remember that God is the true creator. They use the monarchic model of power to exercise control over their children. They are "dazzled" with thoughts of royal power.

Both parents make their children, giving them life and being; therefore, "nobody would deny but that the woman hath an equal share, if not the greater as nourishing the child a long time in her body out of her own substance. There it is fashioned and from her it receives the materials and principles of its constitution."[46] The mother, thus, cannot be denied an equal share in begetting the child.

Children are not little adults and have no evil character, Locke argued. Children should be viewed as *innocent* of previous knowledge, free from sin, and deserving of no punishment. Parents and educators should attend to the child as if it were a "tabula rasa," an unmarked slate upon which to inscribe beliefs, behaviors, and knowledge.[47].

Given the opportunity, children can develop two types of identities, one social and one personal. A social identity is acquired through a consciousness of self within a social context. Observations, experiences, and relationships encourage the mind to compare things. When we examine them in time and place we form ideas about who and what we are, making it possible for an identity to emerge, Locke suggested.[48]

A personal identity is different from a social identity in that it is a subjective phenomenon. It emanates from consciousness of processes taking place within the person. It involves a person being able to recognize that there is "something" that is himself, that he might be concerned or happy about—a person who is aware of his own happiness or misery. An intelligent being, a being that reasons, reflects, and can consider itself as itself, can develop a personal identity.[49] In this way, Locke argued for a sense of self independent from one's parents.

About seventy-five years later in France, Jean Jacques Rousseau argued against the mistreatment of children, including the practice of swaddling, in *Julie* and *La Nouvelle Heloise*." (1761) In *Emile* (1762) Rousseau wrote:

> Is there any creature in the world weaker, more unprotected, more at the mercy of his surroundings, more in need of pity, of love, of protection, than a child? Is not this the reason why the first sounds which nature prompts are cries and laments, why she has given him, so sweet and touching an appearance, that all who approach him may sympathize with his frailty and hasten to his assistance?[50]

The practice of swaddling, Rousseau attributed to the desire of wet nurses to avoid trouble.[51] Handing the newborn baby to a wet nurse he considered child neglect. "Do these polished mothers who, escaped from their children, indulge themselves gaily in the amusements of the town know the treatment which their innocent babes in their swathing are enduring in the country?" Rousseau asked.[52] Mothering is a natural instinct that comes with giving birth, Rousseau argued. He believed that the child who is given away to be suckled by another woman misses out on nurturance. "Has a child less need of a mother's tenderness than of her breast?" Rousseau asked. Other women can give the baby the milk, but the tenderness of a mother cannot be given, since it is acquired only through the process of giving birth.[53] Rousseau explained that the tenderness a mother feels while nursing her child will revive her heart. Feelings that had been given up will flow, and make mother and father more dear to one another, "binding the marriage tie more fast."[54]

Inculcating obedience is in the interest of adults, not of children, Rousseau contended. The practice leads to a child being treated as an adult. Man and child should be assigned their own distinct and separate places. A man should be considered a man and the child a child, Rousseau argued. In nature, a child is wholly different from the adult.[55] "As mankind has a place in the world, so has childhood its place in human life."[56]

Boys should be left to grow free. They must be put into situations where they can take risks. Education must "follow nature," that is, it must take into account a child's level of development and his natural interests and activities.[57]

Locke and Rousseau argued against the notion that children are little adults and against physical punishment. They encouraged physical freedom and proposed that the growth and development of children should be the focus of parents and society.

FIGURE 4.9 *Saying Grace.* A middle-class household, where mother and children are fashionably dressed, almost doll-like figures. Their appearance suggests that domestic life is orderly. All emotions seem to be in check. Chardin, 1740. Louvre, Paris. Alinari/Art Resources, N.Y. By permission.

Artists in France echoed Locke's and Rousseau's sentiments. They offered a love-and-happiness model for family interaction. Rather than a burden, children were sources of joy.

In the painting, *Farewell to the Nurse* (1776), Etienne Aubry (1745–1781) portrays the confusion a child suffers when he is pried away from his wet nurse and placed in the arms of a stranger, his mother. The painting also suggests that a father and mother suffer a loss when they give their baby away at birth. In the scene, the natural father, a fashionably dressed man, stands aloof from the drama taking place in front of him. He stands in marked contrast to the peasant husband, who openly expresses his attachment to the baby. Meanwhile, the unhappy baby squirms to get out of the arms of his natural mother and into those of his wet nurse.[58]

Encouraging the diffusion of the nuclear family ideal in France were other paintings of a conjugal couple and their children in the mid–1750s and 1760s. Ideas of a loving father and a happy, good mother were introduced to the public.[59] Earlier portrayals of domestic life, such as those of Chardin (1699–1779) in the 1740s, show a life that is pleasant and full of simple charm (see Fig. 4.9), in contrast to the emotionality and drama

FIGURE 4.10 *The Bible Lesson.* The father is the central figure in the family. The painting embodies Rousseau's belief that the poor are full of natural virtue and honest sentiment. Greuze, 1725–1805. Louvre, Paris. Giraudon/Art Resource, N.Y. By permission.

that came to characterize the art of the mid-1750s and 1760s.[60] At the same time, these pictures demonstrated the obliviousness of a figure or a groups of figures to everything outside their own sphere. The characters are shown absorbed in each other.[61] Denis Diderot, a renowned critic of French art, pronounced that Greuze's (1725–1805) pictures in the 1750s and 1760s were not simply pleasant to look at, they spoke of cultural preferences and of vital moral issues.[62]

Although some critics dismissed Greuze's work as "pandering to the masses," in his *Un Père de famille qui lit la Bible à ses enfants* (Salon of 1755) (see Fig. 4.10), for example, others during that period disagreed. French art critic abbé de la Porte praised the painting for its artistic merit and at the time described it in this manner:

A father reading the Bible to his children. Moved by what he has just read, he is himself imbued with the moral he is imparting to them; his eyes are almost moist with tears. His wife, a rather beautiful woman whose beauty is not ideal but of a kind that can be encountered in people of her condition, is listening to him with that air of tranquility enjoyed by an honest woman surrounded by a large family that constitutes her sole occupation, her pleasures and her glory. Next to her, her daughter is astounded and grieved by what she hears. The older brother's facial expression is as singular as it is true. The little boy, who is making an effort to grab a stick on the table and who is paying no attention whatsoever to things he cannot understand, is perfectly true to life. Do you not see how he does not distract anyone, everyone being too seriously occupied? What nobility and what feelings in this grandmother who, without turning her attention from what she hears, mechanically restrains the little rogue who is making the dog growl! Can you not hear how he is teasing it by making horns at it? What a painter! What a composer!"[63]

La Porte's commentary, art historian Fried observed, makes clear what he found compelling in the painting—a persuasive representation of the state of rapt attention. The figures seem to be engrossed in what they are doing, La Porte pointed out, calling attention to the absorptive activity of the adults and to the potentially disruptive activities of the two youngest children. Another critic, Baillet de Saint Julien, suggested that the potentially disruptive actions of the two children served to heighten the intense absorption of the other figures, their lack of awareness of being beheld.[64]

To demonstrate the change that had taken place, Greuze's family pictures were contrasted by art historian Carol Duncan to those of Chardin. In Chardin's *Saying Grace* (see Fig. 4.9), painted around 1740, before he integrated naturalism and absorption into his work, the mother and her children seem almost doll-like and their expressions are merely pert.[65]

Children as objects imbued with the powers of nature, rather than that of their parents, was a vision offered by the German painter Philip Otto Runge (1777–1810). *The Hülsenbeck Children*, (1805–1806) (see Fig. 4.11), shows the three young children ages two, four, and five, of Runge's brother's friend Friedrich August Hülsenbeck. Instead of portraying them as was customary, as little adults or cuddly angels, Runge depicts the children here as transmitting a force and vitality whose origin is nature. The children appear as objects belonging to the organic realm of the sun, trees and flowers, observed art historian Robert Rosenblum.[66]

August, age four, and Maria, age five, seem to rise to twice the height of the picket fence behind them.[67] August is wearing a skeleton suit which moves with the motion of the body. A dark shirt with a white collar and calf-length boots complete his attire. He is facing the viewer almost abreast. His left foot solid on the ground and his right foot raised as if poised for action, he is standing on his toes. In his right hand he is holding a twig and his arm is raised as if he is ready to strike.[68]

FIGURE 4.11 *The Hülsenbeck Children.* Runge conceived of children as full of the life force of nature. As organic beings they belong within the realm of animals, trees, and flowers. The boy, August, is shown in a skeleton suit, as he freely moves his arms and legs. Philip Otto Runge, 1805–1806. Kunsthalle, Hamburg. Museum photo.

Maria is wearing a simple, unstructured, short-sleeved, and delicately ornamented dress, which reaches down to just below the calf. With neither a corset nor a bonnet to constrain her movement she seems free. Her hair is short and patterned like artichoke leaves or sunflower petals.[69]

These two young giants are pulling with what seems a heroic force a wheelbarrow barely containing their two-year-old brother Friedrich, who is clinging to a stalk of a wild clamp of sunflowers. His face is glowing and his stare intense.

Runge had studied botany, and for him plants and children manifested earthly evidence of nature as a spiritual force. Children whether young or old contained biological truths and symbolic mysteries.[70] In his art, Runge attempts to provide a new symbolic language of what is important in art, nature and religion, observed Rosenblum.[71]

The ideas of philosophers and artists had a limited impact on the style of nineteenth-century children's clothes. There seem, however, to have been two exceptions. The new reason for dressing babies and young children completely in white was to emphasize innocence. Infants' limbs were no longer considered "limbs of Satan," suggested costume historian Clare Rose (1989).[72]

The skeleton suit was developed in England around 1780. It was a jumper-coveralls garment for boys ages two to four. [73] It had a very high waist, narrow shoulders, and full trousers. A slit in the side along each seam allowed the back to be let down. There was also a front fly which closed with a buttoned flap. A favorite feature was the buttons trimming the outfit. They were often in flat mother-of-pearl or brass. The skeleton suit enabled boys to play, jump, and run. Since it was different from anything girls or women wore, it enabled boys to learn of their gender identity earlier. In 1787 a German fashion magazine advertised the skeleton suit as "functional and comfortable clothing for children based on the ideas and theories of John Locke."[74]

Notes

1. Elizabeth Ewing, (1977) *History of Children's Costume*. New York: Charles Scribner's Sons, p. 32.

2. Lawrence Stone, (1977) *The Family, Sex, and Marriage in England, 1500–1800*. New York: Harper and Row, p. 409.

3. Stone, op. cit., p. 410.

4. James Laver, (1960) *Viyella*. Nottingham, England: William Hollins, p. 7.

5. Percy Macquoid, (1923) *Four Hundred Years of Children's Costumes, From the Great Masters 1400–1800*. London: The Medici Society, p. 99

6. Michael Mann, (1986) *The Source of Social Power*. Cambridge: Cambridge University Press, p. 459.

7. Phillipe Braunstein (1988) "Towards Intimacy: The Fourteenth and Fifteenth Centuries," in Georges Duby, ed., A *History of Private Life: Revelations of the Medieval World*, trans. Arthur Goldhammer. Cambridge, Mass.: Belknap Press of Harvard University Press, pp. 577–578

8. In an illustration called *A desco da parto* (c. 1430), Tuscan School, the boys have stripped to their shirt and hose for ease of movement. In Jacqueline Herald, (1981) *Renaissance Dress in Italy*. London: Bell & Hyman, p. 62.

9. Jacques Gelis (1989) "The Child: From Anonymity to Individuality," in Roger Chartier, ed., A *History of Private Life*, vol. 3, trans. Arthur Goldhammer. Cambridge, Mass.: Belknap Press of Harvard University Press, p. 309.

10. Gelis, op. cit., p. 310.

11. Ibid.

12. A popular children's story constructed around this theme was Frances Hodgson Burnett's (1886) *Little Lord Fauntleroy* (New York: Charles Scribner's Son's). It tells of a seven-year-old American boy, Cedric Errol, born in New York City, who is taken to England to the home his father had been banished from because his older brothers had been expected to continue the family line. They, however, had died, and so had his father. Now the American-born Cedric is to inherit the family title and estates, to become a member of the nobility. Throughout the story the child is portrayed wearing clothing in the style of the aristocracy: over-the-knee breeches, a soft white lace collar, wide white cuffs, and shoulder-length flowing blond hair.

13. Stone, op. cit., pp. 42–43

Also, in 1762, there were 15,351 births; burials for children under the age of five during that year numbered 10,659. G. F. Still, (1931) *History of Pediatrics*. London: Oxford University Press, pp. 455–456.

14. Stone, op. cit., pp. 42–43.

15. Stone, op. cit., p. 88.

16. Mann, op. cit., p. 460.

17. Macquoid, op. cit., 'p. 1.

18. Ibid.

19. Macquoid, op. cit., p. 99.

20. Macquoid, op. cit., p. 98.

21. Ewing, op. cit., p. 45.

22. A statement by Bishop Butler, quoted in Ewing, op. cit., p. 32.

23. Ewing, op. cit. p. 32.

24. Ewing, op. cit., p. 33.

25. Ibid.

26. Erik H. Erikson, (1962) *Young Man Luther*. New York: W. W. Norton, p. 67.

27. Erikson, op. cit., p. 78.

28. Erikson, op. cit., pp. 82–83.

29. Ewing, op. cit., p. 37.

30. Quoted in Ewing, op. cit., p. 37.

31. Stone, op. cit., pp. 161–162.

32. Stone, op. cit., p. 162.

33. Ibid. Also, Jo B. Paoletti and Carol L. Kregloh (1989) "The Children's Department," in Claudia B. Kidwell and Valerie Steele, eds., *Men and Women Dressing the Part*. Washington, D. C.: Smithsonian Institution, p. 25.

34. Stone, op. cit., p. 160.

35. Paoletti and Kregloh, op. cit., p. 25.

36. Ibid.

37. Norah Waugh (1954) *Corsets and Crinolines*. Boston: Boston Book and Art Shop, pp. 17–19.

38. Stone, op. cit., p. 162.

39. Stone, op. cit., p. 162.

40. Stone, op. cit., pp. 405–406.

41. Stone, op. cit., p. 410.

42. Herman W. Roodenburg "The Autobiography of Isabella Moerloose: Sex, Childbearing and Popular Belief in Seventeenth Century Holland," *Journal of Social History*.

43. Roodenburg, op. cit., p. 524.

44. Stone, op. cit., pp. 163–164.

45. The essay is aimed at refuting the doctrine of absolute monarchy founded on divine right, as expressed in the book *Patriarcha* (1680) by Sir Robert Filmer. John Locke, (1690/1953) *Two Treatises Of Civil Government*. New York: Dutton, p. x; p. 36.

46. Locke, *Two Treatises of Civil Government*, op. cit., p. 39.

47. Locke, (1693), *Some Thoughts Concerning Education*, quoted in Jo B. Paoletti, Carol L. Kregloh, op. cit. pp. 24–25.

48. John Locke (1690/1979)*An Essay Concerning Human Understanding*, ed. Peter H. Nidditch. Oxford: Clarendon Press, pp. 187, 328–348.

49. Locke, *Human Understanding*, op. cit., pp. 341–342.

50. *Jean Jacques Rousseau: Emile, Julie and other Writings*, (1964) ed. R. L. Archer and S. E. Frost. Woodbury, New York: Barron's Educational Series, p. 37.

51. Rousseau, op. cit., p. 72.

52. Ibid., p. 72; also, *Emile* Book 1.

53. *Emile*, Book 1, op. cit., pp. 72–73.

54. *Emile*, Book 1, op. cit., p. 74.

55. Rousseau, op. cit., see Biographical Note.

56. Rousseau, op. cit., p. 89.

57. Rousseau, op. cit., p. 11.

58. Carol Duncan (1973) "Happy Mothers and Other New Ideas in French Art," *Art Bulletin* 55, p. 575.

59. Duncan, op. cit., p. 577.

60. Duncan, op. cit., p. 570.

61. Michael Fried (1972) *Absorption and Theatricality: Painting and the Beholder in the Age of Diderot*. Berkeley: University of California Press, p. 66.

62. Fried, op. cit., p. 3.

63. La Porte's description of the painting as quoted by Michael Fried, op. cit., p. 10.

64. Fried, op. cit., pp. 11, 122.

65. See Fried, op. cit., pp. 13–15.

66. Robert Rosenblum (1984) *19th-Century Art*. New York: Harry N. Abrams, p. 85.

67. Ibid.

68. Ibid.

69. Ibid.

70. Rosenblum, op. cit., p. 84.

71. Rosenblum, op. cit., p. 86.

72. Clare Rose, (1989) *Children's Clothes Since 1750*. New York: Drama Book Publishers. Reference in the Victoria and Albert Museum.

73. In the nineteenth century Charles Dickens described the skeleton suit in this manner: "A skeleton suit, one of those straight blue cloth cases in which small boys used to be confined . . . [giving their] legs the appearance of being hooked on just under the arm pits." Quoted in Rose, op. cit., p. 53.

74. Quoted in Rose, op. cit., pp. 52–53.

5

Children's Clothes in Colonial America, 1609–1800

In Colonial America[1] parental social rank and secular and religious aspirations guided the choice of children's attire. Children were dressed in
miniature versions of adult clothing, and a child's social identity, for the
most part, was based on that of the parents.[2] In those areas where parents
desired the trappings of nobility and aristocracy, the well-to-do insisted
on their children wearing sumptuous, fashionable attire. The Puritans
based their orientation to clothes in part on the Calvinist belief that economic success suggested being among the "elect" (those designated by
God to achieve salvation); and that stylish appearance reflected righteous
conduct. They dressed their children in the latest adult style.[3]

Quakers, Mennonites, and Moravians dressed their children according
to the precepts of their churches—plain and austere. Decorations, such as
ornate buttons, braids, ribbons, plumes, laces, shiny surfaces, and bright
colors, anything that would give the appearance of vanity or luxury, was
shunned. Moreover, throughout the Colonial period their attire bor-
rowed sparingly from changing fashions, modifying their established
sober style only slightly.[4]

From the beginning children's dress was intertwined with ideology
and had symbolic significance. Except for Jonathan Edwards (1703–1758)
and other religious thinkers who emerged in the early part of the eighteenth century preaching the "utter depravity of man," for most of the
Colonial period settlers shared Calvinist beliefs regarding children.[5] In
particular, they believed that the infant child was intrinsically limited by
its heritage of sin, and that sin expressed itself "in excess" or pride of
will. Salvation, it was thought, depended on the parents' strict training in
the ways of the Lord and on the child's absolute obedience. The pleasure-
loving child would surely be on the road to perdition.[6] Breaking the
child's will, they believed, was essential to upholding moral virtue.

Grownups were relentless in getting children to sit and stand erect. Children were assigned adult-like responsibilities, boys at the age of six or seven[7] and girls at the age of three or four.[8]

In Boston, standard advice to parents on how to control their children was to teach them to fear death and eternal damnation. The following example is from the diary of Samuel Sewall of Boston. In 1690 a nine-year-old boy died of smallpox. Sewall thought it was a good opportunity to teach his eight-year-old son Samuel about death. He warned his son that he needed to prepare for death. Later that day the boy burst into a bitter cry and said he was afraid that he was going to die. Nine years later, in 1696, Sewall's fifteen-year-old daughter, Betty, also burst out crying. She explained that she was afraid she was going to go to Hell, because her sins had not been pardoned.[9]

Differences between the costumes children wore in Colonial America and those worn in Europe were quite minor, observed costume historian Alice Morse Earle.[10] The styles of children's clothes in America during the colonial centuries were much like those in England, France, and Holland. For example, boys in America wore lace collars that had a straight edge. Lace collars worn by children in England were in the Van Dyck style; they had a deeply pointed edge (as a painting of the Duke of Orange reveals). Boys of French descent were drawn to French fashion— wigs, swords and ruffles—and Dutch boys' fashionable attire had wider pants than those worn by other boys.[11] By the stylishness and sumptuousness of their dress children of the well-to-do could be distinguished from poorer children regardless of their country of origin.

In his study "Infancy and Childhood in the Plymouth Colony," however, John Demos suggested that infant attire may have been less restrictive in America and that mothers were more nurturing. He found an attitude of concern and tenderness towards infants and no evidence of swaddling or otherwise binding the child to restrict movement.[12] The infant wore a smock, some type of linen, and was kept warm under several layers of woolen blankets. It appears that a baby's nourishment consisted entirely of breast milk and infants seem to have had easy access to their mothers' breasts. Demos attributes this sympathetic attitude towards infants to the high mortality rate during the first year of life (approximately one in ten).[13]

Infants were often more elaborately dressed than older children. It began before birth, when the mother prepared and embroidered special garments. Christening was a major event and the formalities were observed even by the austere Pilgrims. The event was celebrated on two accounts, as a sacrament of the church and as a family landmark. It was a time of rejoicing, good wishes, and gift-giving. Lavishness and expense characterized the christening dress.[14]

This was in contrast to the experience of Protestants in the Swiss city-state of Zurich. Ordinances of 1612, 1637, and 1650 limited the celebration of baptism by controlling expenditure. Both gifts and festivities were restricted. Costly materials such as satin and silk, and ornaments of gold, silver, ribbons, or feathers were prohibited. Money gifts were also restricted.[15]

In America, the ceremony involved the minister dressing the child in a white robe, called a chrismale or a chrisome, that had been anointed with sacred oil. If the infant died within the month of the ceremony he or she would be buried in the robe and called a chrisome-child. The robe was also called a bearing cloth or christening sheet.[16]

A christening blanket was also part of the ensemble. It was usually made of silk, often richly embroidered with a text from the scriptures, initials, emblems. It was often lace bordered. The christening blanket of Governor Bradford of the Plymouth Colony is owned by a descendant. It is still whole and unfaded. It is made out of rich crimson silk, with sprays of flowers in pink and yellow embroidered six inches apart. A whole inventory of clothing—a cap, apron, bib, cuffs, shirts, petticoats, and mittens—were part of the christening attire.

White is the color of the lily and usually symbolizes purity.[17] Yellow was also a desirable color, because a golden yellow is the emblem of divinity[18] and therefore proper for pledging the child to God. Scarlet or crimson laid over the head was said to keep an infant from harm.[19]

As in Europe, babies were considered unwisely and improperly dressed without a close-fitting linen or lace cap. It was thought that caps protected babies from earaches. Hence, babies wore caps day and night, and for days at a time.[20] Often the cap was attached to the baby's clothes.[21] Caps, like the other elements of an infant's attire, were starched stiffly. Sometimes the entire cap was padded, but most often the padding came in a thick roll that circled the head; it was called a "pudding" cap. The padding protected the head from injury if the baby fell. Leading strings, a long dress, aprons, collars, and cuffs were the other elements of a young child's wardrobe.

Suggesting further that care, nurturing, and protection characterized early mother-child interaction (before the age of six) are the hanging sleeves and leading strings. Long hanging sleeves were at the back of the arm and fell to the skirt's hem. These sleeves were held by an older person to help the young child walk, run, or climb. Leading strings were ribbons, often made of linen or satin and decorated with crewel embroidery, and sewn to the back of the dress bodice.[22] Outdoors, leading strings were often tied to a tree or fence post. Measuring five feet in length, leading strings gave the child space within which to play.[23]

FIGURE 5.1 *Jacques De Peyster.* He wears the style of an upper-class Dutch child, a dress and a lace-trimmed apron; a large lace capelet covers the shoulders. The dress, made out of silk, has a contrasting color sash with a jeweled fringe. A chain dangles from under the sash, to which a toy rattle is attached. Anonymous Dutch artist, 1631. Collection of James De Peyster Jr., N.Y.

The Dutch had brought with them the custom of dressing young children in long "hanging sleeves."[24] There is evidence that Mary, Queen of Scots, made a pair for her baby, James, future king of England.[25] The popular and insistent use of hanging sleeves became a metaphor used in literature and in common speech. Earle told the following story. When Benjamin Franklin was seven years old he wrote a poem, which he sent to his uncle. His uncle responded with the following:

> *'Tis time for me to throw aside my pen*
> *When Hanging-Sleeves read, write and rhyme like men.*
> *This forward Spring foretells a plenteous crop*
> *For if the bud bear grain, what will the top?*[26]

Hanging sleeves came to mean innocence and youth, but they also referred to second childhood and a romance sought by an older man.[27] In 1720, Judge Samuel Sewall, of Boston, who was about seventy-five years old, wrote to another old gentleman whose widowed sister he desired to marry. He wrote:

FIGURE 5.2 *Margaret Gibbs*. She is painted in a fashionable French-style dress, which indicates the family's wealth. Anonymous, 1670. Collection of Mrs. Elsie Q. Giltinan, Charleston, W. Va.

I remember when I was going from school at Newberry to have sometimes met your sisters Martha and Mary in Hanging Sleeves, coming from their school in Chandlers Lane, and have had the pleasure of speaking to them. And I could find it in my heart now to speak to Mrs. Martha again, now I see myself reduc'd to Hanging Sleeves.[28]

The range of clothing styles available to older children was narrow. A boy wore an underdress with ankle-length skirt until he was about six years of age, when he was dressed in adult-style male costume, a buff coat and breeches. On occasion buttonholes and pockets were outlined in braid. Though these adornments were useless, the effect was that of an adult coat.[29] A boy's outfit sometimes included a small-scale sword,[30] and he was encouraged to strut and act as manly as he could.[31] Children's necks, however, were spared the ruff that at the time was in style.[32] Reports from the period note that in order to play, boys took off the long coats and sometimes the vests and loosened the tight waistband. This caused the shirttail to fly and the breeches and stockings to fall.[33]

Girls' dress (see Fig. 5.2) mimicked that of their mothers. They were put into stays when they were four. Many wore stays that were stiffened with wooden busk to assure an erect carriage. Sometimes at about six or seven girls would be strapped to a "backboard" so that they would stand and walk erect. They wore hats and carried accessories like their mothers—fans, for example. Their shoes were made out of delicate leathers and silks, with the same type of high heels that their mother wore. Girls were discouraged from running and playing. Many primly sat for hours.[34]

The Virginia Planters

The planters of Virginia came to America during the reigns of Queen Elizabeth I and King James I. They focused on agriculture, in hopes of instituting an aristocratic way of life. When they arrived they were wearing the current British mode, which was influenced by the "Spanish bombast" style. It consisted of a padded trunk, hose stockings reaching the knees, a doublet made of stiffened materials tapered to the waist, and a white linen shirt. Close-fitting sleeves were sometimes attached at the shoulders and lace cuffs adorned the wrists. A pleated ruff or a wide upstanding collar encircled the throat.[35]

Manufacturing was not allowed in the colonies in the seventeenth and eighteenth centuries. Fashionable attire was costly. Under British mercantile policy the colonies were to serve as suppliers of raw materials and consumers of British manufactured goods.[36] The planters exchanged their agricultural products in England for fashionable attire for their children and themselves. Measurements and details were communicated to their agents in England.[37]

Members of the planter class ruled their estates as feudal lords in medieval Europe did, often using physical force on their slaves. As the planters grew richer they built houses "as large and pretentious as their wealth allowed".[38] They were built on or near some navigable water way with their own landing stage and their own ships.[39] Once a year in late spring or early summer the tobacco ships nosed up, unloading bales of stuffs and chests of fine clothing, made to measure by English tailors and French dress-makers, for the planters and their children. Their agents in London arranged payment for last year's crop. The American homespun linens and woolens that existed in 1675 were considered too coarse and the local tailors "too inexpert for an exacting taste."[40] Social pressure on the planters and parental pressure on their children was such that parent and child had to get new fashions every year for each shipment of tobacco.[41] (We are referring, of course, only to the upper class or gentry.)

The New England Merchants

The merchant class of New England (1620–1675) had its roots in the Puritan communities of England, which were compact, versatile, and democratic.[42] The Pilgrims, the first Protestants to arrive, were poor and had suffered religious persecution, and to outfit their expedition they mortgaged themselves to a group of London merchants for a term of seven years. They set themselves to the task of clearing and planting; to working out their destiny in the New World. The Pilgrims' revolt against all excess and worldly show found its principal expression in dress. Their garments conformed in general shape to the prevailing fashions in England, but being short of money, they wore the older fashion of rigid doublet, trunk hose, and ruff. Their clothing, moreover, was stripped of all the elements associated with loose-living gallants of the royal court.[43] They abstained from handsome fabrics, such as silks, satins, and velvets, in favor of leather jerkins and breeches made of strong cloth canvas, leather, wool, a cotton called broadcloth, and fustian.[44] Moreover, their garments, for the most part, were stripped of all ornaments: braids, ribbons, laces, large decorated buttons. In the early years they filled in with makeshift hide and fur. Little girls, like their mothers, wore a skirt and bodice and a heavy cloak with a hood.[45]

The Puritan exodus from England took place about ten years after that of the Pilgrims in 1620. A high proportion of the Puritans were educated and wealthy. They were landowners, merchants, yeomen, tenant farmers, preachers, and professional men. They arrived well equipped to carry on with their trades and professions. The wealthier ones brought with them servants, laborers, and household gear, and wore the latest fashion in rich, sober colors—a longer and looser doublet, breeches, and a falling collar.[46]

The Puritans believed that dress had a moral effect: To dress orderly and well in the prevailing style helped to preserve the morals of the individual and the welfare of the community.[47]

Puritan preachers denounced extravagance in dress. They exhorted the flock against excess in dress and absurd extremes, such as "petticoat-breeches." The church published lists of prohibited garments, such as big floppy boots and beaver hats, which were expensive. The attempt was unsuccessful. Anyone who wanted to wear them wore them.[48]

The severe garb of the Pilgrims, the more religiously zealous group, is often ascribed to the Puritans. The Puritan members of the merchant class wore, by and large, sumptuous attire just like the planters of Virginia colony, the high fashions of England and France. It was the dress of the clergy that was severe and that conforms to our present-day image of "Puritan dress."[49]

The quality and style of clothing of the children of the well-to-do Puritans was just as rich as the dress of the children of the nobility in England and that of the planters in the south. It was also just as cumbersome. The five-year-old Daniel Ravenel, for example, wore a frock with spreading

FIGURE 5.3 *Young Man with Deer.* A portrait of a De Peyster family member. Painted according to the courtly model, the trimmed and ornamented costume indicates high social rank. Attr. Gerardus Duyckinck, 1730–1735. New York Historical Society.

petticoats that touched the ground (see Fig. 5.3 for a similar costume), tight-fitting, trim waistcoat with silver buttons and lace, as Earle observed.[50] Made of rich velvet or brocade, and lined with heavy black buckram, the bodice of girls' dresses was stiff, heavy, and unwieldy. Richly laced and petticoated, the dresses were too long for walking.

Between 1640 and 1780 fabrics made in America were of hemp, flax, wool, cotton, and some silk. Luxury fabrics, such as brocades and damask, had to be imported.[51] Restrictive legislation by England on the import of luxury fabrics to New England created occasional problems, but these were sometimes solved through smuggling. After 1750 importing became more difficult and the colonists found it prudent to produce their own essential clothing, borrow it, or wear any kind of hand-me-down. The shortages encouraged local production of elaborate fabrics, including lace.[52] Homespun fabrics (loosely woven, hand-loomed in the home from uneven hand-spun yarns) were always available. The quality of homespun fabrics in America was nearly identical to the quality of homespun fabric in England, because materials and equipment were the same. The ban on luxury importation in 1768, moreover, encouraged the senior class at Harvard to decide to wear only American-made garments. Students at Yale followed suit. In the next year they voted to wear garments made out of homespun fabrics for commencement.[53]

When cravats became popular, lace began to disappear from little children's collars and collars were made out of muslin or lawn ruffle. When the cravat went out of fashion towards the end of the century, it was replaced by the stock, a high-wrapped neck band, and the combined stock and the ruffle tended to swallow up the boy's neck. The smaller boys were relieved of the stock, and the ruffle-edge neck band of the shirt was allowed to fall open. There was no fastening of any kind for the shirt and it was cut to be open to about the navel. The amount of the chest that was exposed depended on how high the vest or coat was buttoned. By the third quarter of the eighteenth century this style had been adopted by boys into their teens and worn with an increasing degree of exposure. If no vest was worn, the shirt would fly open.[54]

The shoes were made in smaller sizes than those of men, and they were probably heavier and less comfortable to wear, Warwick suggested.[55] There seem to have been two types of shoes: leather shoes for wearing and silk ones, which were often embroidered and beaded, for display on formal occasions. At home children went about barefoot. Like the adult style, boys' shoes had buckles. During the middle years of the eighteenth century their style, size and shape changed frequently. By the end of the century, as the use of buckles by adults came to an end, so did their use in children's wear. Liveried boys and serving girls were supplied with shoes for formal events.[56]

Like adults, boys wore breeches. Before 1730 the vent at the back of the breeches was closed by lacing or buttons; later, a buckle was employed. It was customary for boys to wear their vest long during the normal round of schooling and church-going, so the breeches were hardly visible. Smaller boys, when not wearing a vest, wore a sash around the waist to hold in the very full shirt.[57]

Throughout the seventeenth and eighteenth centuries daughters of the wealthy class, like their mothers, were dressed in voluminous skirts (often lined with coarse fabric and sewn with thread as coarse as shoe thread, often home-spun), and high-heeled shoes, the same type of heels worn by their mothers.[58] They were made out of delicate leathers and silks. The girls were rigidly corseted in stays and the sunbonnet was sewn around the youngster's head.

Among the merchant class, the degree of control a father had over his son's future affected the clothing the child wore.[59] Members of the merchant class had the interest and the means to acquire fashionable attire and require their children to wear it.[60] In Salem, Massachusetts, the merchant class was dominant around the year 1800. Its power rested on success in shipping and commerce, sociologist Bernard Barber observed.[61] They created alliances and partnerships through marriage, which were then extended to politics.[62] The father was considered a patriarch, the governing authority. He engaged in entrepreneurship, such as sending out ships on long voyages that sometimes took two or three years. Children's clothes among the well-to-do in America helped preserve the family's status and maintain its rank. Girls were expected to learn all they needed to know from their mothers and later from their husbands. The son working at his father's side was one way that boys gained the skills of buying and selling, or making things.[63] Children of merchants or craftsmen, however, often prepared for life under the oversight of someone not connected to them by kinship.

The boy who wished to follow the craft that occupied his family stayed home and continued to dress in the manner worn in their country of origin.[64] With extensive periods of apprenticeship and an emphasis on occupation as family property, the young had little autonomy in their daily lives. Children being trained by relatives remained within their family of orientation longer, encouraging tight social networks, which also encouraged a traditional style of dress.[65]

Many sons did not wish to follow their fathers' calling. Some were boys who were born on the farm and had no wish to follow the plow. Others simply preferred to move on to something different: "In the wish to quit the parental roof the motives of doing better in life and of displaying individuality were intertwined," observed Oscar and Mary F. Handlin.[66]

Some chose the military. During the American Revolution, for example, boys as young as nine wore state militia uniforms. As drummers for the infantry, they dressed in the uniform of the regiment in which they served.[67] Military uniforms that boys wore were also replicas of those of the adults.

The Middle Colonies[68]

The middle colonies—New York, New Jersey, Pennsylvania and Delaware—were ethnically and religiously diverse. The family's religious identity and its rank determined a child's appearance. New York City, which in 1623 was called New Amsterdam, was run by the Dutch West India Company, which had been given control over Dutch trade in America. Thirty families arrived. Nearly all were Walloons—Protestant refugees from Belgium. Their clothes were like those fashionable in France and England, playful and flirty (Cavalier fashion). The doublet was shaped to the waist with a low waistline, to which was attached a series of small tabs, coming to a point in front. Under the doublet was a linen shirt with an upstanding collar that had a scalloped edge. The closely fitting sleeves had a wide cuff made to match the neck pieces. A fairly large falling ruff surrounded the neck. A three-quarter length cloak

FIGURE 5.4 *Charles Calvert.* Aristocratic style for both the young master and his African-American servant. John Hesselius, 1761. Baltimore Museum of Art. Museum photo.

hid the wings or rolls at the shoulder. Other garments worn were breeches, linen hats, and floppy boots.

On their estates along the Hudson River valley Dutch settlers wore fuller and more loose-fitting attire. Those of rank carried swords suspended from belts or baldrics—a wide sash of silk or leather worn over the right shoulder and fastened on the left hip.[69] Variety in color and trim, and buttons, stripes, and ribbons characterized their appearance.

Dutch authorities attempted to regulate the production of clothes, not their consumption.[70] Legislation on June 7, 1629, titled "CHARTER OF FREEDOMS AND EXEMPTIONS TO PATROONS," grants the Dutch ownership, use, and control over large parcels of land along the Hudson River. Article XXIX of the document states, "The colonists shall not be permitted to make any woolen, linen or cotton cloth, nor weave any other stuffs there, on pain of being banished."[71] The provision affects the manufacture of clothing. It establishes a dependency upon imported cloth, its color and style.

William Penn formally launched his colony, Pennsylvania, in 1681 as a Quaker experiment in government. Penn welcomed industrious carpenters, masons, shoemakers, and other manual workers. What attracted a heavy inflow of immigrants was the land policy which made it possible to acquire substantial holdings and to engage in serious farming. There was also no restriction on immigration. The presence of several thousand "squatters," Dutch, Swedes, English, and Welsh along the banks of the Delaware River and the fact that he signed a treaty with the Indians made the task of establishing the colony easier.[72] The "Quaker explosion" occurred between 1650 and 1690 when groups of Quakers immigrated from England and settled in Maryland, Long Island, Rhode Island, and in the southern colonies of Virginia and North Carolina (in addition to Pennsylvania).[73]

George Fox (1624–1691) started Quakerism in England. The basic principle of Quaker dress was no ornament, but it was unrelated to salvation.[74] Fox's style of dress was similar to that worn during the period of Charles II. Charles wore a feather in his hat, which Fox eliminated. Fox also preferred a plain linen band to the lace ties. His breeches had no points. His stockings were homespun and his shoes had no ribbon roses. Like King Charles, however, Fox carried a cane (a sign of leadership).[75]

Quakerism has been described as the "extreme statement of the Reformation."[76] Its basic belief was that a person must open to the Inner Light, a Light identified with Christ himself. The belief in an Inner Light empowered the Quakers. They formed a new breed of preachers and actively engaged in conversion. They approached people on the street and, uninvited, spoke in church services, where they had captive audiences. Most Quakers were convinced of the ultimate equality of all men before God. They shocked officials by treating them as equals rather than in an obsequious manner. They refused to doff their hats when addressing supposed superiors, to pay "Hat Honor."[77] Because of their belief in nonviolence, a Quaker carried no sword.[78]

Innovation in dress was interpreted as evidence of one's concern with worldly matters, causing much anxiety to a Quaker meeting. The story is told of a young girl whose father brought her an umbrella from his travels. She carried the novel gift with great pleasure and delight. The meeting to which she belonged became alarmed and the Overseers spoke to the worldly-minded father. During the controversy one woman Friend said to the young girl, "Miriam, would thee want that held over thee when thee was a-dying?" The offending umbrella was relegated to seclusion.[79]

It was easy to identify Quaker girls. They wore dresses that seemed well-made, with hoods, cloaks and bonnets. A bonnet could have folds or plaits or be flared.[80]

Friends belonging to the first generation of Quakers, moreover, refused to have their portraits drawn or painted. They preferred to be remembered by their deeds, recorded in their journals and in other publications.[81] Between 1750 and 1850, however, silhouettes, or shadow pictures, came to be accepted. Shadows belong to the natural world, it was argued. Light from the fireplace cast the "cat's dark silhouette on the wall."[82]

Other sects who advocated sober dress like that of the Quakers were the Mennonites, the Dunkards, and the Amish. They wore plain drab or brown garments with no buckles or buttons. They used hooks and eyes to fasten their garments and came to be known as "Hookers."[83]

Around 1700, new immigrants came to Pennsylvania fleeing religious persecution, economic oppression and the ravages of war in Europe. Most were from Protestant sects, such as Scotch Presbyterians, Huguenots, and communicants of the Dutch Reformed Church.[84] Many immigrants settled in rural areas and farmed large expanses of land. Their skillful farming resulted in significant production and a heavy surplus, allowing for exports of grain and other foodstuffs. The middle colonies came to be known as the "bread colonies."

Rural life in Colonial America led to a discontinuity with the past and, usually, to social isolation. The foreign settlers believed that they could recreate the old traditions and new continuities in America.[85] They brought their wives over as soon as they could, or got married and had children. They expected to teach their children the skills with which to make their livelihoods, how to find shelter from the elements, and how to guard against the perils of daily life. The well-regulated family was the staunchest defense, as was religion.[86]

The new settlers of the middle colonies were an important source of religious ferment. Periodic religious revivals began in 1734 and swept through the colonies. The first such phenomenon was called the First Great Awakening. The Awakening gave wide currency to the idea that all men were equally sinners before God, and that God offered grace to the commonest of men.[87] It was an emotional evangelical message that emphasized gaining salvation through a personal commitment to Christ. The authority of the Bible was delivered through dramatic preaching, rather than by a formal ritual.[88] Princeton, Hampden-Sidney, the University of Pennsylvania, and Rutgers had their roots in the Awakening.[89]

Farming encouraged the wearing of clothes that were simple and practical. The basic style, however, was an imitation of European traditions. Climactic conditions and the need to dress up modified everyday attire.

Up to the crawling age boys were naked indoors and were wrapped in blankets when carried outdoors in cold weather.[90] From one to five years old the daily dress was a shift. Hanging sleeves continued to be attached to younger boys' dresses. If the weather was colder a jerkin (jacket) was worn over the shift. Another garment was like a coverall that was open in the crotch but closed again around each leg. The open crotch of this garment was covered by the tails of the shift.

When an event required dressing up, "the dress of boys was a strange hybrid. The upper part was a miniature doublet (a jacket stuffed with wool or cotton and quilted). The lower part was a full skirt. Older boys wore a buff coat and some wore skilts (knee-length Dutch breeches; they were very full and fit snugly at the waist, requiring no suspenders)."[91] Dress-like coats continued for the younger boys into the third quarter of the eighteenth century. When boys reached the age of breeches the long coats continued as a style, lasting until they were wearing trousers. With the advent of trousers the coats of five- to ten-year-old boys were shortened to create a style. (In the country the coat was still long in 1789.) Tightly closed necklines characterized the appearance of boys of eight and nine. The neckline was topped with a ruffle or a ribbon tie. By the end of the century boys were wearing tied neckcloths.[92]

In general, the clothing worn by children of tenant farmers, freemen, servants, and sailors was similar to that worn by their counterparts in their mother countries.[93] European regional and folk costumes also made their way into the United States. They often had to be adapted to available fabrics.[94]

One common outfit worn by workers was a knitted type of shirt, called a jersey today. Popular among adults in France since the tenth century and in England since the eleventh, they seem to have come to England with William the Conqueror in 1066. The shirt was striped and had a round neckline, long sleeves, and a body long enough to cover the waistband of the breeches, reaching the mid-buttock. It had no openings over the chest. Although there is no evidence of knitted fabrics in portraits, by 1683 knitted garments were a major industry in Germantown, Pennsylvania. Little girls were taught to knit, and "knitting tiny garments" for newborns was commonplace.[95]

Small girls up to the age of four continued to wear caps, some of which were very elaborate in form and others surmounted by large hats. Girls older than five had a variety of hats. Those most depicted are broad-brimmed, low-crowned hats. For the summer they were made out of straw and trimmed with wreaths of flowers, as in France, where trimmings became particularly extravagant after 1760. Yards and yards of wide ribbon were used for hats for girls of all ages; and other hats were made of puffs of lawn-like fabric (linen). The later years of the eighteenth century were a milliner's heyday, a high point of the art that has not been reached again.[96]

Colonial Schooling

A Massachusetts law of 1642 observed that many parents greatly neglect the training of their children in "learning and labor" and other employment which may be profitable to the commonwealth. The law required that at least one person in each town be charged with the responsibility for children's education. Within a generation other New England colonies followed this example.[97]

While in school children wore aprons over their fashionable dress. Two types of aprons were popular. One style, called a "pinner," was a combination of an apron with a pinned-up bib. The Harvard College record of expenses for 1677 mentions "Linnen Cloth for Table Pinners," which suggests that Harvard students had to wear bibs at commons.[98]

The second style of apron, called a "tier," had sleeves, covered the arms and the upper and lower body, and buttoned in the back. "You had to wear sleeved tiers as you had to have the mumps," concluded Earle.[99] Children had to endure the wearing of them with as much patience and fortitude as they could command. Wearing aprons was a custom children loved to outgrow, and thoughtful parents "would not make you suffer it long," observed Earle.[100]

There was no customary age for school attendance and no established sequence took a child from one level to another. Parents sent their children to academies for a variety of reasons that made schooling more advantageous than apprenticeship or job experience.[101] Academies offered instruction in English, Latin grammar, writing, arithmetic, manners, ideals, and skills. They also offered custodial services. Sometimes the decision to send a child to the academy grew out of the parents' inability to discipline an unruly youth at home. Josiah Quincy (1744-1775), who was only six when he arrived at Andover Academy, was said to be "noisy, heedless and troublesome."[102] Physical punishment was often the means of dealing with unruly children. To Andover's Uncle Sam Taylor (the principal) every boy was considered guilty until proved otherwise. Taylor consciously relied on terror as a means of pedagogy. At home children also had to learn self-denial and self-control in all matters. These lessons were often emphasized by force. "Whip and pray and pray and whip," a friend advised a mother, Ann Carter Lee.[103]

Warm, workday clothing, pants and a shirt, a long jacket and a hat out of homespun fabric were customary in the lower grades. Boys attending the more expensive academies started school later and wore better tailored clothes of finer fabrics, with buttons and frills.[104]

Some parents were willing to toil patiently to make the lives of their children more rewarding. They perceived college and education as the way of achieving the finer things in life, clothing included. Francis Wayland, president of Brown, noted that poor families worked hard so that their sons and brothers would go to college. They would then be able to "dress in clothes such as they never wore, eat from a table such as they could not spread, devote themselves to quiet study while they were exhausted with labor."[105]

Children's clothing introduced the child into a system of meaning, further helping them to differentiate between their own group and that of the other. A child's clothing, for the most part, acted to enhance the development of a personal worldview. Clothes helped to generate a sense of belonging, a sense of social identity.

Notes

1. The different stages of development of children will play virtually no part in this chapter. The fact that the child was viewed as a miniature adult and dressed in miniature versions of adult attire, together with rigid paternal control, a demand for piety, and the early training of the growing child for adult work prevented the recognition that children undergo distinct levels of development. The character desired for a child of any age was the same. Hence, there was little substance to set off one stage of growth from another, as Wishy observed. Bernard Wishy, (1968) *The Child and The Republic: The Dawn of Modern American Child Nurture*. Philadelphia: University of Pennsylvania Press, p. x.

By the end of the eighteenth century, however, parental orientation towards children changed, and children were being trained to exercise judgment and become self-reliant. "As soon as he can sit at a table he chooses his own food, and as soon as he can speak he argues with his parents on the propriety or impropriety of their directions," criticized a visitor from England. Quoted in George R. Clay, (1960) In "Children of the Young Republic," *American Heritage*, April, pp. 46–53.

Only after the father could no longer train his son, in the second half of the nineteenth century, did distinction between different age groups emerge. William Byron Forbush identified three stages of development in a boy's life. *Infancy* is from birth to about six; *childhood* is from six to fourteen; *adolescence*, from about fourteen to manhood. Forbush, (1901) *The Boy Problem*. Boston: Pilgrim Press, p. 7.

2. Estelle A. Worrell, (1980) *Children's Costume in America 1607–1910*. New York: Charles Scribner and Sons, p. 9.

Costume historians Edward Warwick, Henry C. Pitz, and Alexander Wyckoff, however, who wrote earlier (in 1965), claim that well into the eighteenth century there are so few portraits depicting children that the problem of reconstructing children's dress in Colonial America is a severe one. This difficulty is compounded by the dearth of detailed reports and the meager number of artifacts.

Edward Warwick, Henry C. Pitz, and Alexander Wyckoff (1965) *Early American Dress*. New York: Benjamin Blum.

3. Worrell, op. cit., p. 22.

4. Warwick, et al., op. cit., pp. 200–201.

5. Harry J. Carman, Harold C. Syrett, and Bernard W. Wishy, (1960) *A History of the American People*. New York: Alfred K. Knopf, pp. 98–100.

6. Wishy, op. cit., p. 11.

7. John Demos, (1973) "Infancy and Childhood in the Plymouth Colony," in Michael Gordon, ed., *The American Family in Social-Historical Perspective*. New York: St. Martin's Press.

8. Girls were employed in the productions of cotton. Warwick, et. al., op. cit., p. 239.

9. Lawrence Stone, (1977) *The Family, Sex, and Marriage in England, 1500–1800*. New York: Harper and Row, pp. 173–174.

10. Alice Morse Earle, (1903/1971) *Two Centuries of Costume in America 1620–1820*. Rutland, Vt.: Tuttle, pp. 281–283.

11. Earle, op. cit., pp. 281–283.

12. Demos, op. cit., p. 181.

13. Demos, op. cit., pp. 180–207.

14. Earle, op. cit., pp. 301–303.

15. John Martin Vincent, (1935/1969) *Costume and Conduct in the Laws of Basel, Bern, and Zurich*. New York: Greenwood Press, p. 131.

16. Earle, op. cit. p. 301.

17. George Ferguson, (1954/1977) *Signs and Symbols in Christian Art*. London: Oxford University Press, pp. 33–34.

18. Ferguson, op. cit., p. 153.

19. Worrell, op. cit., p. 20.

20. Worrell, op. cit., p. 8.

21. Worrell, op. cit., p. 9.

22. Worrell, op. cit., p. 20.

23. Worrell, op. cit., p. 23.

24. Earle, op. cit., p. 283.

25. Earle, op. cit.

26. Earle, op. cit., p. 287.

27. Earle, op. cit., pp. 286–287.

28. Earle, op. cit., p. 286.

29. Warwick, et al., op. cit., p. 239.

30. Warwick, et al., op. cit., pp. 7, 12.

31. Warwick, et al., op. cit., p. 9.

32. Warwick, et al., op. cit., p. 240.

33. Warwick, et al., op. cit., p. 242.

34. Warwick, et al., op. cit., p. 241.

35. The chief characteristic of the style was that men's garments had an uncompromising rigid outline brought about by a tight-fitting or corseted doublet (jacket) with collar rising high and topped with a ruff. Men's legs were encased in tight-fitting stockings or tights. There were eleven children, seventeen women

and eighty-four men on board the ship that brought the first settlers to Roanoke in 1587. Warwick, et al., op. cit., pp. 60, 233.

36. Kax Wilson, (1979) *A History of Textiles*. Boulder, Colo.: Westview Press, pp. 233–238.

37. It was the task of the planter's wife to produce the cloth and manufacture the clothing the slaves needed. Each slave had to be provided with two sets of clothing, one for summer and one for the winter. Many wives learned the task after marriage. Catherine Clinton, (1982) *The Plantation Mistress*. New York: Pantheon Books, pp. 26–27.

38. Warwick, et. al., op. cit., p. 57.
39. Warwick, et. al., op. cit., p. 60.
40. Warwick, et al., op. cit., p. 59.
41. Warwick, et al., op. cit., p. 58.
42. Warwick, et. al., op. cit., p. 95.
43. Warwick, et. al., op. cit., pp. 95–96.
44. Wilson, op. cit., pp. 18, 245.
45. Warwick, et. al., op. cit., p. 96.
46. Warwick, et. al., op. cit., pp. 98–100.
47. Warwick, et. al., op. cit., p. 100; Worrell, op. cit., p. 22.
48. Warwick, et. al., op. cit., pp. 109, 110, 116–117.
49. Warwick, et. al., op. cit., p. 99.
50. Earle, op. cit., p. 288.
51. Wilson, op. cit., pp. 235–238.
52. Wilson, op. cit., p. 235.
53. Wilson, op. cit., p. 239.
54. Warwick, et. al., op. cit., p. 240.
55. Warwick, et. al., op. cit., p. 241.
56. Ibid.
57. Warwick, et. al., op. cit., p. 242.
58. Earle, op. cit., pp. 285–286.
59. Oscar Handlin and Mary F. Handlin, (1971) *Facing Life: Youth and the Family in American History*. Boston: Little, Brown, pp. 15–23.
60. Bernard Barber (1973) "Family and Community Structure in Salem," in Michael Gordon, ed., *The American Family in Social-Historical Perspective*. New York: St. Martin's Press, pp. 102–104.
61. Barber, op. cit., p. 102.
62. Barber, op. cit. p. 104.
63. Handlin, op. cit., p. 28.
64. Warwick, et. al., op. cit., p. 235.
65. Barber, op. cit., pp. 104–105.
66. Handlin, op. cit., p. 29.
67. Worrell, op. cit., p. 29.
68. Historical discussion in this section is based on Thomas A. Bailey and David M. Kennedy, (1988) *The American Pageant: A History of the Republic*. Lexington, Mass.: D. C. Heath, pp. 36–37.
69. Warwick, et al., op. cit., p. 135.
70. Warwick, et al., op. cit., pp. 132–133.

71. Henry Steele Commager, ed. (1968) *Documents of American History.* New York: Appleton-Century-Crofts, p. 19.

72. Bailey and Kennedy, op. cit., pp. 34–35.

73. D. Elton Trueblood, (1966) *The People Called Quakers.* New York: Harper and Row, p. 24.

74. Amelia Mott Gummere, (1968) *The Quaker: A Study in Costume.* New York: Benjamin Blom, p. iii.

75. Earle, op. cit., p. 600.

76. Trueblood, op. cit., p. 3.

77. Trueblood, op. cit., p. 43.

78. Warwick, et al., op. cit. p. 203; Gummere, op. cit., p. 13.

79. Gummere, op. cit., p. 50.

80. Earle, op. cit., pp. 606–607.

81. Anna Cox Brinton, (1964) *Quaker Profiles Pictorial and Biographical 1750–1850.* Lebanon, Pa.: Pendle Hill, p. 1.

82. Brinton, op. cit., p. 3.

83. Earle, op. cit., p. 612.

84. Bailey and Kennedy, op. cit., p. 21.

85. Handlin, op. cit., p. 13.

86. Handlin, op. cit., p. 14.

87. Carman, Syrett, and Wishy, op. cit., p. 101.

88. H. Paul Chalfant, Robert E. Beckley, and C. Eddie Palmer, (1994) *Religion in Contemporary Society.* Itasca, Ill.: F. E. Peacock Publishers, p. 137.

89. Carman, et al., op. cit., p. 101.

90. Warwick et al., claim that infants were swaddled in America as they were in Europe. The evidence offered, however, is from a 1650 French painting by George de La Tour. Warwick, et al., op. cit., pp. 248–251.

91. R. Turner Wilcox, (1969) *The Dictionary of Costume.* New York: Charles Scribner, p. 322.

92. Warwick, et al., op. cit., pp. 248–249.

93. Warwick, et al., op. cit., p. 100.

94. Warwick, et al., op. cit., p. 99.

95. Warwick, et al., op. cit., p. 240.

96. Warwick, et al., op. cit., p. 246.

97. Commager, op. cit., pp. 28–29.

98. Earle, op. cit., p. 314.

99. Ibid.

100. Earle, op. cit., p. 314–315.

101. Handlin, op. cit., pp. 103.

102. Handlin, op. cit., p. 103.

103. Handlin, op. cit., pp. 74–75.

104. Warwick, et al., op. cit., p. 253.

105. Handlin, op. cit., pp. 119–120.

6

Children's Clothes in the United States, 1800 to 1860

Prior to 1800, life for most children was difficult. The home was designed for adult living. There was no attempt to make the home safe for children by screening fireplaces, covering wells, or blocking stairways. Infants slept in a cradle that was located amid the noise and bustle of daily life. Older children slept wherever there was space, with parents, siblings, or servants, and took their meals standing at the table, or seated on the floor. Households frequently included servants, apprentices, and older siblings. Someone kept an eye on the youngest children, and when necessary, there was physical intervention—holding the baby back. Accidents were common and accepted as inevitable. There was little privacy.[1]

The home was often the location of the family's enterprise, a farm or shop to which children had to contribute.[2] Family members were the primary influences in most young people's lives. Children were regarded as miniature grown-ups and expected to go through their formative years as quickly as possible. They had little time, opportunity, or resources to think about different styles of dress. A rapid assimilation of the child into adult society was expected. Indecorous words or deportment had to be carefully restrained and physical punishment was employed.

On the southern plantation it was believed that correct behavior lays the foundation of the social order. Parents insisted on strict adherence to form and decorum. In a letter to his daughter Polly, dated 1813, Bolling Hall wrote, "It would make my heart bleed within me if I was to hear you were doing anything wrong—the distress which any improper conduct of yours would occasion in the trust of your parents would be indescribable."[3]

Mothers were responsible for the upbringing of younger children. They were expected to shape the moral character of their offspring.

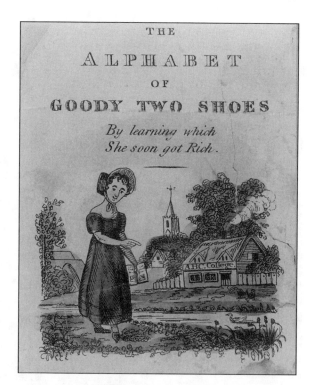

FIGURE 6.1 *The Alphabet of Goody Two Shoes.* Cover illustration. Moral: Learning to read leads to economic success. The child wears an adult-style Empire dress. Artist unknown, 1828? (Inscribed Susan H. Bunting, January 12, 1829.) Chester County Historical Society, West Chester, Pa.

"Their highest priority was to rear Christians worthy of God's grace."[4] Although the father represented the ultimate authority, it was the mother who dispensed the actual punishment. She carried out the unpleasant task of discipline. In a letter from February 7, 1819, a mother wrote to her brother complaining about the behavior of her two-year-old son: "His father spoils him bad enough and thinks him the smartest child in the world. . . . I have all the whipping to do."[5]

Adult European fashions were the basis for children's attire, and the clothes were often designed to reflect parental status and rank. This practice reflected the larger cultural concern for maintaining social order by making social class hierarchy visible. Children of wealthy professionals, merchants, and planters could follow the rhythms of fashion. The clothes for their children were made according to the child's measurements by tailors and dress-makers in England and Paris (see Fig. 6.1). Complexity of design, intricacy of detail, sumptuousness of fabric, and perfection of style determined their cost. Choice of dress was mostly prescribed by the adults, and children's appearance approximated that of the grown-ups. Boys who labored in the fields or worked on plantations or barges wore trousers.[6] Girls wore skirts or dresses.

FIGURE 6.2   "Mother and Child Making a Pie." From *The Alphabet of Goody Two Shoes.* The girl standing on a stool is holding an apple. Her mother is rolling the dough for a pie. The girl wears an Empire dress that reaches the calf, as well as simple pantelets with no ornaments. Artist unknown, 1828? (Inscribed Susan H. Bunting, January 12, 1829.) Chester County Historical Society, West Chester, Pa.

In 1800, the United States was still an agricultural nation. Only six percent of the population lived in towns. Both in the North and in the South the common productive unit was the rural household. Children took an active role, working next to their parents. Allowing children the leisure to have a childhood was a luxury few adults could afford. While boys helped in farming tasks, girls were involved in activities such as processing and preserving food (see Fig. 6.2), candlemaking, soapmaking, spinning, weaving, shoemaking, quilting, rugmaking, and the many other activities that took place on the domestic premises.[7]

As the nation flourished, reform campaigns of all kinds sprang up. There was not "one reading man without a scheme for a new utopia" observed Ralph Waldo Emerson in 1837. One important movement in the

1820s and 1830s involved a change in the conception of the sinful child. Influential Protestant ministers, such as Nathaniel W. Taylor, Lyman Beecher, and Charles G. Finney, introduced the notion of choice. They preached that sin was not original. The decision to do wrong was freely willed. If men and women could freely commit evil acts they could also repent and reform.[8] Sin was "in the sinning."[9] Locke's conception that human beings are born as blank slates gained general acceptance.[10] There was thus no religious rationale for the physical punishment of children and no reason for rejecting fashionable dress.

Another source of style in addition to social class and work attire were clothes that revolved around a distinct social identity, such as the religious ideology of the Quakers, and the lifestyle of the semi-nomadic "fringed people" of the frontier, who for pragmatic reasons required their garments to be made out of leather.[11]

Children's Clothes

Clothes were expensive. Children of the poor were often identified by clothing that lacked lace and was tattered or mended. Even among the well-to-do a child's clothes were planned with growth in mind. Tucks were built in, as well as deep hems and drawstrings that made it possible to loosen things up. It was customary to have two categories of clothes, ordinary ones for around the house and formal, newer ones for Sunday and other formal occasions. A garment was often refashioned by cutting off the worn-out section or by patching the garment. When it was no longer useful, the garment was given away to the poor. Before it was given away, however, all ornament and trimming were removed and saved for future use.[12]

Fashion plates that arrived from England and France showing the latest fashion were often copied by those with fewer resources. Dressmaker or mother mimicked the style. The design, however, was simpler, quality of fabric was secondary, and the fit was less exacting.[13]

Until mid-century toddlers, boys as well as girls, wore pliant, simple dresses that were easy to care for and wear. The neckline was low. A small sleeve was attached at the lower armhole. The hemline was plain. On their feet they wore little slippers in black, red, or a pastel color.[14] Some wore no socks,[15] and some no shoes at all.

City youngsters wore an underbody (an undershirt) and simple trousers. These ankle-length pantaloons were loose fitting and had a drop-front construction. The top was buttoned onto the pants, or the outfit was sometimes held together by a drawstring. Boys' trousers were thus either buttoned onto waists, in the case of young children, or held up by suspenders. At first suspenders were just two separate straps that buttoned to the trousers. By 1850 they had double elastic fasteners on the ends. Sometimes only one suspender or brace did the job. In hot weather, or when playing, boys wore the trousers without a blouse or a jacket.[16] Boys opened the shirt they wore only over the chest and not all the way down to the shirt's bottom.[17]

The Quaker style was plain and austere. Stories were told about the ways young Quaker girls attempted to circumvent the rule against ornament. After leaving home girls picked red cherries from the tree and decorated their plain straw hats. They were careful to discard the cherries before they went back into the home. [18] Prepubescent children, it seems, were allowed to roam the countryside without much restriction.

Between 1818 and 1858 pantelets were in fashion for boys and girls. Two sisters whose parents were Quakers wanted a pair of pantelets, which, because of their ornamentation, they were not allowed to wear. One day early in the morning the girls woke up and decided to make them themselves. They took a sheet from the bed and proceeded to make two pairs of pantalets. Busy sewing they did not hear their mother approaching their room. Suddenly the door was open and mother was at the door. "The two little quakeresses" never got the chance to wear the pantalets.[19]

For everyday wear thrifty mothers (except Quakers) made pantelets out of stout calico, while for dress occasions pantelets were white and trimmed with embroidery and lace. Occasionally they were embellished with ruffles.[20] The quality of fabric (velvet vs. cotton), design, and trimmings identified parental wealth, rank, sometimes political[21] or religious orientation, and sometimes mourning. No lace or embroidery was placed on children's pantelets when the children were in mourning. In general, pantelets were made from the same material as the dress.[22]

Fashionable Attire For Boys

Despite some accusations of immorality, fashions from England and France became important sources of style. Boys' attire, however, appears to have had a less confining fit than English versions. At the beginning of the century, for example, the Spencer jacket, popular in England, was adopted by American men, and "boys were seen everywhere in it," reported costume historian Estelle A. Worrell.[23] The jacket in blue, red, or black was sometimes double breasted. Sleeves were gathered in the shoulder and tapered to fit the lower arm. White vests with rounded collars were worn buttoned. Shirt collars, stiffly starched, stood up off the coat lapels, and cravats were tied in a bow. The ties were white for formal occasions, and red or black for informal ones. Long trousers were worn with black riding boots. Hair was parted in the middle with a little wave

FIGURE 6.3 "Willie and Geoffery." The boys are dressed in miniature adult male style. The engraving is from *The Doll and Her Friends: or Memoirs of Lady Seraphina.* Illustrations by Hablot K. Browne, engraved by Baker and Smith. Boston: Ticknor, Reed, and Field, 1852. Chester County Historical Society, West Chester, Pa.

over the forehead.[24] Sometimes the ankle-length trousers had a drop-front construction, which allowed the blouse to be buttoned onto the pants, helping to hold them up.[25]

Between 1820 and 1830 the suit for little boys had many variations in detail. It consisted of a short jacket that was rarely fastened and ankle-length trousers. The blouse had a wide lace ruffle around the open collar. A top hat with black grosgrain ribbon band was worn by fashionable boys (see Fig. 6.3) at this time.[26] During this period buttons were still more for decoration than for fastening. The jacket was worn longer, the vest acquired stripes, and some wore a watch fob on a bright red ribbon. Vests had a small collar and were in white, gray or buff, and worn with long pants. The shirt or blouse underneath had an open collar starched to stand out from the jacket. It seemed more loose around the neck.[27]

"Skeleton" suits, a style that followed the general lines of the body and consisted of a soft shirt buttoned onto a pair of long but loosely fitted trousers, continued to be worn by young boys in the United States, although they were no longer fashionable in England. The skeleton suit in the United States acquired pockets.[28]

As in England, boys up to four years of age and sometimes older continued to wear dresses. Familiar sights in the 1850s were little boys wearing elaborate, colorful dresses in orange, fuchsia, and magenta. They also wore plaid stockings, and the Scottish bonnet was popular in the next two decades.[29]

The Eton suit, with its characteristic short jacket and fitted long sleeves, by 1850 also became a classic in the United States. Rather than a stiff collar, the American version had a white shirt that was soft and had a ruffle-edge. The white pique vest was visible and its ends were pointed.[30]

As in England, in 1850 boys who were under ten years of age began to wear "full short trousers to the knee." Also around this time the style of dress fashionable for boys younger than fifteen became different from that of their fathers. A pronounced differentiation by age began to take place. Boys seven to fourteen sometimes wore the Scottish kilt or the sailor suit.[31] The sailor suit was worn as it had been designed in England.[32] A suit consisting of breeches or trousers and a matching velvet or ribbed silk jacket, or coat, was also fashionable for boys. These garments were often lined with silk. The preferred jacket buttons were filigree silver.

Fashionable Attire For Girls

The dominant style at the beginning of the nineteenth century was the Empire fashion (see Fig.6.4). The dress had simple lines with very little decoration. A satin sash was used to give shape to a dress made of taffeta or soft muslin. The waistline went as high as it could go. The little bodice puffed out at the bosom and was gathered at the neckline. The dress had a low neck and short sleeves. Some trimmed the neckline with frills of lace or muslin.[33] The Empire dress was worn over short pants of cambric and slippers of kid.[34]

By 1835 sleeves had reached extravagant proportions (leg-of-mutton sleeves), but then became less full, and declined in size.[35] In 1836 the sleeves were gathered into three puffs from shoulder to wrist. By 1840 the sleeves reached only to the elbow. Mitts of thread and silk, which were fashionable in the eighteenth century, continued to be in style until about 1830.[36] In the winter a coat with a deep cape was worn over the dress, also a beaver hat. During the summer girls wore straw hats over their caps.[37]

By mid-century girls' fashions became complicated and repressive, like those of their mothers. Waistlines and necklines dropped. Girls wore ostentatious, elaborate copies of adult fashions (see Fig. 6.5), including the corset, stays, full skirt, petticoats and an impractical bonnet.[38]

Between 1810 and 1820 dress necklines were generally wide and low. Girls, particularly farm girls, had to protect the neck from sunburn. Sunbonnets developed. They varied in the depth of brim, fullness of the

FIGURE 6.4   "The Scalded Girl." The girl wears a better fitting and more elegant version of the empire style. She is also wearing a necklace. Her mouth has been scalded by the steaming hot cereal and she has turned to her father (?) for comfort. Her father, who is holding a cup of tea, reaches to comfort her. He seems to have been dressed by a tailor—he wears a well-made suit, a cravat, socks, and shoes. From *The Picture Reader: Designed as a First Reading Book for Young Masters and Misses.* By a Friend to Youth. New Haven: S. Babcock, 1841. Chester County Historical Society, West Chester, Pa.

crown, and size of the neck ruffle. To stiffen them, brims were either starched or quilted, or cardboard was inserted into the lining.[39]

To protect their dresses girls wore aprons. The style was adapted to wherever the waistline was located in fashion. The apron went over the shoulders, crossed in the back, wrapped around the waist, and tied in the front.[40]

Work Attire

Much of the clothing worn by new immigrants was brought with them, made out of coarse European homespun fabrics.[41] Climatic or work needs often dictated some modifications. Parents frequently cut down their own garments to dress their children. At the turn of the century

FIGURE 6.5 "Girls with Dolls." The girls and their dolls are costumed in charming adult fashions. The book from which the illustration comes seems to have been designed to tell about the upper class. From *The Doll and Her Friends: or Memoirs of Lady Seraphina.* Illustrations by Hablot K. Browne, engraved by Baker and Smith. Boston: Ticknor, Reed, and Field, 1852. Chester County Historical Society, West Chester, Pa.

smocks in various colors were popular for boys in city and country (see Fig. 6.6). Children of English farmers wore cream or green muslin; those of German descent preferred black, and the French wore blue.[42] Smocks were popular until the Civil War.

Work attire worn by American boys (see Fig. 6.7), black or white, in rural areas or in the city, among waterfront workers or children of western pioneers, usually consisted of a drop-shouldered full shirt, opening only part way down the front. Trousers had a button-front opening, with the buttons exposed. Trousers often buttoned up along the leg, which facilitated pulling the trouser leg over a boot. Suspenders or braces developed stretch ends after 1836, when Charles Goodyear developed elastic. A jacket was worn over a vest; a scarf was held by a small button and was wrapped around the neck. Cravats and ties changed, as did the collar, but the shirt changed very little. A red bandanna sometimes replaced the scarf. A variety of hats, boots, and shoes were worn with these simple clothes.[43]

The word "bandanna" is an East Indian word meaning tie-dyeing and referred to a large silk or cotton handkerchief dyed in brilliant color spots on a dark ground.[44] The origin of the red bandanna, it is thought, lies in the red cravat brought by French immigrants at the beginning of the nine-

FIGURE 6.6 "Boy in Smock." A child wearing a smock with pantalets. From Estelle A. Worrell, (1980) *Children's Costume in America.* By permission.

FIGURE 6.7 "Boy in Work
Clothes." Boy's trousers
buttoned with suspenders.
From Estelle A. Worrell,
(1980), *Children's Costume in
America*. By permission.

teenth century. Worn by artists or cowboys, it was a functional object and became a distinctive American folk symbol of egalitarianism.[45] Red bandannas were worn throughout the country and by boys of all social classes. The bandanna was useful for wiping perspiration, and it could be pulled up over the nose in the fields or on the trail to keep dust out, tied around the head and neck to soak up sweat, or tied over the ears in winter for warmth. In an emergency it could be a tourniquet or a bandage; and it could be a washrag or towel if needed. Young boys also used bandannas for fist fighting; it made an effective weapon when folded and knotted.[46]

Many of the garments considered work attire in the nineteenth century, such as the bandanna, trousers with button-front opening, suspenders, hat, and boots, were later romanticized and acquired the designation of "folk style."

Frontier Clothing

Between 1800 and 1840 hundreds of traders and trappers swarmed to the undeveloped wilderness of the American West, often with children in tow. Even among fur traders in the wilderness children's attire imitated that of adults. The northern Indians relied heavily on animal furs or hides for clothing. Fur-bearing animals were skinned and eaten, and the fur was dressed. Indian women tanned the hides and made them thick or thin, soft or hard as they wished. When European goods became available they bartered fur and leather for woolen blankets and cloth from England, as well as beads, which until the first half of the nineteenth century were manufactured in the glass factories of Murano, Venice. The Indians discovered that wet wool cloth was more comfortable than leather, which sticks to the skin. Moreover, a blanket could be worn in a variety of ways, making it possible for an Indian to change his or her appearance.[47]

For the Europeans, the Indians were the source for moccasins, buckskin jackets and leggings—the fringed clothing the fur traders and voyageurs wore (see Fig. 6.8). The Indians and others, however, called them the "fringed people," because of their preference for fringed buckskins, which were sometimes decorated in motifs of a local Indian tribe.[48] These men often had Indian wives and were accustomed to bringing their women and children with them every time they broke camp. Their children wore clothing modeled after that of the adults.[49]

Toys

Children continued to play with the toys and games that had amused children through the centuries—balls, hoops, kites, marbles, stilts, tops,

FIGURE 6.8 *Fur Traders Descending the Missouri.* The voyageurs are wearing
drop-shoulder shirts open only part way down the front, made of colorful thick
cotton. Worn by fishermen and hunters, these shirts are designed to allow
freedom of movement. The fabric may have been brought from France.
Bingham, 1845. Metropolitan Museum of Art, New York.

wooden horses, and a cup-and-ball game (the ball was tossed and caught
in the cup) (see Fig. 6.9).[50] Toys were either made at home or produced as
a sideline by ordinary tradesmen.[51] They were usually individually
handmade, and to order, from wood, clay, or metal. Whittling, that is,
shaping a piece of wood by slowly paring it with a knife, was almost a
national pastime. Some consider it folk art.[52]

The rich might have toys made in silver or porcelain.[53] Dolls may not
have been intended as toys. At times they were three-dimensional fashion plates displaying the latest fashion.[54] Dolls were also used to com-
memorate weddings and other great occasions.[55]

Elias Howe's invention of the lock-stitch sewing machine in 1843 made
it possible for more urbanized mothers to make clothes for their children
more cheaply. With the growth of railroads and canal-boat travel in mid-

FIGURE 6.9 Jumping Rope. Jumping rope, flying a kite, walking on peg legs and spinning a top are the games boys play. The boys are wearing jackets and pants made of coarse fabric. They are dressed alike. "Boys at Play," from *The Picture Reader: Designed as a First Reading Book for Young Masters and Misses.* By a Friend to Youth. New Haven: S. Babcock, 1841. Chester County Historical Society, West Chester, Pa.

century new supplies of cloth became available, and new types of garments became possible. *Godey's Lady's Book* of 1859 offered fashion paper dolls to enable young girls "to develop design taste and ability."[56]

Schooling

Public school precluded the development of an indigenous style of dress for children. Public schools were places where the orphaned and the poor received their education.[57] They wore school uniforms.

There was a spirit of unity and "nationalism" in the United States after the Revolutionary War.[58] Soon after 1800, however, several waves of religious revival emerged.[59] The evangelical fervor that dated back to the Great Awakening of 1740 acquired new strength, encouraging Americans to turn to God. It was believed that God acts to reward the deserving, punish the evil, and convert the doubting. As a result, public discourse on the rearing of children and children's clothes became an important part of the cultural landscape. The discussion played a role in keeping the child from engaging in "childish" activities. There were few objects designed expressly for children's use. Middle-class parents sought to limit play in favor of learning and virtue.

Children who were homeless or offspring of indigent parents were thought to require more intensive efforts. In the hundreds of orphan asylums established throughout the Northeast during the middle third of the century children were uniformly dressed. The Rochester (New York) Female Association for the Relief of Orphan and Destitute Children was typical. Initiated in 1837 by church women of mainstream Protestant affiliation it represented a serious attempt to mold those children who would otherwise be "misshapen." Their express purpose was "to rescue these orphans and destitute children from their life of want and sin, and by kind judicious training fit them for usefulness here and happiness hereafter."[60]

Relentless regulation of dress and learning characterized the various educational systems existing in the United States in the first half of the nineteenth century. Many patterned their structure after machines. Teachers' behavior within the classroom both "complemented and extended the intrusive mode of child-rearing"[61] practiced in the home. It was generally agreed that teachers are "mental disciplinarians and moral overseers."[62]

Encounters between students and teachers were likely to be physical as well as intellectual. In the East, West, North, and South, in every kind of teaching situation, teachers demanded complete obedience. Children were required to memorize the questions and answers supplied by the teacher. Under the threat of corporal punishment, they refrained from questioning, criticizing, creating, or re-creating meaning.

Recitations were organized so that students would learn independently. In the "loud" schools of the 1830s and 1840s students were forced to learn their lessons in isolation. Teachers sought to isolate students by preventing eye contact among them. "My first teacher" recalled a Pennsylvanian who had attended school in the 1850s, "demanded that students keep their eyes on the books whether they were studying their lessons or not. The placing of desks and benches in a row had the advantage of making it difficult for students to look at one another. No playing or visiting was tolerated. A breach of that rule resulted in a heavy . . . stroke from the master's open palm."[63]

Teachers demanded silence. Whips of quince, birch, maple, or hazel were prominently displayed. Whipping posts too were silent but forceful admonitions to potentially disruptive and inattentive students. It was thought that schooling could not proceed without the recognition of the full authority of the teacher.[64]

Children in urban settings were segregated into communities marked by ethnic, religious, racial, and economic similarity.[65] School reformer Joseph Lancaster provided a model that countless teachers learned. He created a mentoring system in which students at all times were responsible to a designated authority. No minute of the day was left unexplained and no student unattended. "A place for everything and everything in its place," was his motto. There were monitors to take attendance, monitors to keep order, and monitors in charge of monitors. Students who failed to toe the line were punished for improperly placed hands or feet. Students were required to keep themselves in a sort of handcuffed state.[66]

Students in low-cost primary schools in urban settings were enclosed in a rigid world of regulated time and space. Since learning to read and write was done in private, attending school for urban children was an asocial experience.[67]

In rural areas learning to read and write often began at home in the evening or in a slack season—winter or summer. Some students began to attend school to learn catechism. Together students recited prayers and learned to repeat hymns. At home they read biblical passages aloud to their families. The written word, thus, was incorporated into a face-to-face community of oral discourse.[68] Even school architecture typically reflected the face-to-face characteristics of cultural transmission in rural communities. Before the 1860s country school houses resembled amphitheaters, with benches surrounding a central space, a stove, and a teacher.[69]

Proceeding from the assumption that an orderly mind and a regimented body were somehow connected, teachers in rural settings maintained order by regimenting the students physically. They required them to literally "toe the line"—line up in a perfect line along cracks in the wooden floor. In addition to whips, dunce caps, wisdom stools, and a lazy boy's corner were reminders of the perils of an error, intellectual, moral, and social.[70]

Children of New York City's poor could attend infant schools. Children were taken in at "two years of age and even less."[71] Infant schools were run by a charitable organization known as the Infant School Society. Students were marched in a lockstep with much rigid formality to and from the classroom. The classroom itself (see Fig. 6.10) was structured like an ancient amphitheater. The three-year-olds, dressed in uniforms, sat on the wide steps while the teacher stood on the ground below.

Bernard McQuaid, who was raised in the Prince Street asylum and rose to be a bishop of the Catholic Church, distrusted orphanages. The relationship that prevailed in the asylum was like that in a prison between keepers and inmates, he believed. It was an institution without the love that tied fathers and mothers to their children.[72] School advocates and

FIGURE 6.10   Infant School in New York. Orphan children as young as three wore uniforms supplied by a charitable organization known as the Infant School Society. 1825. New York Public Library Picture Collection.

factory owners believed that for orphans and for children laboring in factories these schools introduced moral nurture when none was available. A boy deprived of parents and a home they considered to have been in total want.[73] For many children with parents schooling was only an occasional activity.[74]

Concern for children's moral development is also evident in books written for boys and girls. Authors claimed that unquestioned truths of morality and religion led to personal fulfillment. This happy goal could only be achieved if in thought and in deed the child gave his parents complete obedience. "A child's pleasure should be to please his parents."[75] Cheating is of no use. God and conscience are always there.[76] Jacob Abbot's books warned that life is a trial. The world is a place of temptation in which one must make right prevail.[77]

Child-Rearing Theories

In the early 1830s, authors of newspaper columns blamed fashionable attire for "corruption in the home."[78] Fashionable attire, they claimed, violates "proper republican simplicity and Christian order."[79] Fashionable attire has made the child into a "lawless" creature. Children dressed in such attire grew up artificial and spoiled, more like a "household pet, or live doll."[80]

FIGURE 6.11   *The Pet.*
A new conception of
children appears in art.
Children are creatures
of nature, imperfect,
vulnerable, and in need
of nurturing, like the
cat. The girl's dress is
falling off one shoulder
and she only has one
shoe on. John Thomas
Peele (?), 1850s.
National Academy of
Design.

A Christian neo-orthodoxy mounted an attack on the idea of the child as inherently pure and deserving of happiness. The new moralists believed that parents must break or beat down the inherent "willfulness" of the child as soon as it began to appear. Parental insistence on obedience should be viewed as a direct confrontation with original sin.[81] The president of Amherst College, Herman Humphrey, in *Domestic Education* (1840) wrote that the young resembled twigs who would grow crooked unless bent in the proper direction.[82]

Criticism and analysis of children's behavior became a popular topic of discussion in the daily press during the 1830s. English sociologist Harriet Martineau, in *Society in America* (1837), complained about the spoiled, corrupt, and unruly children in America; however, she admired "the independence and fearlessness of (American) children."[83]

In a *Treatise on Domestic Economy* (1842), Catharine Beecher rejected the idea that fashion is responsible for the misbehavior of children and suggested that the unruly behavior of American children may be related to the openness of American society, to social mobility. She argued that in *Democracy in America*, Alexis de Tocqueville had pointed out that in a society organized around one's origin of birth a high degree of order exists.

All ranks and classes are fixed and each person is educated to fit within a particular social category. This ensures that people remain within the class in which they were born. This kind of social control is lacking in the United States. The unruliness of children may be the result, the "price" Americans must pay for economic opportunity and social freedom.[84]

Foreign observers from England and Germany also noted that children in the United States enjoyed a greater degree of freedom than children in Europe. English observer Mary Duncan, however, argued that excessive liberty underlies children's unruly behavior. She remarked, "To see sensible people smile with secret admiration at the spirited exhibition of rebellious will on the part of their offspring excites in the English mind, a sense of lurking danger."[85] Fredrika Bremer (1853) suggested that the cause of children's unruly behavior is disorder in the home,[86] including mothers who show their love to their children "principally by spoiling them."[87]

A range of advisers on child care appeared in books and newspaper columns, calling on parents to bring up a child who is fully powerful in will and perfectly pure in spirit, characterized by ascetic individualism and a deep belief in God.[88] A large number of child-rearing manuals were published during this period. Many were so popular that they went through several editions and remained in print for fifty years.[89]

Physical Punishment

Contradictory views prevailed regarding children exercising "free will." Some educators claimed that control of children's behavior was necessary. Physical punishment was required. They argued that life would inevitably be marked by unhappiness and strife. John S. C. Abbott, *The Mother at Home* (1833), provides an anecdote typical of contemporary advice literature on how to punish. Young Mary, who defied her mother's "mild and judicious" injunction about playing with the Bible, is caught defying her. Despite the child's promises that she will never repeat the offense, her mother "seriously and calmly punishes her. She inflicts real pain—pain that will be remembered."[90] Then she says to her daughter, "Mary, it makes me very unhappy to have to punish you." She reminds Mary that she has disobeyed God as well as her mother. A little solitude will deepen the impression, Abbott suggests. Together, mother and daughter then pray for the child's forgiveness.[91]

Educator Horace Mann (1796–1859), on the other hand, proposed that the use of the rod should be limited in the common schools of Massachusetts. "Educate, only educate enough, and we shall regenerate the criminal and eradicate vice; through schools we shall teach mankind to eradicate passions and develop their virtues."[92] Some, like William Alcott

(1833), for example, suggested that punishment would never be necessary if good examples were set for children by their peers;[93] others suggested that the rod should be used only for extreme misbehavior.[94] Others, who were religiously orthodox, such as Hubbard Winslow and Matthew Hale Smith, refused to give up corporal punishment, reported Lyman Cobb in his book *The Evil Tendencies of Corporal Punishments* (1847).[95] Those who insisted that sometimes the rod would have to be used suggested that it be combined with a "You cannot know how much this hurts *me*."[96]

Notes

1. Karin Calvert (1984) "Cradle to Crib: The Revolution in the 19th-century Children's Furniture," in Mary Lynn Stevens Heininger, Karin Calvert, Barbara Finkelstein, Kathy Vandell, Ann Scott Macleod, and Harvey Green, eds., *A Century of Childhood*. Rochester, N.Y.: The Margaret Woodbury Strong Museum, pp. 33–34.

2. Oscar Handlin and Mary F. Handlin, (1971) *Facing Life: Youth and the Family in American History*. Boston: Little, Brown, p. 71.

3. Quoted in Catherine Clinton, (1982) *The Plantation Mistress: Woman's World in the Old South*. New York: Pantheon Books, p. 101.

4. Clinton, op. cit., p. 48.

5. Quoted in Clinton, op. cit., p. 48.

6. Alice Morse Earle, (1903/1971) *Two Centuries of Costume in America 1620–1820*. Vol. II. Rutland, Vt.: Tuttle pp. 764–765.

7. Ann Douglas, (1978) *The Feminization of American Culture*. New York: Alfred A. Knopf, p. 50.

8. Heininger, et. al., op. cit., p. 2.

9. Sydney E. Ahlstrom (1973) *Religious History of the American People*. New Haven, Conn.: Yale University Press, p. 420.

10. Among the many books written on the subject, see Theodore Dwight's *The Father's Book* (1834), Lydia Maria Child's *The Mother's Book* (1844), and S. C. Abbott's *The Mother At Home* (1833).

11. E. Lisle Reedstrom, (1992) *Authentic Costumes and Characters of the Wild West*. New York: Sterling Publishing Co., p. 25.

12. Estelle A. Worrell (1980) *Children's Costume in America 1607–1910*. New York: Charles Scribner and Sons, p. 33.

13. Worrell, op. cit., p. 34.

14. Worrell, op. cit., p. 71.

15. Worrell, op. cit., p. 85.

16. Worrell, op. cit., pp. 59, 74.

17. Worrell, op. cit., p. 72.

18. Elisabeth McClelland (1904/1973) *Historic Dress in America 1607–1870*, vol. 2. New York: Benjamin Blom, p. 302.

19. McClelland, op. cit., p. 303.

20. McClelland, op. cit., p. 303.

21. Earle, op. cit., p. 770.

22. Earle, op. cit., p.777.

23. Estelle A. Worrell, (1980) *Children's Clothes in America 1607–1910.* New York: Charles Scribner and Son, p. 56.

24. Worrell, op. cit. pp. 55–56.

25. Worrell, op. cit., p. 59.

26. Worrell, op. cit., pp. 63–64.

27. Worrell, op. cit., p. 66.

28. Worrell, op. cit., pp. 70–71, 67.

29. Worrell, op. cit., pp. 99–100.

30. Worrell, op. cit., pp. 70–71.

31. McClelland, op. cit., p. 320.

32. Nora Villa, (1989) *Children in their Party Dress.* Modena, Italy, Zanfi Editori, p. 20.

33. McClelland, op. cit., p. 311.

34. Worrell, op. cit., p. 56.

35. McClelland, op. cit., Vol. 2, pp. 295–299.

36. McClelland, op. cit., vol. 2., p. 299.

37. Worrell, op. cit., p. 72.

38. Thorstein Veblen, (1899) *The Theory of the Leisure Class.* New York: Macmillan Company, p. 209. Also, Stella Bloom, ed., *Fashions and Costumes from Godey's Lady's Book.* New York: Dover Publications. Between 1837 and 1869, see pp. 1, 30, 31, 32, 50, 52, 64.

39. Worrell, op. cit., p. 72.

40. Ibid.

41. In 1800, the population of the United States was 5,300,000; by 1860 the census showed more than 31,400,000. The gross area of the nation when Jefferson came to power was 892,000 square miles; when Lincoln arrived in Washington for his inauguration in 1861 he was president-elect of a nation of more than three million square miles. American national wealth in 1800 was approximately $2.4 billion; by 1860 the figure had increased nearly sevenfold to $16.16 billion. Harry J. Carman, Harold C. Syrett, and Bernard W. Wishy, (1960) *A History of the American People.* New York: Alfred A. Knopf, p. 501.

42. Worrell, op. cit., pp. 41–42; Also, the term blue-collar worker grew out of the blue smocks worn by French factory workers, who brought the idea to America.

43. Worrell, op. cit., pp. 95, 101.

44. R. Turner Wilcox, (1969) *The Dictionary of Costume.* New York: Charles Scribner, p. 16.

45. Worrell, op. cit., p. 97.

46. Worrell, op. cit. p. 102.

47. Robert C. Wheeler, (1985) *A Toast to the Fur Trade.* St. Paul, Minn.: Wheeler Productions, p.62.

48. E. Lisle Reedstrom, (1992) *Authentic Costumes and Characters of the Wild West.* New York: Sterling Publishing Co., pp. 23–25.

49. Wheeler, op. cit., pp. 17–18 ; In Canada, employees of the Hudson Bay Company tended to dress their children, who were often of mixed blood, in fash-

ionable European style. See Sylvia Van Kirk, (1980) *"Many Tender Ties": Women in Fur-Trade Society, 1670–1870.* Winnipeg, Manitoba: Watson & Dwyer, pp. 225, 239.

50. Bernard Barenholtz and Inez McClintock, (1980) *American Antique Toys.* New York: Harry N. Abrams, p. 28.

51. Jac Remise and Jean Fondin, (1967) *The Golden Age of Toys.* Greenwich, Conn.: Edita Lausanne, p. 12.

52. Remise and Fondin, op. cit., p. 15.

53. Ibid.

54. Remise and Fondin, op. cit., pp. 11–12.

55. Remise and Fondin, op. cit., p. 12.

56. Quoted in Worrell, op. cit., p. 86.

57. Paul Monroe, (1940) *Founding of the American Public School System.* New York: Macmillan, Chap. 8.

58. Carman, et al., op. cit., pp. 219–220. Donald Weber (1988) *in Rhetoric and History in Revolutionary New England* suggests that the evangelical ministry shifted to political rhetoric when promoting independence from England. By 1800 they felt safe to return to religious concerns. New York: Oxford University Press.

59. Meredith B. McGuire, (1997) *Religion, The Social Context.* Fourth edition. Belmont, Calif.: Wadsworth Publishing, pp. 238–239.

60. Heininger, et al., op. cit., pp. 9–10.

61. Barbara Finkelstein, (1974) "Pedagogy as Instrument of Intrusion: Teaching Values in Popular Public Schools in Nineteenth-Century America," *History of Childhood Quarterly* 27, p. 348.

62. Finkelstein, op. cit., pp. 352–353.

63. Finkelstein, op. cit., p. 365.

64. Finkelstein, op. cit., pp. 355, 357.

65. See Thomas Bender, (1978) *Social Change in America.* New Jersey: Rutgers University Press; Diane Ravitch and Ronald K. Goodenow eds. (1983) *Schools in Cities: Consensus and Conflict in American Educational History.* New York: Holms and Meier.

66. Barbara Finkelstein and Kathy Vandell, (1984) "The Schooling of American Childhood: The Emergence of Learning Communities, 1820–1920," in Heiniger, et al., op. cit., pp. 70–71.

67. Finkelstein and Vandell, op. cit., p. 68.

68. Finkelstein and Vandell, op. cit., p. 67.

69. Finkelstein and Vandell, op. cit., p. 67.

70. Finkelstein and Vandell, op. cit., p. 68.

71. Monroe, op. cit., p. 372.

72. Handlin, op. cit., p. 81

73. Diane Ravitch, (1974) *The Great School Wars, 1805–1973: The History of a Battlefield for Social Change.* New York: Basic Books.

74. Finkelstein and Vandell, op cit., p. 65.

75. Peter Parley, (1835) *The Parent's Present.* Boston: Light and Horton and W. Thomas, pp. 43–44. 50.

76. Parley, op. cit. p. 50.

77. For example, Jacob Abbot, (1841) *The Rollo Code*. Boston: Crocker and Brewster. In *The Rollo Code* (1841) Abbot advised children that youth was a time of preparation for adulthood. Watching for failings, shunning corrupting influences and bad companions, and remembering that punishment would follow immoral or improper conduct, the child would be able to improve himself. His books were popular among boys and girls.

78. Wishy, op. cit., p. 14.

79. Ibid.

80. Quoted in Wishy, op. cit., p. 14.

81. Wishy, op. cit., pp. 5, 10.

82. Heininger, et al., op. cit., p. 4.

83. Harriet Martineau, (1837) *Society in America*, vol. 2. New York, p. 271. Also quoted in Wishy, op. cit., p. 13.

84. K. K. Sklar, (1973) *Catharine Beecher: A Study in American Domesticity*. New Haven, Conn.: Yale University Press.

85. A. W. Calhoun, (1918) *A Social History of the American Family*, vol. 1. Cleveland: A. H. Clark, p. 55.

86. Fredrika Bremer, (1853) *The Homes of the New World*. Vol. 2, p. 455.

87. Quoted in Wishy, op. cit., p. 13.

88. Wishy, op. cit., p. 4

89. Historian Joseph Kett has pointed out that during the 1820s many young married and unmarried couples moved from rural America to the cities. Separated from the advice of their elders or more experienced family members they sought the advice of experts. They constituted the prime market for these publications. In Heininger, et al., op. cit., p. 4.

90. Heininger, op. cit., p. 4

91. Heininger, op. cit., p. 4

92. Quoted in. Carman, et al., op. cit., p. 515.

93. William Alcott, (1833) *A Word to Teachers*. Boston: Allen and Ticknor, p. 27.

94. Jacob Abbott, (1841) " Punishments," *Mother's Assistant*, February, pp. 74–77.

95. Lyman Cobb, (1847)*The Evil Tendencies of Corporal Punishments*. New York: Newman.

96. Cobb, op. cit., pp. 32–33.

7

Children's Clothes in Nineteenth-Century England

Nationalistic and economic concerns helped shape the character of children's clothes in nineteenth-century England. The new styles of dress introduced children to patriotism, school, and work. The styles prepared children for the roles they would play as adults; for the first time it was expected that they would have their *own* roles rather than continue those of their parents.[1]

In the first half of the century, the kilt and the sailor suit reflected the government's desire to expand its political designs. Age-specific attire introduced children to differentiation and specialization, characteristics associated with the development of science, technology, and industry.[2]

In the second half of the century, in the public schools, where children of the upper class and the rising bourgeoisie went, school uniforms became required. They encouraged obedience to those in authority and to rules. The uniform also encouraged self-restraint. It thus imbued future administrators and bureaucrats with the qualities they would need to control the far flung posts of the British Empire.[3]

The Kilt

Made of tartan cloth, the kilt had been Scotland's traditional dress. In the nineteenth century, the kilt was used to support England's national interest, and the garment as well as the cloth acquired two contradictory symbolic meanings: conformity and rebellion.[4]

The two contradictory meanings stem from the history of the relationship between England and Scotland. It was the English government in the eighteenth century that defined the kilt and the cloth from which it is made, tartan, as signifying rebellion. For many centuries the making of the plaid fabric or tartan in the Highlands was a small-scale production.

It mostly supplied local needs.[5] Highland women made the yarn using a spinning wheel of the saxony type, which they carried around to use in spare moments or, often, concurrently with other domestic tasks. Later they wove the yarn into cloth whose design consisted of a grid, a systematic ordering of both line and color. The wool cloth produced on the Highland looms was finely woven. It was effective as clothing by day and used as a blanket at night. The colors were clear and bright, and the patterns were bold and clearly defined.[6]

The costume made out of this fabric was the ordinary dress of Highland peasants. Its roots are much speculated about.[7] The kilt initially consisted of a colorful piece of cloth used to wrap the whole body, with an easy swathe across the shoulder and a skirt-like lower portion. The skirt was short enough to be appropriate for crossing rivers. In the eighteenth century this one-piece garment was developed into an outfit consisting of two parts: the plaid over the shoulder, and the kilt, a pleated skirt.

The kilt and the tartan cloth of which it was made acquired symbolic significance in 1747. Through the Act of Disarming the Highlanders, adults and children, were prohibited from carrying arms and wearing tartans. The Stuart dynasty that had ruled both England and Scotland until the Glorious Revolution of 1688 had been Scottish in origin, and when the Stuart claimant to the throne, Bonnie Prince Charlie, attempted to regain the crown from the Hanoverian dynasty in 1745, he made Scotland his base of operations. The Highlanders especially rose up to support him, and after his forces were defeated and he had fled the country, the kilt and tartan were outlawed as signs of disloyalty to the House of Hanover. At the same time, the rebellious Highland clans were forbidden to bear arms.[8]

Forty years later the English royal family recast the image of tartan. The Act of Disarming was repealed in 1782. In exile on the Continent, bankrupt, sick, and with no real heirs, Bonnie Prince Charlie was no longer a threat.[9] (He died in 1788.) The popularity of the *Works of Ossian*, purporting to be founded on original Highland documents, demonstrated a public interest in the inhabitants, mountains, and islands of Scotland. In his visit to Edinburgh in 1782, King George III wore tartan, symbolically incorporating Scotland into England.[10] In 1789 the king's three sons were painted in Scottish dress.[11] From folk attire the kilt became a costume worn for ritual and ceremony.

An interest in kilts and in Scotland further increased after the publication of Sir Walter Scott's poem *The Lady of the Lake* (1810), inspired by his travels through the Highlands.[12] Scott took charge of the ceremonies that welcomed King George IV to Scotland in 1822. The king covered himself in yards of tartan and Sir Walter Scott wore a kilt. During this visit the myth of a clan tartan emerged, the idea that a particular design of tartan was associated with a specific clan, and worn as a means of identity. With the promotion of this idea in reference and other books, not only have tartans proliferated, but their categories expanded. Some clans "acquired" lighter and brighter *dress tartans* suited for formal occasions; and some a *hunting tartan* associated with day and the outdoors. Forty-five different patterns of tartan were identified, and sketches of them appeared in McIans's *Costume of the Clans*. The book was dedicated to Queen Victoria with her permission. These sketches were later incorporated into James Logan's book, *The Clans of the Scottish Highlands* (1845–1847), and published in London by Ackerman & Co. The book was dedicated to Queen Victoria for "her patronage of the Highland's cloth and costume."[13] The Queen granted her permission for the dedication.

Queen Victoria's first visit to Scotland was in 1842. "No holiday taken by a distinguished person had such tumultuous consequences," English historian Antonia Frazer observed.[14] By 1845, the passion for tartan, the clans, and "the things Highland" soared, explained Frazer. As public interest and demand for tartan increased, tartan was no longer the dress of "northern barbarians" or political dissidents. The visually striking uniform of the Forty-second Regiment wearing the Black Watch design became famous, triggering questions about the kilt and the tartan cloth and contributing to the kilt becoming considered the "national uniform" of Scotland.[15] Tartan in the form of kilts, skirts, shirts, and pants became fashionable. Parents and their children traveled to Scotland to learn more about the clothing and the fabric, the myths and the romance. The fabric's vibrant colors, together with its practicality and endurance, resulted in its increased popularity among children around the world. The production of the fabric in the traditional way, in largely pastoral and domestic settings, could not meet the increased demand. Machine production, however, made tartan cheap enough to use even for school uniforms.[16]

Queen Victoria played an important role in decreasing the rebel symbolism of the tartan in a more direct way. She dressed her children in kilts and had them painted by Winterhalter in 1849. In 1852, *Lady's Newspaper* reported, "The costume worn by the Prince of Wales, when at Balmoral, has set the fashion of adopting the complete Highland costume."[17] Worn by English monarchy only in Scotland, the kilt was relegated to the category of ceremonial dress.[18] Queen Victoria's use of tartan to line the interiors of Balmoral castle (opened in 1855),[19] further deflated its rebel symbolism.

The Sailor Suit

Much of the clothing available to boys in the nineteenth century had a stiff collar. The sailor suit did not. It was loose around the neck, making

FIGURE 7.1   Max Rhodes in a plaid outfit. Boys under the age of seven were still wearing dresses. Doris Langley Moore, *The Child in Fashion*, 1953. 1864.

it possible for children to play. Children liked the outfit. Since it was a copy of a military uniform, wearing it imbued the child with a sense of significance. Adults liked the outfit too. Adult-like costumes make the child look "cute." The sailor suit became popular among children throughout the world.[20] The sailor suit made its appearance at a time when the government was making a concerted effort to upgrade and modernize seafaring by offering the industry major support (patronage).[21] In the 1840s Queen Victoria ordered a little sailor suit for her eldest son, the five-year-old Albert Edward, Prince of Wales (later Edward VII) (see Fig. 7.2). The tailor who outfitted the sailors of the Royal yacht made it, and a painting by Winterhalter in 1846 popularized it. The trousers were white, wide-legged with a front flap much like the one popular since the late eighteenth century. The tunic (shirt) was tucked into the trousers and had a blue collar edged with white tape. A black silk handkerchief and a straw hat completed the outfit. The costume was considered an exact replica of the uniform worn by British sailors.[22] Wearing a reproduction of adult clothing carries with it a special charm, the charm

FIGURE 7.2   Prince Albert Edward in a sailor suit. 1851. Bibliotheque National, Cabinet des Estampes, Paris. Photo Flammarion.

of the unexpected. The prince looked cute. The outfit's characteristics enticed many parents and children throughout the world.[23]

Increasing the popularity of the sailor suit in the middle of the nineteenth century was the continued association of sailors with heroism. The exploits of the Naval Brigades in the Crimean war (1854–1856) were much publicized and so was the awarding of the Victoria Cross to Joseph Trewavis in 1855. Regular fleet reviews, moreover, helped convert royal support into more broad-based enthusiasm. The sailors who manned these ships were the custodians of Nelson's triumphs and the bearers of strange tales from across the seas. "The sailor who stepped off some snorting and puffing steamship with a parrot on his arm was every schoolboy's hero," observed David Marcomb.[24] He explained that the sharing of the hardship, discomfort, and danger of life at sea was full of romance.[25]

Further support for sailor outfits came from the classic novels *Treasure Island* and *Robinson Crusoe*, which were based on seafaring, and the maritime motifs in the comic operas of Gilbert and Sullivan. Nautical images were popular in the home, too. Seascapes were portrayed in paintings, in mass-produced prints, potteries, and glassworks. All were manufactured for the domestic market.[26]

Diversity characterized the appearance of sailors until the middle of the nineteenth century, when an official uniform was instituted. It was authorized after the Crimean War (1854–1856) with the professionalization of the occupation.[27] In 1837 most of the officers had come from wealthy families. For their promotion they relied largely on influence and patronage. Their training took place at sea. Like officers, most seamen entered as volunteers, often encouraged by payment of a bounty. They too were trained at sea. In 1851 Queen Victoria's government retired large numbers of senior officers, and the Royal Naval Reserve began to draw officers and men from the merchant service and train them. These specialized courses created career sailors. An occupational structure developed and with it seafaring uniforms.[28] The image and prestige of the sailor suit was further enhanced when it was recommended by a dress reform movement called the Aesthetic Movement.

Sailor suits dominated childhood. A sailor suit for three-, four-, and five-year-old boys came with a pleated skirt.[29] For older boys it came in pants. Girls wore sailor-style dresses with pleated white skirts. Many middle-class parents sought the sailor suit for their children. Together with military uniforms and confirmation suits, the sailor suit became a stock outfit in the repertoire of costumes offered in manuals for "Outfitters and Clothiers of Juveniles." As soon as the sewing machine became practical in the early 1890s the sailor suit, whether for boys or girls, was quickly selected for production by the ready-to-wear market.[30]

Age and Class

New technology, new capital, and access to new sources of energy required businessmen, mechanical inventors and investors to develop an orientation to social life that was goal-directed: "rational, industrious, and distinctly sober."[31] The industrial system fostered the development of special social groupings which were organized around knowledge and skill.

Schoolmasters too approached education in a more systematic way. They tied education to the calendar year. They organized school classes according to calendar age and wrote sequenced textbooks.[32] Postman described it in this way: "The mastery of the alphabet and mastery of all the skills and knowledge that were arranged to follow constituted not merely a curriculum but a definition of child development." Postman then suggested that age-grading and childhood emerged with the economy's need for rationality and industriousness.[33]

Age became an important determinant of a child's clothing in the early part of the nineteenth century, whereas in the past children were considered immature adults, and a boy of four or five, and sometimes younger, graduated immediately to adult-style dress. An age sequence developed; a boy's style of dress was determined by his age. As boys advanced in age they graduated from one style of clothing to another.

Boys from four to six, who had been wearing the skeleton suit since 1780, no longer did so by the 1820s. Their clothing reverted back to tunics and petticoats; to styles similar to those worn by mother and sister.[34] They were turned into young children again. The new fashion of pantalettes, moreover, hindered their ability to participate in active play. It was difficult to participate in games without dirtying their garments.[35]

A slightly older boy, however, wore a short jacket over trousers. The trousers later in the century were replaced by above-the-knee or below-the-knee knickerbockers.[36] Boys, moreover, wore some version of a hat from early childhood to manhood. Two popular styles were a hat with a high, stiff crown and narrow brim in straw or beaver and a softer, lower crowned, wider-brimmed style.[37] Older boys preferred the top hat. Prior to going to boarding school, boys might be dressed in playful clothing (see Fig. 7.3).

The emphasis on age-appropriate dress led to a rise in the need for tailors and tailoring skills.[38] In *A Practical Guide for the Tailor's Cutting Room* (1850), Joseph Couts reported that in 1809 he and an associate, Duncan McAra, developed a tape-measure designed to encircle the child's body, enabling him to make measurements exact. The increase in demand for a new and better fit required special measuring devices for a body type and age group, and the industry developed new ones in 1818, 1832, and 1840.[39]

In addition to age and figure, the tailor must take into account the image the child is to convey, Couts instructed. In a question and answer form, Couts offered illustrations and detailed instructions on what measurements were needed, how to get them, and whom the tailor should seek to please. A mother's opinion, for example, was of consequence mostly in the outfit the tailor made for the five-year-old, the first made by a tailor. With the outfits made by the tailor for the older sons, it was the father who must be satisfied.[40]

Couts used fashion-plates to demonstrate age differences in dress.[41] A seven-year-old boy was shown wearing a one-piece tunic which seems to a be a transition garment between "petticoats" and trousers. Older chil-

FIGURE 7.3   Adam Pearson in a black velvet knickerbocker suit, 1874. Boys' attire between nursery years and boarding school portrayed parental wealth. Knickerbockers started being imported from the United States in about 1860. The suit is similar to the Little Lord Fauntleroy outfit that became fashionable ten years later. Fashionably dressed boys and girls wore shoes with heels and pointed toes, buttoned boots, or gaiters. Doris Langley Moore, *The Child in Fashion*, 1953. By permission.

dren's outfits should be styled to convey a distinct attitude. The clothing of an eight-year-old boy should convey "neat smartness;" that of a twelve-year-old boy should make him appear "as having liberty." It should convey self-satisfaction. The twelve-year-old, moreover, was shown holding his hat under his arm rather than wearing it on his head and seemed sure of his good-looking appearance. The youth's trousers are close-fitting at the waist and hips. The jacket and pants are of the same color, be it blue, brown, or dark green. The vest, however, according to Couts, must be of a lighter shade. A "young gentleman"—a youth older than fourteen?— however, is "self-willed," Couts warned. There is a swagger about him. Couts advised, "Don't be surprised at anything he asks. It is better to be conciliatory, to approve all that he says. His father will set him straight."[42] "Young men's" suits are informed by adult fashion and style. A boy's style of clothing became a means of enhancing the child's passage from one age group to another, each with its own attendant rights and responsibilities.

In the past boys had learned about the clothes they would have to wear and the skills they would need as adults by assisting their parents, becoming apprentices, studying under tutors, attending a secondary school, or receiving higher education in a university.[43] By the late 1700s, the advancement of science had led to a technology based on science. New technologies in the fields of textile manufacturing, transportation, agriculture, and many others, required knowledge of science. Employment in these fields became increasingly dependent on educated engineers and scientists[44] who also learned about expected attire.

In the beginning of the nineteenth century, specialization of labor and mobilization of capital with a view to profit encouraged a clear distinction between the wage-earning class and members of the middle class, those who acquired wealth and owned the means of production—the bourgeoisie.[45] As economic opportunities increased, it was necessary for the bourgeoisie to educate their children to positions that did not exist in the world into which the children had been born.[46]

Children of the wage-earning class were often part of the labor force by the time they were seven.[47] The boys wore trousers and smocks, and the girls wore much plainer clothes (see Fig. 7.4). In portrayals of them, their clothes often appear ill-fitting, tattered, and frayed, and their feet are often bare.[48] In the first part of the nineteenth century children whose parents were members of the middle class, the bourgeoisie, went to a private school sometime between seven and nine, and later could attend the university.[49] An education for one's offspring became important. It constituted a means of acquiring and renewing the technical abilities the family possessed. By opening branches in different countries and cities sons helped create a solid network of social and commercial relations. The expression "family business" meant that kinfolk provided the technical knowledge, the commercial outlets, and the capital. Duty to family encouraged many industrial families to abstain from birth control so as to increase the number of their members.[50]

Self-Restraint

In the second-half of the nineteenth century, the clothing of the young acquired a new function, that of preparing them to become future citizens. The young had to learn the complex code of rules, customs, and relationships appropriate to future "empire-builders and . . . gentlemen."[51] They had to learn to stifle their emotions, which could not be "simply sweated out in the burst of adolescent pluck," observed sociologist Edgar Z. Friedenberg.[52] The young had to develop the ability to relate to many different kinds of people, to work in situations where those around them would mostly be of a different race and class. They, thus, had to be instilled with the ability to withstand loneliness and isolation.[53]

The male business suit was designed to create human beings who would regard themselves as members of an organization rather than as

FIGURE 7.4   *The Park Bench.* Social class distinctions. A fashionably dressed girl in a well-designed hat, blouse, skirt, jacket, buttoned boots, and an umbrella. The other girl on the bench is in a plain dress, pinafore, and laced boots. She is poor. F. P. Shuckard, 1870.

persons or individuals.[54] An emblem of rationality and of holding one's personal feelings in check, the male business suit stood for respectability. It indicated membership in the middle class, whose members were expected to reject feelings of compassion. The suit's structure and dark color suggests emotional distance, rationality, and self-restraint.[55] Charles Dickens's novel *Dombey and Son* (1846–1848), set in the 1840s, refers to the emotional impact this type of suit often had on family interaction. It also demonstrates the importance to the rising middle classes of creating a family business. The firm is named in part after Mr. Dombey's son, Paul, then merely an infant. One of the illustrations that accompanies *Dombey and Son*[56] depicts the home environment as severe and characterized by duty. Mr. Dombey is seated on a chair; his back is straight, rigid, and cold, and his face is pinched and tiny-mouthed. He faces away from the wet nurse who is holding his son. His demeanor is detached, like a man not at home in his own home.[57] Wearing the formal, dark suit he would wear at a business meeting, he holds a prideful posture.[58] His daughter, who is standing behind her father's chair, is cowering. Mr.

Dombey could not acknowledge the loss of his wife either to the wet nurse or his daughter.[59] Dressed in the nonuniform uniform of the business class, he was unable to express his own feelings of loss, engage his children, or feel pity for them.

The Eton Suit

The Eton suit became the school's uniform after the middle of the nineteenth century. The rise of organized team games led to team clothes and *then* to school uniforms, observed costume historian Elizabeth Ewing.[60] The wearing of the Eton suit as a uniform signified duty and service and was instituted to support educational reform motivated by the desire to expand the British Empire.

The history of the Eton suit is an example of a change in the role of children, children's clothes, and the educational system. Eton was founded as a charity school in 1440. The boys at that time were supplied with the Tudor-style robe, which was long and had a hood. The robe was worn over regular clothing. The purpose of the charity uniform was to inform the public of the low status of the children who wore it.[61] It also enhanced the self-image of the benefactor. To raise funds for the schools the wearers of charity dress were paraded through the streets, before audiences, and at the annual dinners of the Philanthropic Society. In order to win over the public's heart the charity dress had to look attractive. The students believed the uniform branded them as poor.[62]

Charity uniforms belonged to the school and were often manufactured on the premises by schoolgirls, who were put to work sewing them in needlework classes. The uniform, often in the style of a cassock, looked like a monastic habit, and the children who wore it were expected to conduct themselves with the iron discipline of the monks.[63] Charity children remained charity children even after they had grown up. Boys who left the Foundling Hospital for example, were given a document inscribed as follows:

"You were . . . quite helpless, forsaken, poor and deserted. But of charity you have been fed, clothed and instructed."[64]

By at least 1560 the school was no longer for orphans alone. Letters found from Eton students to their parents from that date and again in 1719, reveal that children ask their parents for shirts, a stomacher, boots, stockings, garters, and for money to pay shoemakers' and tailors' bills. The letters make it clear that there were no uniforms at Eton and no required attire for over 200 years.[65] The students wore simple suits of wool, muslin, or cotton. Students whose family needed their help often took a part-time or half-time job before they reached fourteen. Their job became their source of identity, pointed out Stephen Spender.[66]

Around 1798 Eton became a secondary school for members of the upper class. These were fee-paying students who adopted what came to be known as the Eton *suit*.[67] It consisted of a short jacket without lapels in blue cloth, trousers, a pale yellow waistcoat, and a black tie tied in a sailor knot. At the time, many students wore their own version of the Eton suit, particularly those who were new, and those who resided off-campus, in town. They wore breeches instead of trousers, red-tail coats, a cravat tied in a bow, a stick-up collar, or a brown jacket with gold buttons, and some wore top hats.[68]

At the beginning of the nineteenth century, display of personal fancy, costumes of velvet, and intricate artistry still characterized the clothing of the children of the aristocracy. Eton students of 1812, boys of twelve and thirteen, for example, were still dressing in a style reminiscent of the aristocracy. It consisted of a jacket and trousers, often in contrasting colors, a blue or red jacket, for example, with fawn or white trousers and waistcoat in matching or contrasting cloth. The jackets usually opened at the cuff and had ornamental rows of buttons on each side of the opening. Some boys wore short-tail coats, body-hugging pants (called pantaloons), waistcoats, shirts, bow ties, and low shoes or boots. Boys who went to private boarding schools often took with them a large wardrobe. A boy going to the Charterhouse School in 1826, for example, took with him a variety of shirts, stockings, handkerchiefs, nightshirts, and nightcaps.[69]

Around 1846 Eton instituted a dark coat and trousers with either a turn-down or stick-up collar, the Eton short jacket, and a top hat as its required attire, its "uniform." Initially the collar could be loose, floppy, and comfortable. Later, nearly every boy, even when in sports clothes, wore the stiff white Eton collar, which enclosed the neck like a vice. Stricter requirements came about around 1860. "Some curb must be placed on individual eccentricities in dress," was the explanation.[70] In 1846 the Eton suit required the top hat. Students' appearance was subjected to careful regulation and part of the students' education entailed learning to accept the new restrictions on dress.[71] However, the Eton suit with the top hat made the person look taller and more important. The image was envied and widely copied (see Fig. 7.5). It was an image the ruling class of the British Empire needed to exercise their authority, Spender suggested.[72]

Until the mid–nineteenth century, the public schools were anarchic places. The young aristocrats dressed as they wished and played their games in whatever battered and worn gear they had at hand. Along with compulsory games, stricter supervision of students' lives, and the broadening of the classical curriculum, all new at mid-century, uniformity of dress was firmly established, replacing anarchy with order, as John Rae, former headmaster of the Westminster School, pointed out.[73] Moreover,

FIGURE 7.5   Eton collars with Norfolk jackets, below-the-knee shorts, and boots are worn here by the students at the Stratford Board School in 1899. Elizabeth Ewing, *History of Children's Costume*, 1997. By permission.

the uniform also delineated rank and privilege within the school, identifying a hierarchy of authority, John Rae added. The uniform informed the new student of the deference he owed to those who were his seniors. The number of "done" (closed) buttons up the blazer and the angle at which the straw hat was worn were some of the unwritten signals. The school uniform thus identified social class and encouraged obedience to tradition and rules and regulations.[74]

The Eton suit became required attire as the passion for games developed. The style, which consisted of a stiff collar and the top hat, was unyielding. The contrast between the white collar and the dark jacket and trousers was striking.[75] Involvement in games kept the young occupied. This new level of involvement was necessary because the schools had expanded their curriculum and enrollment. Eton and the other public schools had increased the years of required schooling by three or four. A student stayed in school until about seventeen or eighteen years of age. Enrollment was also increased to include the children of the striving middle classes. This expansion of schooling resulted in teenagers being isolated from the real world, an increased period of dependence deferring entry into work and marriage.[76]

To prevent the potentially disruptive consequences of such social moratoria, the public schools were reshaped along the lines of what Erving Goffman called "total institutions," observed John R. Gillis.[77] The schools were places of "residence and work where a large number of like-situated individuals, cut off from the wider society for an appreciable period of time, together led an enclosed, formally administered round of life," and as such had a powerful shaping effect on all those who passed through regardless of background.[78] Upon entry to school, students were stripped of their original identity. Cut off from the outside in these single-sex schools, the students were in effect deprived of access to civic and economic freedoms possessed by children of other classes. These deprivations were compensated for by the prospect of elite status that the school offered to their graduates and by the diversions of debate clubs and team sports.[79]

Through "the cult of games," middle- and upper-class youth developed patriotic devotion to duty and service. The public schools were called upon to help staff colonial outposts and military cantonments, observed John Springhall.[80] An Eton head explained it in this way:

> What we in public schools aim at . . . is a man who has learnt *not* to consider his own interests as important as those of the institution he serves, who believes rightly or wrongly, that there are some great and solid virtues which his country possesses, and is anxious that its reputation should not suffer in his keeping.[81]

The clothing of the well-to-do students attending the other secondary schools mimicked Eton's style. The image was desirable, and the suit, or at least a distinct part of it like the stiffly starched collar, was widely copied. Other schools too, like Harrow and Rugby, adopted the Eton style. Parents, believing that the Eton suit encouraged a boy to develop the demeanor of a gentleman, dressed their boys in the Eton suit. It became the boy's Sunday best and was often also worn to parties. Seeking to convey a sense of dignity, choirs too adopted the style.[82] Their imitation was "complete with the hard and shiny topper and stiff white collar."[83] Rather than indicating a future occupational role, the attire indicated a particular orientation to social life—a stiff upper lip.[84]

While for upper- and middle-class adolescents the public school helped defer entry into the adult world, the average state-educated youth left school and made the transition to being a wage-earner. The part-time jobs they might have held as students had to be replaced by full-time work, usually in their mid-teens.

Girls: Fashion and School Uniforms

Not until girls in public school started playing sports and wearing uniforms did girls' attire and that of adult women diverge.[85] The change was slow and in 1914 it was still common for a girl to receive a large part of her schooling in the parental home. Many girls, however, were educated in small schools of six to eight students, which parents liked because they provided a sheltered intimate environment. These schools helped girls internalize the idea that femininity entails self-sacrifice, and that it was womanly to be modest, retiring, and attentive to others' needs. These schools emphasized social training.[86] Parents expected their daughters to grow up decorative and marriageable. They believed that the "gentler graces" and winning qualities of character would "be their best passport to marriage."[87]

Creating a "gentlewoman" was the goal of a school in Hampstead run by a Mrs. Ottley. She expected her students to develop the qualities of "modesty (deference to men), service, and forgetfulness-of-self." There was no reading the newspaper or discussing politics in the school.[88]

Girls wore a simplified version of the prevailing adult female fashion. In the beginning of the nineteenth century the Empire fashion was desirable. It was a loose-fitting long dress in white cotton or muslin with a sash tied in a bow in the back, often in color. In 1806, for example, girls' dresses were in a style similar to the dresses they wore as infants.[89] A girl's attire was a simplified version of the one worn by her mother. The color and texture of their dresses depended on the time of day and the season. In the summer they wore gingham in the morning and white in the afternoon; in the winter it was a light woolen fabric throughout the day. Because of the dress's low neck and short sleeves, when they went outdoors they wore a cover; a short jacket, called a spencer, or a short cape, called a tippet, and a bonnet. Trousers reaching the ankles replaced the customary petticoats.[90]

When the Empire style was no longer in fashion, girls' dresses continued to be like their mothers, and their clothes became cumbersome and confining. Skirts widened; in 1838 petticoats had to be worn and the long narrow trousers slowly became shorter and wider. By mid-century they appear as a little more than embroidered frills visible beneath the hem of the dress.[91] Later fashions required girls' dresses to be of heavier fabrics and darker hues, and worn with several petticoats. Respectable women of all ages had to wear them.

Around 1838 corsets became fashionable; [92] little girls were expected to wear them, too. Sometimes they were compelled to sleep in bone corsets so as to acquire the much admired slender waist. The fashion of the crinoline led to tight lacing. In order to wear the crinoline gracefully it was necessary to have a really small waist. Lacing impeded the use of one's limbs. Girls wore hoops, and elaborate headdresses, and from the tenderest years were encased in stomachers (wedge-shaped pieces of wood inserted into the dress bodice to hold the body flat and straight). As a result girls grew languid and listless and often suffered from curvature of the spine.[93] "In vain the medical profession thundered against the evils of tight lacing."[94]

In the second half of the nineteenth century, the pioneer headmistresses of the public schools for girls introduced clothing that made it possible for girls to play sports. This daring innovation was based on the principle *mens sana in corpore sano*, a healthy mind in a healthy body. Girls' schools established games, gymnastics, and uniforms. In a novel published in the 1860s, the narrator, who had been sent to a boarding school, describes the uniform she wore to play sports as consisting of blouses and knickerbockers. The blouse descended below the knee and was trimly tied at the waist. The knickerbockers were long and ample and tied to the ankles.[95]

The girls' public schools prepared their students so that they could proceed to the university and then to the professions. Students in these schools tended to adopt elements of dress worn by male students. Some wore shirt blouses with stiffly starched Eton collars; others adopted the attire worn by boys' hockey and cricket teams, sailors' shirts and caps. Roedean girls wore a boy-inspired sailor blouse and a striped dickey with their skirts. In many schools the sailor straw hat became the school's identifying signature, worn even away from sports and games.[96]

One of the first girl's schools was founded in 1850 by Frances Mary Bass (1827–1894). The North London Collegiate School for Ladies, which she founded,[97] she believed should have physical training like calisthenics—musical gymnastics—for it improves the figure and carriage. When the school was rebuilt in 1873, the name was changed from "Ladies" to "Girls," illustrating the increasing emphasis on age distinction. It included a gymnasium about 100 feet long and about 40 feet high where gym classes were held. Miss Bass sought to have a school uniform which would be graceful and rational, but she never attained this desire, wrote her biographer Annie E. Ridely. She disapproved of corsets and tight clothing and advocated clothes that hung from the shoulders.[98]

In 1858 the headmistress of Cheltenham Ladies College, Dorothea Beale (1831–1906), banned stays and boots and shoes with pointed toes and high-heels and offered to introduce parents "to harmless substitutes."[99]

"Dress may be a trifling thing, but even from childish days it has worried me. I wanted to be free to run, jump, and climb trees," wrote Dame Louise Lumsden, the headmistress of St. Leonards from 1877 to 1882. As headmistress she introduced a 'games uniform' whose main features were a blue knee-length tunic, knickerbockers or trousers to just below the knee, and a leather or webbing belt.[100]

Fashionable attire in 1890 consisted of a heavy corseted dress, which was particularly restrictive and unsuitable for sports. To introduce Olympic games and competitions, Mary Bass was able to introduce a uniform for sports, a gym tunic made of a navy blue serge designed to hang down from the shoulders, leaving the waist completely free. Nothing more than a straight unconstricting bodice was worn under it. It became a general school uniform and lasted for many years.[101]

In her memoirs, Sarah Burstall, the headmistress of Manchester High School for Girls, recalls that parents objected to and resisted school uniforms. They viewed them as the badge of a charity school and a social degradation. It was very long before "the uniform gymnastic tunic ... became possible for us."[102]

Uniformed Youth Movements

In the second half of the nineteenth century, lower middle-class and some working-class adolescent boys still free from adult roles were organized into youth groups by middle-class men committed to patriotic values. The British Boys Brigade, the Catholic Boys Brigade, and the Boy Scouts, for example, were all dressed in uniforms.[103] The Boys Brigade was started in Glasgow, in October 1883, by local businessmen active in the Volunteers, a British part-time military force.[104]

Mostly from working-class families, these boys were expected to relinquish their preference for spontaneity in favor of patriotism, rationality, and self-restraint.[105] Each of the groups had its own characteristic dress: a particular style of cap, a belt, and a haversack, an over-the-shoulder bag.[106] Also organized into youth brigades were occupationally committed adolescents such as shoeblacks, pavement sweepers, and rag collectors.[107] The activities they engaged in included life-saving, woodsmanship, outdoor survival, and seamanship.[108]

Children's clothes in nineteenth-century England supported societal goals. Uniforms made possible the training of boys for bureaucratic and militaristic services, contributing thus to the society's economic and political welfare. Fashionable attire supplemented by gym outfits broadened choices of activities available to women. Educated women were viewed as able to pursue aesthetic and intellectual activities, raising the standards of culture for society as a whole.[109]

Notes

1. Stephen Spender, (1948) "The English Adolescent," *Harvard Educational Review* 18, no. 4, pp. 228-239.

2. Martine Segalen, (1996) "The Industrial Revolution: From Proletariat to Bourgeoisie," in Andre Burguiere, Christiane Klapisch-Zuber, Martin Segalen,

Francoise Zonabend, eds., *A History of the Family,*. trans. Sarah Hanbury Tenison. Cambridge, Massachusetts: The Belknap Press of Harvard University Press pp. 393–396; Ibid., p. 392.

3. Spender, op. cit., pp. 229-230.John Springhall, (1986) *Coming of Age: Adolescence in Britain 1860–1960.* Dublin: Gill and Macmillan.

4. Antonia Frazer, (1979) Preface to James Logan, (1845-1847/1980) *The Clans of the Scottish Highlands.* London: Chancellor Press, p. xxi.

5. James D. Scarlett, (1990) *Tartan: The Highland Textile.* London: Shepheard-Walwyn, p. 7.

6. Ibid.

7. The earliest indisputable reference is from 1582. In *Scoticorum Historia,* George Buchanan wrote of the Highlanders, "They delight in variegated garments, especially striped, and their favorite colours are purple and blue. Their ancestors wore plaids of many different colours and numbers still retain this custom, but the majority, now, in their dress, prefer a dark brown, imitating nearly the leaves of the heather, that when lying upon the heath in the day, they may not be discovered by the appearance of their clothing." Quoted in Scarlett, op. cit., p. 11.

8. Scarlett, op. cit. pp. 35. Scarlett also tells us that the 1747 Act resulted in the manufacture of tartan leaving Highland villages for factory villages on the Highland fringes where the fabric was made in great quantity for the British army and for export to the colonies. Being bright, cheap and durable, it was popular for dressing slaves. p. 14, pp. 34-35.

9. Bonnie Prince Charlie's brother was a priest and had no interest in claiming the throne.

10. Scarlett, op. cit., p. 15. Some writers claim that Sir Walter Scott and Robert Burns staged the visit, encouraging the king to wear the kilt.

11. Antonia Frazer, (1979) Preface to James Logan, (1845-1847/1980) *The Clans of the Scottish Highlands.* London: Chancellor Press, p. v.

12. Sir Walter Scott's writings are commonly described as reflecting Romanticism—the new spirit in architecture, art, and literature in the late eighteenth and early nineteenth centuries, which often involves a nostalgia for the past. The Romantic aesthetic of "long ago" and "far away" is conveyed in locales and settings that indicate the passage of time. The underpinnings for Romanticism are attributed to the writings of French philosopher Jean Jacques Rousseau who advocated a "return to nature" and believed in the concept of the "noble savage." Laurie Schneider Adams (1994) *A History of Western Art.* Madison, Wisconsin: Brown and Benchmark, p. 386.

13. On the attribution page of James Logan (1845–1847) *The Clans of the Scottish Highlands.* London: Ackerman & Co. The book was reissued in 1980.

14. Frazer, op. cit., p. v.

15. Frazer, op. cit., p. xxi; Information also gathered at *Tartan,* an exhibition sponsored by the Scottish Woolen Publicity Council at the Fashion Institute of Technology, October 25, 1988–February 4, 1989.

16. Lytton Strachey, (1921) *Queen Victoria.* New York: Blue Ribbon Books p. 264; Elizabeth Longford (1964) *Queen Elizabeth Born to Succeed.* New York: Harper and Row p. 237

17. Elizabeth Ewing, (1977) *History of Children's Costume*. New York: Charles Scribner's Sons, pp. 180–181.

18. Scarlett, op. cit., p. 40.

19. Strachey, op. cit., p. 237.

20. Ewing, op. cit., p. 87.

21. This increased patronage came about because of the political and military significance of British sea power, as seen in the Battle of the Nile in 1798, and the Battle of Trafalgar in 1805 in which the French navy was crushed, making it possible for the British to drive the French out of Portugal in 1808.

22. David Marcombe, (1985) *The Victorian Sailor*. London: Shire Publications, p. 4.

23. Marcombe, op. cit., pp. 6-7.

24. Marcombe, op. cit., p. 6.

25. Marcombe, op. cit., p. 3.

26. Marcombe, op. cit., pp. 6–7.

27. Marcombe, op. cit., p. 25.

28. Marcombe, op. cit., pp. 17–25.

29. Ewing, op. cit. pp. 127–128

30. Ewing, op. cit. p. 87

31. John Harvey, (1995) *Men in Black*. University of Chicago Press, p. 130.

32. Neil Postman in the *Disappearance of Childhood* (1982) argued that the tie between education and calendar age took time to develop. Prior to the printing press childhood evolved unevenly. Where literacy developed there were schools and books. Initially classes or grades were based on the ability of students to read. The unyielding linearity and sequential nature of printing led to the reordering of thinking; after that the concept of childhood rapidly developed. New York: Laurel Books, pp. 42, 45.

33. Postman, op. cit., p. 45.

34. Clare Rose, (1989) *Children's Clothes Since 1750*. New York: Drama Book Publishers, p. 91. Elizabeth Ewing points out that the change proceeded slowly (op. cit., p. 46).

35. James Laver, (1951) *Children's Fashions in the Nineteenth Century*. London: Batsford Press, pp. 2–3.

36. Rose, op. cit., p. 91; Ewing, op. cit., p. 172.

37. Ewing, op. cit., p. 176.

38. In England, there was a close association between tailors who custommade clothes and the clothing industry with its ready-made clothes until about the 1840s. After that establishments developed that carried only ready-to-wear. The invention of the sewing machine around 1846 revolutionized the method of manufacture. The production of all classes of ready-to-wear apparel increased at an enormous rate. Tailors who made custom-made clothing attempted to compete by using cheaper labor. Jesse Elizabeth Pope, (1905/1970) *The Clothing Industry In New York*. New York: Burt Franklin, p. 12.

39. Joseph Couts, (1850) *A Practical Guide for the Tailor's Cutting-Room*. London: Blackie and Son, pp. 8–12.

40. According to Couts, tailors began with boys of about six, though they were still wearing dresses. At this young age it is the parents that the outfit must

please. It consists of a jacket, a shirt, and a cotton velvet skirt worn over a petticoat. The skirt is plaited and the shirt and sleeves are often tight. Three rows of buttons ornament the jacket. The dress resembles "ladies riding polka"— women's riding outfits—except that the skirt is about knee-length and close-fitting trousers are worn underneath. They are strapped down under shoe or boot. Couts, op. cit., pp. 11, 56.

41. See Couts, op. cit.

42. Couts, op. cit., p. 56.

43. "Education Today," *World Book Encyclopedia*.(1994) Chicago: World Book, Inc., p. 101.

44. Ibid., p. 100

45. Segalen, op. cit., pp. 379–384.

As Segalen pointed out, at the beginning of industrialization the industrial entrepreneur could not meet the growth in demand from his factories. He distributed the necessary materials among the peasant-craftsmen working in a family context. In England, until the 1840s, large quantities of industrial production continued to come out of family workshops and a diversity of working-class families.

46. Segalen, op. cit., p. 394.

47. Segalen, op. cit., pp. 383–384; 393.

48. Examples: Alexander Antigna, *The Fire*, Salon of 1850–51; Joseph Everett Millais, *Christ in the House of His Parents*, 1850; George Frederick Watts *The Irish Famine*, 1849–50; and William-Adolphe Bouguereau's *Indigent Family*, Salon 1865. In Robert Rosenblum, (1984) *19th-Century Art*. New York: Harry N. Abrams.

49. Secondary schools designed for upper-class boys offered a liberal arts program based on Latin and Greek sources. Until the 1800s, secondary schools provided for most upper-class European boys, except for those who attended the universities.

"The Rise of Universal Public Schools," *World Book Encyclopedia*. Chicago: World Book, Inc., pp. 100–101.

50. Ibid., p. 394.

51. On January 1, 1877, Queen Victoria was proclaimed the Empress of India. In Queen Victoria, (1926) *The Letters of Queen Victoria. Second Series. A Selection From Her Majesty's Correspondence and Journal Between the Years 1862–1878*, ed. George Earle Buckle. New York: Longman Green, pp. 514–516.

52. Edgar Z. Friedenberg, (1959) *The Vanishing Adolescent*. Boston, Beacon Hill: Beacon Press, p. 5; Spender, op. cit., p. 236.

53. Friedenberg, op. cit., p. 5

54. Harvey, op. cit., pp. 228–239.

55. Ruth P. Rubinstein, (1994) *Dress Codes: Meanings and Messages in American Culture*. Boulder, Colo.: Westview Press, p. 41

56. By Dickens's regular artist, "Phiz" Harlot Knight Brown. In Harvey, op. cit., p. 137.

57. Harvey, op. cit., p. 136.

58. In Dickens's novel *Dombey and Son*.

59. A. O. J. Cockshut, (1962) *The Imagination of Charles Dickens*. New York: New York University Press, pp. 98–99.

60. Ewing, op. cit., p. 116.

61. Alexander Davidson, (1990) *Blazers, Badges and Boaters: A Pictorial History of School Uniform*. London: Scope Books, pp. 11–17.

62. Davidson, op. cit., p. 16.

63. Davidson, op. cit., p. 11.

64. Davidson, op. cit., p. 20.

65. Ewing, op. cit., p. 113.

66. Spender, op. cit., p. 239.

67. Identified by Reverend Wallace Clare. In Ewing, op. cit., p. 113.

68. Ewing, op. cit., p. 114.

69. Ewing, op. cit., p. 174.

70. Wallace Clare, quoted in Ewing, op. cit., pp. 113–114.

71. Davidson, op. cit., p. 87.

72. Spender, op. cit., p. 235.

73. John Rae, Forward, Davidson, op. cit.

74. Ibid.

75. James Laver, (1960) *Viyella*. Nottingham, England: William Hollins.

76. John R. Gillis, (1973) "Conformity and Rebellion: Contrasting Styles of English and German Youth, 1900–33," *History of Education Quarterly* Fall, pp. 251–252.

77. Gillis, op. cit., p. 251.

78. Erving Goffman, (1961) *Asylums*. New York: Garden City p. xiii.

79. Gillis, op. cit., p. 252.

80. John Springhall, (1977) "Youth, Empire and Society: British Youth Movements, 1883–1840." *International Review of Social History* 16 (part 2), pp. 138–140.

81. Quoted in Davidson, op. cit., p 10.

82. Ewing, op. cit., pp. 115–116.

83. Laver, op. cit., p. 6.

84. Middle-class parents saw the education received in public schools as a passport to success in professional and public life. Carol Dyhouse, (1981) *Girls Growing Up in Late Victorian And Edwardian England*. London: Routledge & Kegan Paul, p. 40.

85. Ewing, op. cit., p. 117.

86. Carol Dyhouse, (1981) *Girls Growing up in Late Victorian and Edwardian England*. London: Routledge & Kegan Paul, pp. 41–43.

87. Dyhouse, op. cit., p. 43.

88. Dyhouse, op. cit., p. 47.

89. Ewing, op. cit., p. 194.

90. Ewing, op. cit., pp. 195–198.

91. Ewing, op. cit., p. 198.

92. Margaret Braun-Ronsdorf, (1964) *Mirror of Fashion: A History of European Costume 1729–1929*. New York: McGraw-Hill, p. 46.

93. Braun-Ronsdorf, op. cit., p. 3.

94. Braun-Ronsdorf, op. cit., pp. 4, 5, 7.

95. Ewing, op. cit., p. 117.

96. Laver, op. cit., p. 6.

97. Ewing, op. cit., p. 119.

98. Ewing, op. cit., p. 121.

99. Ibid.

100. Ewing, op. cit., p. 122.

101. Ewing, op. cit. pp. 118–124.

102. Quoted in ibid.

103. John Springhall, (1971) "The Boy Scouts, Class and Militarism in Relation to British Youth Movements, 1903–1930," *International Review of Social History* 16 (part 2), pp. 140–150.

104. Springhall, (1977), op. cit., p. 39.

105. Springhall, (1971) op. cit., pp. 139–140.

106. Springhall, op. cit., pp. 14–15, 25.

107. Olive Anderson, (1971) "The Growth of Christian Militarism in Mid-Victorian Britain," *English Historical Review* 86, 46–72.

108. Nathan Joseph, (1986) *Uniforms and Nonuniforms: Communication Through Clothing*. New York: Greenwood Press, p. 120.

109. Carol Dyhouse, (1981) *Girls Growing Up in Late Victorian and Edwardian England*. London: Routledge & Kegan Paul, pp. 58, 60.

8

Middle-Class and Other Children: Children's Clothes in the United States, 1860–1918

By mid-nineteenth century, the hold that moralists, Calvinists, and the Puritans had on the upbringing of children had weakened.[1] Calvinism in its old virile sense was slowly disappearing. Minister Henry James Sr. (b.1842) complained that American Protestantism was moving slowly towards "a sad condition of decline."[2] Religion was being replaced by "a feeble Unitarian sentimentality."[3]

Evangelical religion, with its pleading to embrace God with the heart not with the mind, reinforced positive ideas about the nature of childhood among the faithful.[4] Church authorities, moreover, supported ties of affection between mothers and children.[5] There was thus a general shift away from focusing on children's "innate tendencies to wickedness" and the idea of original sin. Children were neither intrinsically divine nor innocent.[6]

There was, moreover, a reassertion of faith in economic opportunity. After the Civil War Americans eagerly speculated on the growth of towns and cities, rushed into all kinds of business enterprise, and embraced many of the economic opportunities which opened up. Fueling the economy were mining, manufacturing of iron and steel, construction, and large projects, such as the transcontinental railroad, rather than farming and trade. The rise of industry brought unprecedented prosperity to several groups: businessmen, the new urban middle-classes, and many immigrants.[7] Work increasingly shifted away from the farm to urban areas, separating the father from his family. Fathers who left home to earn a living often did so at an office, becoming entrepreneurs or salaried employees.[8]

Scientific thinking, technological innovation, industrial production, new communication systems, and economic success came together during this period, generating changes in attitudes towards children, child-rearing practices, and clothes for children.[9]

Unlike the past, when the father introduced his son to crafts, farming skills, or commerce, few fathers could introduce their sons to the tasks performed at the new workplace. Clerical, mechanical, and mathematical operations skills were needed, and these were not easily divisible into manageable parts which children could master.[10] The distinction between what was considered truly important in adult society and what children were actually capable of doing became clear. Little boys and girls played at feeding animals and at using tiny brooms and dustpans but were no longer expected to contribute to the economic resources of the household. Children in the middle-class households were clothed, fed, and educated, but they didn't labor. They became endowed with sentimental value, and parents sought to pass on to their children whatever privilege they had gained.[11]

Child-Rearing Practices

While men immersed themselves in business, they left all other areas of life to their women. The home became a place where the husband rested after the strain of labor, and where the children stayed until they left home. Women's lives revolved around making the home a place of beauty and tranquility. Since fathers were likely to be away at work, it was mothers who took care the family's financial affairs, managed the household, brought up their children, and took responsibility for their clothing.[12]

Adult fashion decreed the choice of material, color, style, and skirt's width. Girls' dresses were simplified, shorter and frillier than those worn by their mothers. The size of the garment and its tightness of fit suggested that a limited degree of activity was allowed.[13] In the 1860s, rich color wool dresses trimmed with black velvet, with full skirts supported by stiffened petticoats, were worn by mothers and daughters. Like their mothers, girls were expected to cover their heads. Girls younger than ten wore hats with low crowns and wide-flapping brims; those older than ten wore hats in the style of "a mushroom, turban or pork-pie."[14] *Godey's Lady's Book* and *Harper's Bazaar* illustrated the fashions of the day, including pantalets with embroidered ruffles that covered the legs to the ankle (see Fig. 8.1), or skirts that met the top of the boot. Like their mothers, girls wore morning frocks, school dresses, visiting and dancing frocks, and a variety of outer wrappings for all sorts of weather.[15]

Younger boys wore tunics and skirts (see Fig. 8.2). Older ones were often dressed in styles originated in Europe, often derived from army or navy uniforms (see Fig. 8.3). Trousers had the bold front or the very new

FIGURE 8.1 Miss Johns. An eight-year-old girl is dressed in party attire. It is a two-piece outfit: an off-the-shoulder blouse in a shimmering dark color, a ballroom-style white skirt in bands that glisten, and ornamental pantalets. Her shoes are flats. From a carte de visite, 1861–1863, by Broadbent & Co., Philadelphia. Chester County Historical Society, West Chester, Pa.

front fly. It seems that boys wore a fly-front on trousers before it was commonly used on men's garments.[16] Braces or suspenders were worn over the shirt when these were tucked inside the trousers. Shirts had dropped shoulders, a soft collar that exposed the chest, and a loosely tied cravat.[17] Popular pant styles for the children of the affluent were just below-the-knee pants with Norfolk or Brighton jackets, or a sailor blouse. Sometimes boys wore tailored suits with collar and tie like their father.[18]

What middle-class children actually wore reflected the family's fortune. Women's magazines continued to urge that children's clothes should be "of equal consequence as those of the grown up members of the family."[19] Buying clothing for their children was a sign of love (see Fig. 8.4). Lacking in inherited or inheritable wealth, members of the rising middle-classes used consumption to demonstrate their economic success. Any new style that appeared in France and England was adopted by middle-class parents, who on Sunday and other formal occasions dressed their children in fashionable attire, creating a sense of connected-

FIGURE 8.2   William Husted, Jr. The development of practical, middle-class style: the boy is wearing a skirt with ornamented pantalets, hose, and laced boots. From a carte de visite, 1858–1866, by E. Woodward, West Chester, Pa. Chester County Historical Society, West Chester, Pa.

FIGURE 8.3   J. Pusey Passmore. By the age of five or six little boys could be dressed in male-style dress. The style here may be based on the style of military uniforms, replete with buttons on the jacket and breeches. From a carte de visite, 1871–1874, by E. S. Marshall. Chester County Historical Society, West Chester, Pa.

FIGURE 8.4   Howard Frees. A young boy three years of age is wearing a loose-fitting comfortable dress. From a carte de visite, 1877–1886, by Ralph F. Channel, Phoenixville, Pa. Chester County Historical Society, West Chester, Pa.

ness and forging new social identities. Their clothes helped anchor them to a world characterized by consumption.[20]

Children in middle-class homes were seen as deserving their own space, their own eating utensils, and even their own furniture. The infant spent the first few months in a bassinet in the adults' space. Then the child was moved to a room they called the nursery and placed in a crib with guardrails and bars. Children ate seated in a high-chair, from a set of dishes that differed from those of the adults. The special chair, dishes, and flatware made it easier for a young child to eat without spilling food and disrupting adult meals. Baby carriages, toys, and books were now widely available.[21]

Newspapers, magazines, and advertising[22] depicted children as innocent beings, playful and free.[23] The common belief was that influential adults can shape a child's future conduct. Affection towards the young was what the experts—educators, psychologists, and advertisers—were recommending.[24] Mothers exercised control, but through an open display of affection, kisses, the singing of a song, or permission to play a favorite game.[25] A mother forced to resort to the rod had already failed her children, warned Orson Fowler in 1870.[26] Autobiographies rarely report physical punishment during this period. "Our parents never cared much about punishing us . . ." reported Alice Kingsbury. She recalls that she was spanked only once. She wrote: "Usually when I had a tantrum, my mother took me in her arms and sat in a rocking chair, rocking and singing to me."[27]

Some parents expressed their love and approval in a material form. They rewarded a child with the opportunity of amusement or a break for play, suggesting that middle-class parents approved of their children having fun. Child-sized mugs with appropriate inscriptions, "A Present for a Good Boy," for example, appeared; also tin whistles with patriotic symbols and the words "For a Good Child."[28] Gardener and Company of New York City manufactured a doll-sized chair about 1875 whose back was pierced in a pattern which spelled the word "PET."[29] Such a chair was a gift to a child. The little girl would be the one to read the message as she faced it during play. In mother-child doll play the doll would become the projection of the child—"PET."[30]

In women's magazines children were portrayed as charming extensions of nature's bounty (*Godey's Ladies Book*, May 1862).[31] In the text, the young child is referred to as "kitten," "bunny," "lamb," or "pup"—creatures of nature, soft, cuddly, and playful.[32] Such images were of young creatures, neither fully grown nor tame, doing little but eating, playing, and sleeping. Innocence was considered childhood's most distinguishing characteristic. In popular poetry, for example, a child that had died was portrayed as "a bud that never bloomed."[33]

In the decorative motifs on household accessories, such as napkin rings, match safes, and trivets, figures of children were often interchangeable with those of leaves and flowers, animals and insects, alluding to the idea that children were creatures of nature. Young boys were often shown with angelic faces and characterized as gems and treasures. Advertising and other popular graphic arts often imposed the face of a young child on a flower.[34]

Illustrations of girls reaching school age, about six, portray them as docile and immaculate (see Fig. 8.5). This image perhaps foreshadowed the adult ideal, that women should be the keepers of the home and maintainers of virtue and should stay away from the world of commerce and competition.[35]

At home there were no sharp differences between appropriate conduct and activity for prepubescent boys and girls, autobiographies suggest. Children of the middle class were growing up curious, free-spirited, and less well behaved than before. They touched parlor ornaments they shouldn't have touched, leaned out the windows, balanced themselves

FIGURE 8.5   Sisters Anna and Jennie Eachus. Both are dressed in
ill-fitting practical dresses and pinafores, which are dark in color.
The girl who is standing is wearing unornamented pantalets and
shoes that are laced. The seated girl wears shoes that are buttoned.
The girls' outfits may reflect the fact that during the 1850s and
1860s factory-made clothes became available, and Butternick
introduced full-scale patterns in 1863. Shoes, too, began to be
machine-sewn in 1860. Those who could neither afford handmade
shoes nor produce their own footwear could now wear shoes. From
a carte de visite, 1871–1874, by A. McCormick, Oxford, Pa. Chester
County Historical Society, West Chester, Pa.

on the back of chairs, and performed a variety of tricks, disrupting adult
conversation.[36] By 1864 it was considered bad manners for a mother to
take her children with her on her morning visits,[37] helping to separate the
adult domain from that of the children's.

During play hours children should be unrestrained and unwatched, advised Dr. David Little, managers of the Rochester Orphans' Asylum in 1868. Children would be stronger, happier, and wiser if they were allowed to run, leap, and holler.[38]

Autobiographies of childhoods lived before 1875 also suggest that girls were growing up in an environment that was more friendly than in the beginning of the century. Girls, for most of the week, experienced childhood as a period of physical and psychic freedom.[39] In a book published in 1897, Carolyn Briggs complained that while growing up in Northampton, Massachusetts, once a week she lost her accustomed freedom to Sunday strictures: "At sunset Saturday night, the straightjacket was put on . . . [and] all the joy of life was set aside."[40] She was buttoned into a child's corset, fashionable outfit, and white gloves. After dinner on Sunday, she reports, all her nice clothes were taken off and she was allowed to run "like a young calf in the meadow back of the house. . . . I thank God for that every year of my life."[41]

Freedom to play outdoors and experience a vigorous outdoor life was often recommended by physicians for girls who suffered from tuberculosis or were otherwise physically frail. As a result some girls could spend their days completely as their brothers did, unfettered by the accoutrements of fashionable attire. Girls climbed trees, jumped off stable roofs, fell into rain barrels, fished in the horse trough, dirtied and tore their dresses.[42]

Reaching puberty meant an end to freedom.[43] The end of free-spirited childhood was marked by the demand that the girl switch into restrictive female attire. Nineteenth-century women identified freedom with childhood and clung to it as long as they could, Louisa May Alcott suggests. In her books *Little Women* (1868) and *Jack and Jill, A Village Story* (1880) she tells about the regret her heroines felt at having to leave childhood behind.[44] The popularity of the books over several generations suggests that generations of girls sympathized with the character Jo's plea, "Let me be a little girl as long as I can," and her wish that "wearing flatirons on our heads would keep us from growing up."[45]

Caddie Woodlawn, a popular historical novel for children by Carol Brink, published in 1935, describes the life of a girl growing up on a farm in Wisconsin in the mid–1860s.[46] The girl ran free with her brothers, but her two sisters did not. Caddie's father hoped that the outdoor life would improve her fragile health. At the time of the story Caddie is twelve and approaching puberty. Her mother has punished Caddie alone for an act of meanness in which Caddie and her brothers had conspired.[47] The mother thus indicates that this was a behavior inappropriate for a girl. Repeatedly, Caddie's father explains that she has reached an age where her life must change and exalts the role that women play. It is women, he tells her, "who keep the world sweet and beautiful. Women's task is to teach men and boys gentleness and courtesy and love and kindness. It is a big task . . . harder than cutting trees or building mills or damming rivers."[48] "How about it, Caddie, have we run with the colts long enough?" Caddie's father asks.[49]

Toys

The word toy in the sense of a plaything exclusively for children has its origin in the nineteenth century.[50] Toy historians consider the period between 1860 and 1914 as the Golden Age of toys.[51] The Census Bureau listed 47 toymakers for 1850; by 1880 there were 173. The jump in the number of toymakers reflects the changed agenda for children.

Milton Bradley, a toy maker from Springfield, Massachusetts, saw toys as a means of teaching the child through play. He viewed play as "the child's equivalent of the adult job."[52] In 1861, he began developing child-oriented toys for kindergartens. Craftsmen and skilled mechanics applied their skills to the design of toys; they were produced in quantities never dreamed of before and some at prices that even factory workers could afford. Street vendors often sold them.[53]

Replicas of real objects, like moving vehicles for example, were expensive and designed for the children of the well-to-do. They were often modeled after coaches, cannons, toy soldiers, and the doll houses had furniture and crockery of the kind the children's families used. For example, a child could have a handmade horse-drawn coach called a Carpenter Tally-ho. Its cost was about four dollars.[54] In 1870 three to four dollars was a weekly salary for many workers. A toymaker working for Francis W. Carpenter Company in 1889 earned $8.50 for a sixty-hour week.[55]

Having cars and engines that really worked introduced children to the identity of privilege; to the reality of what Mark Twain called the Gilded Age. Toys made of materials such as tin, lead, leather, rubber, and wood were affordable.[56] Technology was such that sheets of metal could now be rolled and these could be clamped, punched, cut, folded into shape, printed with designs, and equipped with tools, creating a world in miniature. Mechanisms such as springs or gear-wheels were simplified and placed in miniature trains and trolleys so that they could be used for play. Pleasure wagons, coaches and buggies, service carts of all kinds such as peddlers' wagons, or ice, coal, and grocers' wagons, all drawn by horses, were popular. Along the same lines, several pieces of equipment used by the fire department were reproduced as toys. Fire engines like real ones were housed in firehouses made by Crandall, Reed, and Ives.[57]

Also popular were bell toys, transportation toys, dolls, push-pull toys, balls, marbles, hoops, tops, squeak toys, musical toys, puzzles, board games, mechanical moving banks and ordinary still banks, in addition to animals, from beetles to Noah's Ark to rocking horses. Toy collectors identify the following categories of toys: "Symbols of Freedom," "Toys to Grow On," "Familiar Animals," "Fairy Tales and Fantasy," "The Circus," and toys for sports and recreation.[58]

The craze for teddy bears, which began in 1905, peaked in 1908, and continues still, made people aware that children like to cuddle soft, fuzzy animals. They offer children a sense of comfort. Advertisements for a new style of pajamas designed to keep a child warm and comfortable at night (they had a drop seat and moccasin feet) showed a sleepy child in the pajamas, holding, hugging, or dragging a soft toy bear named, like all teddy bears, after Theodore Roosevelt.[59]

The large number and variety of toymakers, making toys in a large range of prices, suggest that making toys was profitable. Adults and children viewed them as important.[60]

Urban Environment

Urban areas had turned into "walking" environments where people could live within walking distance of their place of work. There were horse cars, trolley cars and, later, streetcars, whose surfaces were increasingly covered with advertisements.[61] Advertising encouraged consumption.[62] The success of advertising encouraged the manufacture of advertising as an industry.[63]

Consumption was encouraged in yet another way. Where it was too far to walk, horse-drawn omnibuses brought together rich and poor, "men, women and children, in silks and rags—brokers and bankers, tinkers and tailors, laborers and lawyers."[64] Other travel exposed parents and children to variety in style. "Social identity was established through new possibilities of consumption," observed Abelson.[65]

To demonstrate their newly acquired wealth members of the middle-class engaged in what Thorstein Veblen called conspicuous consumption.[66] Children of the middle class wore the kinds of clothes that indicated their life-style: fashionable dress for formal activities and comfortable dress for leisure.[67] The good shoes and sumptuous attire of the affluent (see Fig. 8.7) provided a contrast to the clothes worn by working class boys portrayed by Frank Duveneck (1872) (see Fig. 8.8), Winslow Homer (1871) (see Fig. 8.9), and (in photographs) by journalist Jacob Riis (see Fig. 8.10), who depicted the skimpy, frayed, and torn clothing children of the urban poor wore.[68]

Boston, New York City, Chicago, and the other large cities experienced change. Some of the dry goods stores became dry goods bazaars with their racks and counters displaying immense quantities and a large vari-

FIGURE 8.6   Clara Hipple.
Girls' dresses began to
diverge from adult women's
fashions. By the 1880s in the
United States, girls' attire
took its style from the nursery
and schoolroom. In England
in 1880 this style was called a
nursery blouse. It was made
in a variety of different
materials. 1882. Chester
County Historical Society,
West Chester, Pa.

ety of goods. They also began to boast "amazing" decor: profuse displays
of out-of-season flowers and a dramatic use of color, all designed to elicit
shopping behavior. Macy's, Wanamaker's, and Marshall Field's, for example, held special events, such as openings, promotions, and holiday
and seasonal attractions. With their new sounds, sights, and smells,[69] the
department stores became dream worlds.[70]

The cities absorbed millions of immigrants from alien cultures and immigrants from the countryside. The culture of the new immigrants
spilled into the public spaces, which included theaters, music halls,
parks, and fairs. A rich public cultural life took place on the streets of
American cities. New immigrants competed with the native-born citizens for political and economic power. Moreover, the immigrants had
cultural practices undesired by the locals, such as dancing, drinking, boxing, and pornography.

The segmentation of culture was thought to imperil the very basis of
traditional order. The aristocracy gained new influence with the new in-
dustrialists and the new members of the middle-class, since "following
the lead of the arbiters of culture promised both relief from impending

FIGURE 8.7 George Roberts. A boy wears a well-tailored adult-style suit. From a carte de visite, 1879, by T. W. Taylor, West Chester, Pa. Chester County Historical Society, West Chester, Pa.

FIGURE 8.8 *The Whistling Boy.* A working-class boy. He is wearing a leather apron over his tattered clothing. Frank Duveneck, 1872. Cincinnati Art Museum.

FIGURE 8.9 *The School Room.* Before industrialization. Life on the farm and in the country. Some of the children are wearing boots, some are barefoot and most are simply, even poorly dressed. Winslow Homer, 1871. St. Louis Art Museum. Museum photo.

FIGURE 8.10 Two Ragamuffins, "Didn't live nowhere." Jacob Riis, n.d. The Jacob A. Riis Collection. Museum of the City of New York. By permission.

disorder and an avenue to cultural legitimacy," argued Lawrence W. Levine.[71] There was a three-pronged response from the upper classes to the cultural changes produced by the immigrants: retreating into their own private space, transforming public spaces by rules and systems of taste, and converting the strangers so that they emulated the behavior of the elites.[72]

The urban environment resulted in two new types of schooling. The pre-school or kindergarten (a "children's garden") became popular in many cities in the 1860s and 1870s.[73] Kindergartens embodied the view that young children need to learn in order to develop. They were seen as vulnerable beings in need of protection and nurturing.[74] Rather than the traditional male tutor who saw himself as a drill master, kindergarten teachers were women who viewed themselves as pedagogical midwives. Their goal was to engage children in a way that would help cultivate a morally autonomous human being—self-governed, self-motivated, self-disciplined, and self-controlled. Instructive talk and regulated play were thought to achieve these goals. A tutorial environment was furnished with small round tables and little chairs and filled with toys,[75] where the child was expected to keep busy with the things that interested him or her.[76]

In a kindergarten, children interacted with their peers, had the opportunity to measure themselves against each other and sometimes to even compete.[77] This new interaction was unlike the early part of the century, when young children were educated at home or at church, and a child's interpersonal contact with other children was limited.

Private boarding schools were for older children. They were designed to keep sons of wealthy men isolated from the vice of the city so as to preserve the innocence of childhood, allowing growth "into a pure and responsible maturity."[78] They were designed as a four-year college-preparatory program, encouraging children to remain dependent on their parents through adolescence, concluded historian James McLachlan in his study *American Boarding Schools*.[79] Sons of rich men were educated to self-restraint, rigid self-control, severe frugality in personal style, and the ability to postpone immediate gratification for larger future ends.[80]

The new social class that emerged in the second half of the nineteenth century consisted of men who in the new impersonal urban environment sought to acquire status markers.[81] Establishing a family that would be embraced by the social elite was a possibility, and it became an important goal.[82] Acquiring an elite status involved, in part, keeping one's children from engaging in practices that might undermine one's success. Children born to a family that aspired to inclusion in the upper-class were socialized to incorporate the tastes and attitudes that would make them suitable partners in social relationships that would lead to acceptance in upper-class social events.[83]

Crusades to protect children from vice addressed parental fears that vice would render their children unfit for desirable jobs, social positions, or marriage. Obscenity endangered elite children because moral corruption threatened to topple them from the peak of the social hierarchy, rendering them unfit for respectable society.[84]

With the support of the YMCA, Anthony Comstock prodded Congress to close the loopholes which were present in the Federal obscenity statute of 1872.[85] He wanted a law that would suppress all that he considered vice, including illustrations, advertisements, notices of fancy books and pictures, gambling materials, swindling schemes, and articles on contraception. On March 2, 1873, the bill became a law.[86] Congress made it illegal to send pornography and advertisements of contraceptive devices through the mail; materials which, together with prostitution, new immigrants had made increasingly available.[87] The March 7, 1873, issue of the *New York Journal of Commerce* commented, "Something will be forgiven to a Congress which thus powerfully sustains the cause of morality."[88] On Thursday March 7, 1873, puritan Anthony Comstock received his commission as Special Agent to the Postmaster General, where he controlled what was sent through the mails.[89] Trustees of art museums argued that nude paintings in their collections should not be considered obscene, for they would prepare children to appreciate the fine art collections of Europe.[90]

Boarding schools were founded with the express intent of protecting elite children from vice. They carefully selected their students, and those who attended met mostly their own kind. The schools were establishments where the individual child's needs were ignored.[91] By sending their children to boarding schools, social critic Randolph Bourne maintained, the family became "the deadly enemy of individual will and freedom."[92] After vacation when boys had to return to school, they were often reluctant and had to be persuaded. Many felt the pangs of homesickness even before leaving behind the family's comfort and care.[93]

A girl's purity was maintained by keeping her close to home. Domesticity and maternity were the qualities desired of girls. Girls were married so they could love rather than allowed to marry for love.[94] On her twentieth birthday a girl consciously abandoned the lightheartedness of girlhood and put away "the things of a child."[95]

Industrial Production of Clothes

Increasingly, urban households came to depend for their goods and services, including clothes, on industrial production. Searching for fabric, lining, buttons, even the right color thread to make a particular garment, was taxing; home production of clothes had become a burden.

Advertisements assured women that ready-to-wear and factory-design clothes would often exceed in quality those created by the skill of a woman sewing for herself. Although women did not have to buy, some could not easily resist the seduction. The department store became the place where the gradual shift from a prudent economy to guarded extravagance took place.[96] Ready-to-wear clothes[97] were introduced to the United States by tailors who came from England;[98] they produced ready-to-wear attire and offered it for sale. Although each garment was individually made, its details were shared by others. The garments came in stock sizes, affecting fit, comfort, and appearance.[99] They did, however, offer a choice.

Receiving communion for the first time (at age twelve), is a formal occasion. Around 1890 boys tended to wear either the English Eton suit or the Little Lord Fauntleroy outfit for the occasion.[100] Both ensembles had prestigious undertones. The Eton suit was associated with the English upper classes. The Lord Fauntleroy outfit was based on a story about a little boy whose father believed he had no chance of inheriting the family's title. He moved to America. The American child was found by his grandfather and brought to England to inherit the family title. Illustrations by Reginald Birch for *Little Lord Fauntleroy* (1896), depicted the child in an outfit (see Fig. 8.11) based on an eighteenth-century style designed for children of the nobility. The outfit allowed nineteenth-century children and/or parents to dream of being special, of perhaps being "discovered as noble," as Fauntleroy was. The costume allowed parents to delude themselves that they were of the aristocracy rather than members of the middle class who had acquired wealth—a relatively new social formation. The book was a best-seller; so were a subsequent play and movie of the same name.

In the role of a lord, the little boy is shown dressed in a black or blue velvet suit, a white lace collar, black stockings, and black pointed shoes.[101] His pants are about knee length, his jacket is slightly flared, coming down right beneath the waistline with a single cloth-covered button at the neckline. The shirt is loose around the collar and made of silk or white linen cambric with small buttons.[102] The boy is portrayed hopping and running, suggesting that the suit was comfortable to wear. Because it was made out of expensive fabrics, velvet and lace, it was expensive and considered special occasion clothing. Its sumptuousness illustrated the phenomenon of conspicuous consumption, the use of material objects to demonstrate high social worth.[103] Gradually the attire acquired a negative connotation, as "sissy" attire. The Buster Brown suit had no allusions to the English upper class. It was an American invention. The outfit was worn by a cartoon character created by Richard Outcault (1863–1928) and considered formal attire, to be worn for formal in-

FIGURE 8.11 The Little Lord Fauntleroy suit. Popularized by the Frances Hodgson Burnett novel. This version is in purple plush, rather than velvet; the collar and sleeves are of Irish crochet lace. It was worn by a seven-year-old boy to watch Queen Victoria's Jubilee procession in 1887. Bethnal Green Museum of Childhood, England. By permission.

teractions such as going to school. It consisted of a double-breasted jacket, hip length, and pants tapered to the knee. A small round white collar was attached to a shirt with stud buttons, as all collars of the time were. A loosely made bow tie, a straw hat worn over short hair with bangs, and short boots completed the look. Like the Eton suit, it conveyed propriety and self-restraint. The Buster Brown boot was advertised as "helping correct one's step while lending it a style."[104]

The Reefer, on the other hand, was a coat intended to protect the child from wind and rain. It was short and had straight lines. It was made of heavy fabric similar to the one sailors used. It had a double-breasted front closing, a large squared collar and lots of pockets. It spoke of the sea, pirates, and adventure.[105] Its intended purpose, however, was to maintain and safeguard a child's health so that his school attendance would not be affected.

Other protective garments for children also emerged at the turn of the century. These were elements of dress designed to prevent injury while playing sports: canvas tennis shoes with rubber soles, quilted knickers, sweaters, gloves, mitts, catcher's masks, cleated shoes, leather helmets,[106] and jockstraps.[107] Knickerbockers were Turkish-style trousers developed in England in the 1850s for hunting. In the 1880s they were shortened by being gathered at the knee to keep pant legs from becoming entangled in bicycle spokes.[108]

Girls, too, wanted to ride bikes. Some wore bloomers under dresses. Others adopted the divided skirt (Turkish Trousers), also known as "bloomer-trousers," to be able to ride a bike and more fully participate in physical activity. Velveteen was often used for such suits.[109]

Bicycling required more relaxed warmth than a tailored coat or a jacket could provide. "Bike sweaters" for women and turtleneck sweaters for men protected the neck from drafts. The earliest version of the sweater was a pullover that had a fold-down (turtle) neck and was of a heavy knit. By the turn of the century a variety of open-necked and collarless pullovers emerged, including the coat-sweater or cardigan.[110]

The wearing of sweaters spread. Soon mail-order catalogs began selling them. Worn by newsboys, hikers, and football players,[111] their social meaning and significance changed from a garment for a special activity to an all-around warmth-supporting garment.

Older children's attire may have had an impact on the development of clothes for young children that were simple and easy to wear.[112] (See, for example, Fig. 8.12.) Children and adult styles of dress began to diverge toward the end of the nineteenth century. Children's clothes acquired a simpler line and became less constricting. By the turn of the century, coveralls that fit loosely over trousers emerged. The garment had a front bib and was held by a strap around the neck. It offered freedom of movement. Ad-

FIGURE 8.12   *The Daughters of Edward Darley Boit.* Dress pinafores were
decorated with white muslin with frills and sometimes with inserts of lace and
embroidery. The corsets and crinolines that characterized Parisian fashion
during this period are absent. John Singer Sargent, 1882. Museum of Fine Arts,
Boston. Museum photo.

vertisements, however, suggested that "no other trousers are required."
They urged parents to "Let your boy romp about and play without being
afraid of spoiling his best clothes." The garment came to be designated an
overall and worn as the primary garment instead of being an overgar-
ment.[113] Overalls were made in a variety of colors: blue, black, and red-
blue denim. These overalls were also advertised as bike-riding attire.

   The invention of a rubber diaper-cover made it possible for young
boys to wear these overalls at an earlier age. For the first time in Western
society boys could wear trousers before being toilet trained.[114]

FIGURE 8.13 Coming
Home from Fresh Air
Vacation. Jacob Riis, 1890.
The Jacob A. Riis
Collection. Museum of
the City of New York.
Museum photo.

A girl's yoke dress was practical and comfortable. The dress consisted of a full skirt and bodice cut in one piece and sewn to a yoke. It hung from the shoulders and had no constriction at the waist. In a pamphlet discussing the yoke dress Helen Berry wrote that it was "the first truly child's style of dress in the Victorian age at a time when little girls wore replicas of the dresses worn by their mothers."[115] The dress allowed freer use of the limbs. It was easy to make, fit, and launder. It concealed too thin or too plump bodies, and the length could be adjusted to the one most attractive on the child.

The clothes children of the affluent middle class wore on public occasions helped to establish, maintain, and affirm their privileged social identity.[116] The specialized garments they wore for leisure activities enabled them to take part in new activities and experience new feelings and sentiments.

"The Other"

In contrast to the affluent urban middle-class children (see Fig. 8.7), the poor were dressed in rags and often wore no shoes (see Fig. 8.13). Working-class boys reaching school age acquired a negative stereotypical desig-

FIGURE 8.14   *The Tambourine.* Children dancing in the city ghetto. A variety of ages and styles of dress are seen. Jerome Myers, 1905. The Phillips Collection. Washington, D.C. 1890.

nation. They were described as dirty-faced, wily, "bad," or "mischievous." Real boys must manipulate not only the environment, but friends as well, like Tom Sawyer at the white-wash fence; they must learn the tricks of the trade.[117] If a boy successfully bent the rules, he would be deemed "ingenious"; if caught, he would have to take his punishment "like a man."[118]

In books and magazines working-class boys were admonished to acquire middle-class respectability. The ideal of the self-made man that came into prominence suggested that children find their own fortune. To achieve this goal a working-class boy must leave home, Horatio Alger's books suggested.[119] In *Strive and Succeed* (1872), an image typical of Alger's fiction shows the hero, about twelve, waving his hat to his parents, who are waving back. He is leaving home for a life away from his parents' farm. He is in long trousers, jacket, vest, a white collar, and a bow tie. His appearance is neat and his walk purposeful.[120]

The characters that make up Alger's stories are predictable: a villainous father figure, a gentle and appreciative mother, and a benevolent merchant who takes him in. The hero escapes from the plots laid by his enemies—usually an unholy alliance between a snobbish boy and the villainous father figure.[121]

In Alger's stories, leaving the ranks of the "working class" is signified in a change in dress. The hero's patron gives him a good suit and a pocket watch, which indicate his attainment of a more elevated class position with its required respect for time. Worldly success involved self control, which to Alger meant no smoking, drinking, swearing, or lying. He argued that for the "pure," there is always room at the top.[122] On the other hand, it was generally recognized that purity was not enough. A boy who grew up dirty and ragged must learn to dress neatly and modestly, develop mathematical ability, and acquire a smattering of a foreign language.

In the small rural-agricultural communities in the first half of the nineteenth century, the family's rank determined the child's style of dress.[123] If children needed to affirm their identity, the evidence was all around them, in the people and their buildings.[124] The same was true in the second half of the century. The attire of children of pioneer and country families, for the most part, remained unchanged. Except for churchgoing, a funeral or a wedding, children were ill-dressed. They wore mostly battered trousers and shirts, and worn-out shoes or none at all. Canvas gaiters with buttons at the sides were also popular among them. A wool scarf or a red bandanna and a straw hat or a billed cap completed the outfit.[125]

In *The Adventures of Huckleberry Finn* (1884), Mark Twain (1835–1910) rejects the idea of a poor boy growing up in a rural community and achieving middle-class respectability—the embodiment of success. In the book Huck Finn was occasionally coerced into fashionable dress (see Fig. 8.15). Twain presented him as saying, "The widow Douglas took me for her son, and allowed she would sivilize me; but it was rough living in the house all the time . . . ; so when I couldn't stand it no longer I lit out. I got into my old rags and sugar hogs-head again and was free and satisfied."[126] Like the voyageurs of the early part of the century, Huck Finn sought his fortune on a raft. Later, he had to go back to the house where "She put me in them new clothes again, and I couldn't do nothing but sweat and sweat, and feel all cramped up."[127] Twain related that youngsters smoked, swore, and sought to be free of adult constraints. For their pains children were subjected to physical punishment.

Accompanying the story are illustrations. Huck is usually shown wearing loose-fitting trousers held by suspenders (see Fig. 8.16). They are worn out and in a length that today would be called "floods" or "high-waters"—short either because he is too old for them or to avoid getting the pants wet when he accidentally stepped into a puddle. He is usually barefoot and wears a battered straw hat.

In one particular illustration he is in adult-like pose resting on a bank of a river under a tree, a corn-cob pipe in his mouth, dangling a fishing

FIGURE 8.15 "Huck dressed in his Sunday best visiting his father." His father greets him with, "Starchy clothes—very. You've put on considerable frills since I been away. I'll take you down a peg before I get done with you." E. W. Kemble, 1884. From *Adventures of Huckleberry Finn*, Centennial Facsimile Edition, 1985. Photo, Greg Kitchen.

FIGURE 8.16 Huckleberry Finn. He wears the attire of boys in rural areas and those who worked on river boats. Like many other boys, he wears his pants held up by only one suspender. He also wears a straw hat to protect himself from the sun. From *Adventures of Huckleberry Finn*, Centennial Facsimile Edition, 1985. Photo, Greg Kitchen.

rod into the water. He is at peace and one with nature.[128] Huck didn't work for a living. He was a vagrant and often a crook.

Rural Youth

Twelve-year-old boys did leave home to make their own way. During the Civil War they served as "powder monkeys," assisting Navy men in loading guns aboard fighting vessels. (The usual age of adulthood at that time was marked by marriage and the establishment of another family. This was usually at twenty-four years of age or older.)[129] Powder monkeys were outfitted in flared trousers patterned after sailor uniforms. A yoke with dropped-shoulder line goes across the chest with a small panel or yoke at the neck. A black kerchief is tied in front or back. Some also wore a stiff cap, an early form of Kepi, that had a leather visor and was pushed down in the front.[130]

A cowboy's life was also a means of escaping from a future on the family farm. The first long trail drive took place in 1866 from the "beef bowl of Texas." The goal was to feed a hungry nation recovering from years of civil strife.[131] The pay was meager and the work dirty and hard. But riding a trail offered a challenge,[132] and to many it may have been a rite of passage.[133]

On the East Coast, children became familiar with the characteristics of a cowboy, a frontier hero, through the Wild West pageant. The first memorable pageant was the one in 1884, which starred William Levi Taylor (Buck Taylor), also known as "King of the Cowboys." According to his promoter, William F. ("Buffalo Bill") Cody, Taylor was a Texan and lucky that he grew up at all. He was orphaned when he was eight. His father died during the Civil War. He became a cowboy because that was what one did in postwar Texas.[134]

Theodore Roosevelt identified the cowboy with the "cult of the masculine." He viewed the cowboy as a "man's man"—someone who represents masculine virtues. In 1888 Roosevelt described cowboys as "rough-riders," and called on them to join his regiment during the Spanish-American War.

Cowboys wore utilitarian, ill-fitting clothes in a variety of styles.[135] What the children's wear industry calls "Western Wear," the fancy shirt, jeans, and boots, was a costume created by the author Owen Wister for the movie industry.[136] The costume was popularized and turned into an icon in the vocabulary of images in American popular culture.[137]

By the turn of the century, dressing the children of the less affluent became a goal for companies such as Sears Roebuck. A one piece undergarment called a "Union Suit" (similar to the long-johns adults wore) was designed to conserve body heat. In the fall 1900 Sears Roebuck catalogue it was described as "Glove-fitting, Warm, Comfortable." Union Suits for infants were sold according to how old they were in terms of months.[138]

Inexpensive, factory-made garments for boys were mailed to people out west, those living on farms, and those living in remote mountain areas.[139] The suits for boys were advertised as "custom made." What that meant was that the clothes could be customized by providing the merchant with a child's measurements. The garments were made in smaller adult sizes.[140] The styles were described as "Renewed," following the styles adults had worn the "previous season or two."[141] Boys' suits and girls' dresses were illustrated on pages separate and distinct from the clothes designed for adults.

Magazines addressed to the affluent, however, continued to show boys' clothes on the same page as the clothes for an adult male and girls' clothes next to a fashionable adult woman. Moreover, an industry publication, *The American Cloak and Suit Review* of January 1916, reported, "Practically the only difference between the models featured for women in general and those designed especially for the young girl is that the skirt of the misses suit is worn shorter."[142]

Notes

1. Ann Douglas (1978) points out that the change initially affected the role of the well-bred woman in the Northeast. *Feminization of American Culture*. New York: Alfred A. Knopf, p. 19.

2. Douglas, op. cit., p. 17.

3. Ibid.

4. Mary Lynn Stevens Heininger, (1984) "Children, Childhood, and Change in America, 1820–1920," in Heininger, et al., *A Century of Childhood*. Rochester, New York: The Margaret Woodbury Strong Museum, pp. 1–2.

5. Douglas, op. cit., p. 19.

6. Bernard Wishy, (1968) *The Child and the Republic The Dawn of Modern American Child Nurture*. Philadelphia: University of Pennsylvania Press, pp. 109–114.

7. John G. Cawelty, (1965) *Apostles of the Self-Made Man*. Chicago: The University of Chicago Press, p. 167.

8. Heininger, op. cit., p. 11.

9. Warren I. Susman, (1984) *Culture As History*. New York: Pantheon Books, p. 238; Robert H. Wiebe, (1967) *The Search For Order 1877–1920*. New York: Hill and Wang.

10. Heininger, op. cit., p. 21.

11. Nicola Beisel, (1997) *Imperiled Innocents, Anthony Comstock and Family Reproduction in Victorian America*. Princeton, N.J.: Princeton University Press, p. 6.

12. Elaine S. Abelson, (1989) *When Ladies Go A-Thieving*. New York: Oxford University Press, p. 19.

13. In the beginning of the nineteenth century girls' dresses were simple, in accordance with the dictates of fashion, the Empire look.

14. Elisabeth McClelland, (1904/1973) *Historic Dress in America 1607–1870.* New York: Benjamin Blom, vol. 2, p. 319.

15. Estelle A. Worrell, (1980) *Children's Costume in America 1607–1910.* New York: Charles Scribner and Sons, pp. 111–125.

16. Worrell, op. cit., p. 111.

17. Worrell, op. cit., p. 11; see illustration 135, p. 96.

18. Worrell, op. cit., Plates 6 and 7.

19. Abelson, op. cit., p. 50.

20. Thorstein Veblen, (1899/1957) *The Theory of the Leisure Class.* New York: Mentor Books. Veblen argued that parents in American society dress their children in clothing more expensive then they should so as to encourage higher social evaluation.

21. Heininger, op. cit., p. 19.

22. Susman, op. cit., p. 238.

23. The *New York Times*, December 5, 1897. An art review by Grace Glueck was entitled, "Before the Flowers Fade: The Eden of Childhood." An exhibit curated by David Dearinger at the National Academy Museum in New York City.

24. Douglas, op. cit., p. 48.

25. Heininger, op. cit., pp. 16–17.

26. Quoted in Karin Calvert, (1984) "Cradle to Crib: The Revolution in Nineteenth-Century Children's Furniture," in Heininger et al., op. cit., p. 41.

27. Alice Kingsbury, *In Old Waterbury*, (Waterbury: Matatuck Historical Society, 1942). Quoted in Heininger, op. cit., p. 104.

28. Heininger, op. cit., p. 10, 15.

29. Heininger, op. cit., p. 15.

30. Ibid.

31. Heininger, op. cit., p. 14.

32. Heininger, op. cit., p. 15.

33. Heininger, op. cit., p. 14.

34. Heininger, op. cit., p. 25.

35. Heininger, op. cit., p. 26.

36. Heininger, op. cit., p. 41.

37. Eliza Leslie, (1864) *The Ladies Guide to Politeness and Manners.* Philadelphia: T. B. Peterson, p. 290.

38. Heininger, op. cit., p. 16.

39. Anne Scott MacLeod, (1984) "The Caddie Woodlawn Syndrome: American Girlhood in the Nineteenth Century," in Heininger et. al, op. cit., pp. 98–101.

40. Caroline Briggs (1897) *Reminiscences and Letters.* Ed. G. S. Merriam Boston: Houghton Mifflin, as quoted in MacLeod, op. cit., pp. 100–101.

41. Briggs, as quoted in MacLeod, op. cit., p. 100.

42. MacLeod, op. cit., p. 100.

43. MacLeod, op. cit., pp. 97–119.

44. MacLeod, op. cit., p. 108.

45. Ibid.

46. Carol R. Brink, (1935) *Caddie Woodlawn.* New York: Macmillan, p. 240.

47. Brink, op. cit., p. 97.

48. MacLeod, op. cit., p. 97.

49. MacLeod, op. cit., p. 98.

50. Until then the word was used to describe an adult bauble, a costly miniature such as a piece of silver furniture made by the finest silversmith of the day, or a trifle, an object of little or no value.

In Bernard Barenholtz and Inez McClintock, (1980) *American Antique Toys*. New York: Harry N. Abrams, p. 33.

51. Jac Remise and Jean Fondin, (1967) *The Golden Age of Toys*. Greenwich, Conn.: International Book Society, p. 15.

52. Barenholtz and McClintock, op. cit., p. 33.

53. Remise and Fondin, op. cit., p. 12.

54. Remise and Fondin, op. cit., p. 14.

55. Barenholtz and McClintock, op. cit., p. 34.

56. Barenholtz and McClintock, op. cit., pp. 10, 23.

57. Barenholtz and McClintock op. cit., pp. 29, 10.

58. Barenholtz and McClintock, op. cit., p. 9.

59. Thomas A. Bailey and David H. Kennedy, (1987) *American Pageant*. Lexington, Mass.: D. C. Heath & Co., p. 621.

60. Philippe Ariès (1962) found that for a toy to be popular among children it must have some connection with the adult world. *Centuries of Childhood*. New York: Vintage, p. 95.

61. Douglas, op. cit., p. 66.

62. Ibid.

63. Michael Schudson, (1984) *Advertising, The Uneasy Persuasion*. New York: Basic Books, p. 5.

64. In Schudson, op. cit., pp. 151–152.

65. Abelson, op. cit., pp. 25–26.

66. Quoted in Wiebe, op. cit., pp. 112–113.

67. Children's clothes and consumption can be seen as an important component to creating a social-class identity and a means of self-reproduction among the well-to-do middle class. A most severe example of social class self-reproduction was found in France, where a permanent, largely hereditary industrial proletariat appeared by 1880. Technological changes in post-revolutionary France underlay the emergence of a new social class to whom work and family were key elements to social identity, observed Michael P. Hanagan, (1989) *Nascent Proletarians: Class Formation in Post-Revolutionary France, 1840–1880*. Oxford: Basil Blackwell.

68. Jacob Riis, (1892) *Children of the Poor*. New York: Doubleday.

69. Abelson, op. cit., pp. 42–45.

70. Rosalind H. Williams (1982) observed that France in the late nineteenth century was a pioneer in mass merchandising. The new techniques helped create "dream worlds," transforming consumers' orientation to consumption. *Dream Worlds: Mass Consumption in Late Nineteenth-Century France*. Berkeley: University of California Press.

71. Lawrence W. Levine, (1988) *Highbrow/Lowbrow: The Emergence of Cultural Hierarchy in America*. Cambridge, Mass., pp. 176–177.

72. Levine, op. cit., p. 177.

73. The theory underlying the kindergarten was developed by Ernest Froeble. In 1837 he opened one in Kielhau near Blankenburg in Germany. He is reputed to be the first to recognize that communal life is important in the upbringing of in-

fants. An architect, he designed a series of toys for the kindergarten which he called "Occupations." These consisted of balls, blocks, and colored paper to cut and fold. Antonia Fraser, (1962) *A History of Toys*. New York: Spring Books, p. 212.

74. A display of kindergarten materials at the Philadelphia Centennial Exposition of 1876 drew nearly 10 million people and helped broaden awareness of the vulnerability of young children. Diane Ravitch, (1974) *The Great School Wars; New York 1805–1973; History of the Public Schools as Battlefield of Social Change*. New York: Basic Books, p. 111.

75. Barbara Finkelstein and Kathy Vandell, (1984) "The Schooling of American Childhood: The Emergence of Learning Communities," in Heininger et al., op. cit., p. 75.

76. Kate Douglas Wiggins, (1896) *The Republic of Childhood*. Boston: Houghton Mifflin, p. 115.

77. Finkelstein and Vandell, op. cit., p. 76.

78. James McLachlan, (1970) *American Boarding Schools*. New York: Charles Scribner and Sons, p. 13.

79. Ibid.

80. McLachlan, op. cit., pp. 11–12.

81. McLachlan, op. cit., pp. 117–118.

82. Nicola Beisel, (1997) *Imperiled Innocents, Anthony Comstock and Family Reproduction in Victorian America*. Princeton, N.J.: Princeton University Press, pp. 4–5.

83. Beisel, op. cit., p. 7.

84. Beisel, op. cit., p. 6.

85. Heywood Broun and Margaret Leach, (1927) *Anthony Comstock: Roundsman of the Lord*. New York: The Literary Guild of America, p. 132.

86. Broun and Leach, op. cit., p. 141.

87. Beisel, op. cit., pp. 22, 33–35.

88. Beisel, op. cit., p. 144.

89. Beisel, op. cit., p. 22.

90. DiMaggio, Paul, (1982) "Cultural Entrepreneurship in Nineteenth-Century Boston: Part I, The Creation of an Organizational Base for High Culture in America," *Media, Culture and Society* 4, pp. 33–35; and "Cultural Entrepreneurship in Nineteenth- Century Boston; Part II The Classification and Framing of American Art," *Media, Culture and Society* 4, pp. 303–322.

91. McLachlan, op. cit., p. 13.

92. Quoted in Oscar and Mary F. Handlin, (1971) *Facing Life: Youth and the Family in American History*. Boston: Little, Brown, p. 163.

Sending the child away to school was often experienced as cruel. Many of the students learned to tolerate boarding school life. Finding no stimulus to exercise their power, they became passively obedient. Others, like Stephen Crane, the son of a minister, rebelled. At sixteen years of age he learned to smoke and to gamble and acquired a taste for liquor. At a school for boys and girls, Claverack College and Hudson River Institute, he hit it off with a gang of Indians and adopted the motto: "Do what is forbidden." Children were often emotionally unprepared to return to school after a holiday. Stephen Vincent Benet thought ahead to "the big boy's arm and the twist of shattering pain along his twisted wrist." Handlin, op. cit., pp. 164–165.

93. Ibid.

94. Ibid. First menstruation took place at about fourteen or fifteen. See also p. 6.

95. Barbara Welter, (1976) "Dimity Convictions," *The American Woman in the Nineteenth Century*. Athens: Ohio University Press, p. 3.

96. Abelson, op. cit., pp. 76–78.

97. Before the clothing industry became differentiated into ready-to-wear and custom-made clothing, there were three categories of custom-made clothing. The best was that made inside the shop where the tailor worked on the master's premises. Second best was the clothing created when the tailor took the work from the shop of the master and made it up at home with the assistance of his wife and children. The third grade of clothing was created when the work was given to a contractor, who in turn either let it out to be done at a home of the worker or had it made up in his own workshop. See Jesse Eliphalet Pope, (1905/1970) *The Clothing Industry in New York*. New York: Burt Franklin, pp. 12–13.

98. Ready-to-wear infant attire was available already in the seventeenth century. Ewing, op. cit. pp. 161–162;. Pope, op. cit., p. 10.

99. Ready-to-wear clothing was available in stock sizes.

100. Nora Villa, (1989) *Children in Their Party Dress*. Modena, Italy: Zanfi Editori, p. 26.

101. Frances Hodgson Burnett, (1896/1955) *Little Lord Fauntleroy*. Illustrations by Reginald Birch. New York: Charles Scribner's Sons, p. 147.

102. Many considered the suit too elegant and inappropriate for play. "You are dressed like the little Lord Fauntleroy" became a pejorative expression.

103. According to Thorstein Veblen, in his *Theory of the Leisure Class*, the leisure class emerged during this period. A new upper class, made up of families like the Vanderbilts, the Goulds, and the Harrimans, made visible their newly acquired wealth by showing off their costumes, full of gold and glitter.

Thorstein Veblen (1899/1957) *The Theory of the Leisure Class*. New York: Mentor Books.

104. Quoted in Villa, op. cit., p. 28.

105. Worrell, op. cit., p. 170.

106. Worrell, op. cit., p. 205.

107. Initially called Bike Jockey Strap, it was intended for bike riders. The Jockstrap was invented in 1897 by Charles Bennet of the manufacturing sporting-goods firm Sharp and Smith in Chicago. In 1913 they were made in smaller adult sizes. James Villas (1974) "A Short History of the Jockstrap." *Esquire*, 82 (4) Oct., pp. 235+.

108. Blanche Payne, Geitel Winaker, and Jane Farrell-Beck, (1992) *The History of Costume*. Second Edition. New York: Harper Collins pp. 506, 521, 528.

109. Worrell, op. cit. p. 173.

110. Worrell, op. cit., pp. 169–170.

111. Worrell, op. cit., p. 174.

112. Worrell, op. cit., pp. 170–172.

113. Worrell, op. cit., pp. 170, 209.

114. Worrell, op. cit., p. 193.

115. Helen Berry, (1984) *The Children's Dressmaker, Volume Two: The Versatile Dress of the Nineties*.

116. Michael Hanagan, (1994) in "New Perspective on Class Formation Culture, Reproduction, and Agency," *Social Science History* 18, pp. 77–93, emphasized the importance of understanding identity formation in terms of self-conscious efforts to replicate and reproduce these ties through cultural objects. Among the wealthy middle-class private schools, clothes for recreational activities and protective attire reproduce and support the new identity.

117. Heininger, op. cit., pp. 26–27.

118. Heininger, op. cit., p. 26.

119. A puritanical New Englander who, beginning in 1866, wrote over a hundred volumes of juvenile fiction for boys twelve to eighteen.

120. MacLeod, op. cit., p. 107.

121. John G. Cawelti, (1965) *Apostles of the Self-Made Man*. Chicago: The University of Chicago Press, p. 115.

122. Bailey and Kennedy, op. cit., p. 545.

123. Robert H. Wiebe, (1967) *The Search For Order 1877–1920*. New York: Hill and Wang, p. 113.

124. Erik Erikson, (1950) *Childhood and Society*. New York: W. W. Norton, p. 261.

125. Worrell, op. cit., pp. 129, 133.

126. Mark Twain, (1884) *The Adventures of Huckleberry Finn*. New York: Grosset and Dunlap, p. 2.

127. Ibid.

128. The illustrator was Donald McKay.

129. Philip J. Greven, (1973) "Family Structure in Seventeenth Century Andover," in Michael Gordon, ed., *The American Family in Social-Historical Perspective*. New York: St. Martin's Press, p. 85.

130. Worrell, op. cit., pp. 109, 122, 123, 124.

131. William W. Savage, (1979) *The Cowboy Hero: His Image in American History and Culture*. Norman: University of Oklahoma Press, p. 12.

132. Savage, op. cit., pp. 36, 165.

133. Savage, op. cit., p. 14.

134. Savage, op. cit., p. 110.

135. Savage, op. cit., pp. 64–65.

136. Owen Wister (1902) *The Virginian : A Horseman of the Plains*. New York: Macmillan Company.

137. Savage, op. cit., pp. 64–65.

138. Sears, Roebuck and Co., *Consumers Guide*, Fall 1900, p. 575.

139. Worrell, op. cit., p. 133.

140. The practice of sizing of children's clothes in the United States was based on the manufacturing of Union army uniforms. Records had been kept about men's clothing measurements and later used to size men's clothing. Standardized sizing for children was possible only in the twentieth century, when more data was available about children.

141. Sears Roebuck and Co., op. cit., pp. 456–461; 601–701.

142. *The American Coat and Suit Review, Devoted to the Women's and Children's Ready-to-Wear Trades* vol.2, no. 1 (Jan. 1916), p. 251.

9

Establishing Societal Standards: Children's Clothes Between 1918 and 1950

Increased immigration, sentiments of nationalism, technological innovation, and growth in the sciences conjoined after World War I (1918) and led in part to children being designated the nation's natural resource (see Fig. 9.1).[1] By the end of World War I, there was a change in the paradigm of children's clothes and in childhood itself, the period when future citizens are cultivated for the sake of the common good. Children of all social classes were now being defined as priceless. Among the impoverished urban working class, the death of a child because of disease or malnutrition was considered a waste, a visible and embarrassing anachronism, observed sociologist Viviana A. Zelizer (1985).[2]

A commitment to the welfare of children ensued. A widespread indictment of child labor lead to the regulation of children in the labor force.[3] Compulsory school attendance compelled children, who had formerly been vagrants, child workers, and children of new immigrants, to attend public school.[4] Most children were in school by November 16, 1919, reported the Internal Revenue Bureau.[5] The notion of a child in the labor force was replaced by a noneconomic, educational ideal of school as work, with the child taking home a report card rather than a paycheck.[6]

Laws specified the age for attending school. Chronological age now mattered. Gradually childhood came to be seen as a time when biological, social, and cultural development must take place. Children's clothes such as socks began to be stocked and displayed by age rather than item.

The August 15, 1918, issue of *Vogue* was the first to focus on children's fashions, suggesting that children were important enough to deserve their own space. The notion of children as miniature adults and the wearing of the strict adult fashions of the Victorian era began to ease. The clothes, however, continued to hark back to the European tradition. In

FIGURE 9.1   *Children of the Poor.* These children have been appointed as a
board of elections to oversee elections in the Beach Street Industrial School.
Even as early as 1890, then, poor children were being prepared for citizenship.
Jacob Riis, 1890. The Jacob A Riis Collection. Museum of the City of New York.
Museum Photo.

1921 *The Children's Costume Royal* offered eight different styles of suits for
boys, all in simple or simplified design.[7] For toddlers two to four, there
was a variety of one-piece garments made of tan or white linen. The
blouse was buttoned to the pants and had a scalloped collar and cuffs. A
sleeveless jumper in black velvet over a white blouse had the back straps
buttoned in the front for ease in dressing and a quick diaper change.

The outfits offered for boys eight to sixteen in *The Children's Costume
Royal* were simpler versions of the suits adults wore in the second half of
the nineteenth century, the Norfolk suit and the three-piece suit of navy
blue serge. The fabrics, however, were of a lighter gauge. Judging from
the pictures, they seem to have a looser fit around the neck, and their style
was form-following rather than form-fitting, allowing greater ease in
movement. The pants were often short, conveying the idea that boys were
not fully grown males.[8] In the 1920s large stores like Macy's and the May
Department Stores allocated special space for children's clothes; they furnished clothes for boys and girls from birth through the high school years.

FIGURE 9.2 Children's clothes for modern times. Streamlined and simplified, the styles are designed to meet the need of each age group. *The Children's Costume Royal,* Autumn 1921.

FIGURE 9.3 Children's clothes for modern times. *The Children's Costume Royal,* Autumn 1921.

A lesser quality fabric and less particular fit characterized the clothes of the less affluent. In offering clothes for school and "good clothes" for Sunday, Montgomery Ward sought to be more fashion oriented. To better show the new detail, the pictures in the catalogue used live models.[9] Sears Roebuck was less fashionable. The company was concerned with keeping clothing costs low and bought discontinued lines.[10]

FIGURE 9.4   Children's clothes
for modern times. *The Children's
Costume Royal,* Autumn 1921.

FIGURE 9.5   Children's clothes
for modern times. *The Children's
Costume Royal,* Autumn 1921.

In the countryside, farm boys who had to perform chores had always worn their pants long. In the city, boys under five wore wool outfits consisting of a low-waisted tunic over shorts. Around seven they could begin to wear knickers, a garment initially worn to ride a bicycle. Some boys wore a jacket over knee-length pants.[11] As boys grew older they

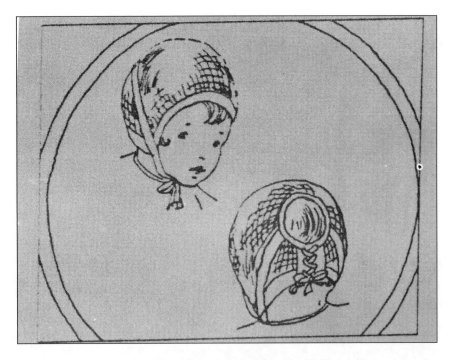

FIGURE 9.6 Ear conformers. Advised for infants. *The Children's Costume Royal,* August 1921.

wore longer and longer knickers. The length of a boy's trousers thus indicated his age.

A new sportswear garment for girls was introduced in 1919, the "Bloomer-Romper." It was advertised as combining "fashion with function."[12] It was anchored at the waist but was loose-fitting, allowing easy movement. Ear conformers were developed for infants to keep the "ears well-shaped and in good position."[13]

Children of The Affluent

Children of the affluent wore mostly imported attire. Sons were often dressed by English tailors. Rowes of Bond Street, a tailor for the British royal family, for example, sent its representative twice a year to New York's Plaza Hotel where the collection was shown and children's measurements taken. The clothes were then made in London.[14]

The "Made in France" label was often sought by mothers for their daughters. The 1920s was an age of opulence. Leather, fur, silk and costly

FIGURE 9.7 Violinist Yehudi Menuhin and his sisters Hepzibah and Yalta, 1928. Skirts, pants, and coats have the short length and straight line that had come to characterize children's clothes. Corbis/Bettman.

woolens were used for children's wear.[15] Dresses made for sizes seven to fourteen were made out of frilly georgette or crepe de chine fabrics. The favorite style was a low-waisted dress with an accordion pleated skirt and sleeves hanging from the shoulders.[16] Artificial flowers and ostrich feathers were used for trim. The industry in its first fashion show offered coats for the "back-to-school" crowd. These were lavishly adorned with fur, beaver, or fox.[17]

The younger children of the well-to-do, the five-, six-,and seven-year-olds, wore shapeless hip-length sweaters paired with pleated skirts and bloomers. Cotton and wool knits were cut like woven fabrics, loosely fitting the silhouette.[18] A black satin coat with scalloped collar that has a sash echoed in a matching bonnet was shown for the two to six-year-old child. Embroidery, red taffeta linings, and Crossed Bertha collars were "must" trimmings for fashionable young girls. Capes were a desirable coat style.[19]

Infants were also dressed in imported clothes. These were "hand embroidered," "beautifully made" long dresses, buntings, bibs, creepers, panties, and jackets. An advertisement in the July 1931 issue of *Earn-*

FIGURE 9.8 Nancy and Van van Vieck. A photograph of upper-class children wearing the matching outfits recommended by *The Children's Costume Royal* of 1921. They are graceful, relaxed, and easy to put on and take off. Newport society children at Southampton, taken in the 1920s. Corbis/Bettman.

shaw's clarifies that these were "the same kinds of garments which used to be an extravagance" (imported from France and Italy), reproduced in Japan and the Philippines, "duplicated at a fraction of the former cost."[20] In July 1931, Eastern Isles Importing Co. advertised "Hand-Made Walking Dresses," dresses for the "Wee Tots" in sizes one to three. The dresses were made of dainty batiste, sheer organdy, and fine voile, with "exquisite" hand-embroidery and hand-smocking and in pastel colorings.[21] These fabrics were "delicate," conveying fragility. The attire was perhaps designed to rouse tenderness in the adults, the desire to protect the helpless child.

Learning to Dress

Fathers, mothers, nannies, tailors, and dress-makers introduced children of the affluent to the realm of clothes. The U.S. Public Health Service, who since 1915 had been providing medical services to all school children,[22] guided nurses, social-workers, and home economists in the help they offered to mothers of public school students. At school and during home visits new immigrant mothers and the poor were offered advice on the mechanics of sewing at home, using hand-me-down clothing, pur-

FIGURE 9.9   A boy in a cowboy suit
for a costume party, and a girl
wearing the early nineteenth-century
Empire style. Reported in *The
Children's Costume Royal* of 1921.
Photo, Greg Kitchen.

chasing used clothing, and what care to use when shopping for new clothes.[23]

The Singer Sewing Machine Company, through its instruction manuals, assisted women, particularly those laboring in poorly paying jobs,[24] in making, remaking, and mending their children's clothes.[25] Since the nineteenth century the company had made it possible for women to acquire sewing machines by selling them on the installment plan. A manual was included, and it supplied detailed instructions on the design and construction of children's clothes.[26] It provided the basic standards of dress for children in the elementary grades in the public school system. Mothers were advised that school clothes must be simple. Fabric should be in neutral tone and even delicate in color. Showiness must be avoided. Children should look forward to school. A new school year should, thus, be ushered in with new clothes. The manual recommended that mothers prepare six dresses, with six pairs of matching bloomers, for the new year.[27] The first day, above all, must be commemorated with a new outfit.[28]

Party dresses made out taffeta, georgette, or lace should never to be worn to school, advised the manual. Party dresses worn for special occasions should be modestly ornamented.[29] The collar and cuffs might be in a contrasting color. Other kinds of trimming, however, should follow adult women's fashion. "Do not use Irish lace when organdie is in fashion," for example. Stringy belts, dangling sleeves, or skimpy shirts were unacceptable.

Boys could be dressed in adult-style suits, or like children, in shirts and pants. The garments should be cut so that they have some ease in the waistline and sleeves. The clothing should have enough fullness to allow the child to move about and sit comfortably.[30]

Other clothing publications during this period, *Simplicity*, for example, focused on merely identifying the latest fashion patterns. By 1935, it was women with growing children who purchased 65 percent of all sewing machines and 68 percent of the washing machines sold by department stores.[31]

Vogue magazine rejected home sewing and encouraged buying readymade clothes.[32] An article titled "Raising the Average" suggested that homemade clothes lack the "intelligence," the "taste level," that buyers for the big stores usually have. "We wish we knew who is most to blame for the lack of artistic feeling and cultivated sense,"[33] the low level of taste in the clothes seen on the street.

The article claimed that wives of well-to-do men trust the stores to provide them with fitting clothes for their children; other women should follow suit. Store buyers usually examine a garment's quality, beauty of line and color, and "good merchandise is not necessarily expensive," the article notes.[34]

Clothing specialists in department stores also offered help to mothers in choosing appropriate dress. The J. L. Hudson Co. in Detroit, for example, instituted "Child Health" as a store promotion feature to help "modern parents meet modern problems of parenthood."[35] In a thousand or more infant departments around the country trained nurses talked to mothers about dressing their children and offered advice. They also met with doctors to find out what clothes they would like their clients to wear. These nurses did not actually sell merchandise but gave talks, advised mothers, and demonstrated new merchandise.[36]

The clothing industry sought to meet consumers' needs better. Columnist for *Earnshaw's* Flora Krauch was sent to observe nursery school children and their needs. She discovered that nursery schools encourage self-reliance. Before they could enter the classroom the children were expected to take off their own outerwear garments: rubbers, heavy snow suits, coats, and leggings.[37] They also put outer clothes on before leaving school. Teachers refrained from helping their students for another reason. They sought to promote children's sense of autonomy. The clothes had been designed by the industry to ease the mothers' chore, but that design was used by teachers and schools to encourage self-reliance.[38]

Home economists focused on raising parental awareness regarding the impact children's clothes had on elementary school students' feelings and actions. In adult classes for parents at the "Y" for example, they were told to ask themselves, could this garment be harmful because it is too shabby, too tight, or too loose? Are the clothes becoming; do the colors complement the child's pigmentation? Will the outfit be enjoyed? The way a child is dressed is an important way of encouraging self-confidence, instructed home economist Florence E. Young.[39]

It is important to dress children in clothing similar to that of their peers. If a child is dressed differently, the other children may pick on the child and say cruel things. A four-year-old boy refused to wear his beret to kindergarten because some first-grade boys had yelled, "Only babies wear berets."[40] It was one thing to allow the child to go ragged around the home, or poorly dressed to a factory or a mine. It was quite another thing to have children compare what they wore with others in their classrooms. Children who are oddly and unattractively dressed are self-conscious and often develop a retiring personality, she advised.[41] It is difficult to be self-respecting when one is dressed in soiled rags and knows it. This hypothesis was tested on a girl living in a poor part of town and wearing dirty, torn clothing. She was given a new, clean dress. From a broken-spirited, listless child "there came forth a saucy, impudent little creature," reported Margaret Story. The child was then given a thorough scrubbing and dressed in a clean, new outfit. A self-respecting and respectful little woman emerged.[42]

School Dress Codes

Public school educators rejected school uniforms in the belief that making choices in dress was an important means of inculcating self-reliance, which would support a democratic society. Students usually came to school wearing ordinary clothes in a large variety of styles four days, usually Monday through Thursday. A more formal attire consisting of a jacket, a white shirt, and blue trousers or skirt was required for assembly day, which was often on Friday.[43]

To participate in gym classes, girls had to wear a newly developed garment called a "Gymee." [44] It was a shoulder-buttoned outfit resembling a child's romper. It had a double seat for cushioning. This garment was usually a part of back-to-school promotions.[45]

Public school students were expected to come to school with washed face and hands, and wearing clean and neat attire. Success in school was partly predicated on a child's appearance. Shabby, torn, or dirty clothing reflected on the child's moral trustworthiness and potential for learning.

FIGURE 9.10 "A Friend Comes to School." For school, girls wear short dresses and boys short pants with a plain or striped shirt. From *Our New Friends,* 1946–1947.

Negative evaluation of a child's appearance was entered into the child's school records, threatening self-esteem and future scholarly careers.[46]

Learning about clothes and dressing up in occupational uniforms was part of the curriculum of schools oriented towards progressive education, that is, schools committed to "meeting the needs of the whole child."[47] To interest children in learning and to enable them to develop social relations,[48] the curriculum drew upon children's life experiences. This often entailed the actual wearing of occupational dress in school.[49] In 1922, the "Little Red School House," an experimental school within the New York public school system, made an effort to make classes informal and related to "real" experience by "doing."[50] Activities were "all important," reported educational historian Sol Cohen.[51] Some two hundred small workers donned overalls and went about "building, hammering, painting, modeling, singing, dancing, constantly creating, and solving problems."[52]

Contributing to the vocabulary of shared images and meanings available to public school children was the iconography accompanying the books used to teach reading, for example, the Dick and Jane stories, a primer used for over forty years to teach school children simple vocabulary.[53] Eighty-five percent of American schools at one time used the book to teach millions of American children. The book was updated every five years until 1965.[54] In the 1946–1947 "Dick and Jane" reader called *Our New Friends* the world is candy-colored. The boys and girls are portrayed as well-scrubbed, neatly dressed, and living in a house surrounded by a white picket fence in an organized, tidy home and neighborhood, in suburbia.

FIGURE 9.11   1946–1947 basic reader print. In the playground children play
with stuffed animals, a ball, a sandbox, a pail and shovel. Boys may wear
overalls or shorts. From *Our New Friends*, 1946–1947.

Uniforms or costumes are used to identify different occupational categories, the tasks they perform, and the idea that distinct social occasions
require a particular type of dress. For example, a policeman in his blue
uniform patrolling the street is happy to respond to children and their
queries. The milkman in white hat and white coverall is delivering milk.
Painters in white bib overalls on ladders are finishing the trim of the
house; moving-men in brown and green uniforms are unloading furniture into the house. The mother cheerfully is doing her housework in a
simple dress and the father is wearing a suit.

The boys in the stories are comfortable in their striped, knit tops and
short pants, the mix-and-match sportswear that became important in the
late 1940s as families moved from the city to the suburbs, making casual
dress acceptable. The girls are in feminine outfits: short bell-shaped skirts
supported by petticoats. The children are busy with friends or playing
with pets, toys, and farm animals. A birthday is a social occasion celebrated with a costume. Pouring rain requires special gear: a rain-slicker,
rubber hat, and boots.[55] The uniforms, costumes and stories offered children a body of images and meanings that became *shared*.[56]

Parochial, Private, and Boarding Schools

Affluent parents believed that the best way to prepare their offspring for the future was to have them attend the proper school.[57] Students in parochial schools, private day schools, and boarding schools were expected to pay tuition. In most, dress codes were established and students were expected to wear the required attire. The wearing of the uniform indicated that personal ideas would be compromised in favor of conformity with and obedience to the those established by the school.[58] For boys it was a dark jacket over knickers or long pants, a white shirt, and a tie. Girls wore a jumper with a white blouse or a knee-length skirt in plaid or navy blue and a white blouse. At Brearly, a private girls' day school in New York City, students wore blue tunics and skirts, an outfit they believed made each look like "a pear."[59] Boarding schools for boys such as St. Paul's, Groton, Exeter, and Lawrenceville, prided themselves on being much like the elite schools in England, including the use of physical punishment. School life was often simple and austere. In some cases students were required to sleep on hard mattresses.[60]

The uniformed appearance and the isolation from the larger society for much of the year encouraged the development of a school spirit and an identity based on the characteristics of the school.[61] The more exclusively people interact with members in a segregated social milieu, the more alike will be their beliefs and behavior, suggested Edwin Sutherland in 1937.[62] Boarding school students were likely to acquire an identity that was international in character and included a sense of entitlement.

Outside of school, when on the beaches and "play grounds," boarding school students should be a source of style for the less affluent, suggested Philip Le Boutillier, president of Best & Co. in the 1920s. Fashion is "an awareness of what is going on around you," and the sons and daughters of the affluent visit European capitals and frolic on their beaches and are more likely to be aware of fashion.[63]

Not only do they follow fashion, they help to create it. What boys in schools such as Buckley, Allan Stevenson, Choate, and Lawrenceville (boarding schools and private day schools) and girls attending Spence, Chapin, and Brearly wear outside of school is important.[64] The sons and daughters of the affluent are likely to take advantage of the latest innovations in style.[65]

Graduates of boarding schools on the East Coast, sociologist E. Digby Baltzell observed, helped to form what came to be known as "the establishment"— individuals in American society who influence the course of social and political affairs.[66] Boarding schools served the function of separating the upper class in America from the rest of the population,

Baltzell suggested.[67] The clothes their children wore functioned as *the* standard for desirable appearance.

American Style

The development of what Europeans identify as the "American style"— clothes that are simple in design, light in weight, practical, moderate in cost, and comfortable—began with infant attire.[68] The attire is often distinguished by devices that make dressing and undressing infants easy: gripper fasteners,[69] zippers, drop seats, and elastic-topped panties, for example.[70] The transformation of infants' attire began after 1918 with the development of mass-production and medical findings regarding children's needs.

Prior to World War I, physical survival or "warmth" underlay the motivational pattern for dressing an infant, reports Margaret Jackson in *What They Wore, A History of Children's Dress.*[71] *Godey's Lady's Book* from 1884 instructs: "Dress children warmly, with woolen flannel next to their person the whole year. By every consideration protect the extremities well. It is an ignorant barbarism that allows the child to have bare arms and feet, even in the summer."[72] Babies wore so many layers that undressing the baby was like peeling an onion.[73] They were clothed in dresses that were long, full, tucked, ruffled, and heavily starched. Infants and children were overdressed.

Well into the 1920s, infants were still being dressed in ornamented long dresses. Those imported were advertised as "hand-made of the world's daintiest silks and needlework,"[74] suggesting that those made locally were less fine. In either case, their length got in the way of the baby trying to creep or stand, particularly those sewn at the bottom, forming a bag.[75]

From the time children began to crawl until the age of five or six, boys and girls wore their hair long. Combing the hair was often a matter of knots and tears.[76] The hair was usually worn in curls. For many that meant using the curling stick. The dampened hair would be wound tightly onto the stick. To achieve the right effect it was necessary to catch all strands of hair right down to the skull.[77] The hair had to be pulled tight. By the 1930s, boys' hair was cut short and that of girls to just below the ears. A close-fitting cap or beret adhered to the head, no matter how strong the wind.[78]

Concerned that dressing infants in several tight-fitting layers of clothes and a long dress that hampered movement encouraged "rage behavior,"[79] behaviorist psychologist John B. Watson criticized these garments. He noted, "Temper is called out many times everyday— in fact every time we dress, undress, or change the newborn. We twist and we roll them to put a tight woolen band around them, and we try not to wrench their arms off while putting on a woolen shirt with sleeves."[80] Moreover, with time things get worse. Since woolen garments shrink with each laundering, the job of dressing and undressing an infant becomes more and more a "gymnastic feat."[81]

Babies who begin to creep or stand must be encouraged. Rubber bloomers or "baby pants" will enable infants to move about freely, advised the Children's Bureau of the United States Department of Labor. It also recommended dressing the infant in a sunsuit, an abbreviated version of the playsuit (a light outfit consisting of a blouse and shorts), making dressing and undressing less frustrating for both parent and child.[82]

Sunsuits and playsuits, moreover, made out of dainty fabrics, were simple to make and cost little when made by the mother. The garment allowed physical mobility and offered maximum exposure to fresh air. It encouraged familiarity with the body never possible before. In 1927 when doctors discovered that sunshine helps to prevent rickets in children, sunsuits, rompers, and playsuits made it possible to leave much of the body exposed to the sun. Though sunbathing was possible in Minnesota, it was particularly practical in California, Miami, Florida, and other sun spots in the United States.[83]

The style rather than the size came to identify toddlers' garments, distinguishing them from children sizes one to three. The stance of the toddler is different from those of older children and adults. Toddlers sway back, walk flat-footed, and in their effort to balance, the stomach protrudes. They still wear diapers. The garments were made full enough to accommodate these distinctions.[84] The "proper fit" must follow the curves of the body. It must allow freedom of movement yet not interfere with the style and lines of the outer garment.[85]

Toddler boys' garments that emerged were more tailored, while those of girls were more playful because they were made of softer fabric such as Swiss shimmering broadcloth and dainty pastels. Rompers, too, were worn by children younger than four. The one-piece garment, consisting of a shirtwaist and bloomers (a variation on the skeleton suit), was made out of heavier gauge fabric that allowed active play. Rompers were sex-specific garments. Those designed for boys were made in strong colors, such as navy blue, and had masculine themes—the nautical look, for example. Those for girls were made of softer cotton and linen and in soft pink and yellow pastels.[86] By 1936 toddlers' garments acquired their own distinct character and became a special category and a sub-department in a children's clothing store.[87]

Popular Culture

New sources of clothing styles and new forces toward shared culture emerged with the depiction of cartoon characters, characters in children's

FIGURE 9.12   Rose O'Neill and her Kewpie Dolls. *Earnshaw's*, 1928. By permission. Photo, Greg Kitchen.

storybooks and in the movies. The chemise silhouette, made popular by the flappers in the 1920s, was designated a party dress for older girls; while yoke dresses, dresses which fell loosely from the shoulders, were offered for younger girls. One of the popular models was called the Kewpie doll dress, after a doll developed by the American illustrator Rose O'Neill.[88] Her dolls had a rotund, ample form, which the yoke dress easily covered. The dress had a large, pleated collar.[89] Aprons were prescribed to protect girls dresses. If made of soft fabrics, they were "easy to make and easy to iron."[90] With the Depression of the 1930s, many could not afford fine imported clothing. To make the new clothes palatable, the John Taylor Dry Goods Co. in Kansas City, in July 1931, used the storybook characters of Little Miss Muffett, Georgy Porgy, and Little Jack Horner to attract customers and sell clothes. The clothes were made out of sturdy fabrics and were simply ornamented. The advertisement said:

> *Please come to see our Story Book Display,*
> *Of children's fashions, colorful and gay,*
> *Made to stand the kind of play*
> *That children like. That's all we'll say.*[91]

FIGURE 9.13
Kewpie Doll dress.
Inspired by Rose
O'Neill's style of
dress. *Earnshaw's,*
1935. By permission.
Photo, Greg Kitchen.

To further divert attention from the quality of the fabrics, seven large open books served as backgrounds for girls' and boys' party ensembles. The girls wore short, just above the knee, print dresses in the Empire style with a contrasting white Peter Pan collar, socks, and Mary Jane shoes. The boys wore dressy suits consisting of above-the-knee pants, a short-sleeve matching shirt, knee-highs or short socks, and shoes. During this period countless Alice-in-Wonderland dresses and pinafores, inspired by the Lewis Carroll classic, were produced and reproduced.[92]

During the Depression, licensing emerged as a new way of embellishing children's clothes. Licensing refers to the use of a fictional character or the name of a celebrity to sell the clothing. Access to movies, radio, and magazines was widely available, and communication, in general, improved across the country. Cowboy and Indian costumes, as well as cartoon characters that started in the newspapers and then were adapted into movie cartoons were used to animate children's clothes. In the form of appliqué, they were unexpected and therefore cute. Whimsical Mickey and Minnie Mouse, lovable Winnie the Pooh, and Rose O'Neill's Kewpies were all considered "personality merchandise." They had to be chosen by the consumer, who at the time was usually an adult. "Personality merchandise" was used to ornament sweaters, coat buttons, clips, and clasps. Disney's cartoon characters began to appear in watches and on fabrics for children's clothes, T-shirts, and sweaters. In the 1920s and 1930s it was Mickey Mouse, Donald Duck, and Snow White. Pinocchio, Dumbo, and Bambi came in the 1940s.[93] Less than cute, yet more popular among children than Mickey, Minnie, were Popeye, the Sailor Man, and his girl friend Olive Oyl.[94] The industry described their effect as "pepping-up" the market.[95]

Mickey and Popeye offered contrasting stereotypes and two distinct aesthetics that informed boys about appearance and behavior. In "Mickey versus Popeye," William de Mille suggested that Mickey is polished, courteous, unselfish, full of desire to help the world; Popeye is sinister, self assertive, worshipping strength rather than justice, determined to dominate rather than to help.[96] Hollywood's glamour advanced the manufacture of girls' clothes. Iserson Imports, an importer and a manufacturer, had specialized in both importing and reproducing quality hand-made and hand-embroidered garments. It was chosen to make a line designed by Hollywood costume designer Orry-Kelly at Warner Brothers under the label "Juvenile Studio Styles."[97]

As the movies became an important form of family entertainment, Shirley Temple and Judy Garland became popular stars.[98] Shirley Temple danced, sang and giggled, and gave the children's apparel industry an image they used: laughing, full of life, and lovable. She was born in 1929 and first appeared in films in 1933. After her first movie, *The Little Colonel*, her popularity was such that the sale of Shirley Temple dolls reached 1.5 million in 1934.[99] Almost every little girl wanted to look like Shirley Temple. In 1935 a dress that fell loosely from the shoulders with a neat Peter Pan collar became the typical young girls' attire. Shirley Temple modeled dresses, coats, hats, sportswear, and bathing suits, all of which were sought out by little girls and their mothers.

The line was imbued with false legitimacy and show-biz glamour when the 1935 fall line of "Shirley Temple Dresses" claimed that the line was designed "right on the lot" with Mrs. Temple, Shirley herself, and members of the film company all lending a hand. [100] Shirley Temple was also the model for raincoats manufactured by Sherman Bros. Rainwear Corporation, which were designed for older girls, as well as infants. Packed individually in "Gay Holiday Boxes," they were suitable for holiday gift giving.[101] Mass-produced by the Rosenau Clothes Co., they were generally affordable.

In 1937 Shirley Temple was older, and she modeled "frocks for older girls."[102] The dress had a little bodice, fitted waistline, little puffed

FIGURE 9.14 Shirley Temple. She is wearing a Shirley Temple dress. With its designer, the owner of the Rosenau Brothers Co. *Earnshaw's*, 1935. By permission. Photo, Greg Kitchen.

sleeves, and a gathered full skirt. The dress came in pastel shades and a variety of fabrics (sheer, silk crepe, and taffeta). The coat she wore and promoted had the typical princess silhouette: fitted throughout the waist with a flared skirt.[103] Her style thus changed from straight falling lines to a fitted silhouette. The dress was promoted under the Cinderella brand (perhaps alluding to the story of Cinderella and the American parable "from rags to riches").

Hilda Jaffe, a children's wear designer of the period, has summarized the changes that followed:

Older girls' attire was simplified further in the 1930s. The corsets were gone and the goal in dressing girls was to dress them as children rather than in the more complex styles their mothers wore. For church and holidays, for example, girls wore "party" dresses which were unbound and easy to wear. They were made of silk, cotton, or a linen and rayon combination. The girl's age was indicated by the length of the skirt. It was shorter for the younger girl and longer for the older one. Boys wore some kind of a jacket and long pants.[104]

The April 1946 issue of *The Girls' and Teens' Merchandiser* reported that the latest Federal Reserve Bulletin noted that despite the Depression, the sale of play clothes designed as play clothes increased between 1935 and 1939, as children wore them rather than worn-out school clothes. Girls and boys were portrayed in trim shorts and a striped shirt of knit fabric. The fabric for girls' outfits was softer in texture than the one designated for boys. Some of the play outfits for girls continued to include bloomer panties with a frill,[105] a decidedly feminine and somewhat childish style.

Boys, however, sought to look more like grown-up adult males. Around 1940 a considerable number of city boys stopped wearing knickers.[106] Boys older than eight began wearing long pants.[107] Bush and London suggested that news reports about World War II led to the change.[108] The assumption was that war makes kids grow up faster.[109] Military style outfits were also offered. They consisted of below-the-hip jackets, long pants, gleaming brass buttons, shirts, and ties. By 1943, these were available to boys in all size ranges.[110]

Child-Rearing Theories

Child-rearing practices were often based on theories offered by experts. The theories applied during this period were those of Sigmund Freud and J. B. Watson. Freudian theory, for example, suggested that at the age of two the child was biologically mature enough to begin to be toilet trained. Starting earlier, Freud warned, could result in trauma, in children who were afraid. They could become excessively orderly or stubborn, which would result in retarding the development of autonomy. Delayed toilet training, on the other hand, might give rise to problems in bowel and bladder control, which would become inimical to the development of work habits.[111] The child able to cope alone with the problems of reality and able to pursue personal aspirations with minimal restriction was the goal.

Breast-feeding versus bottle-feeding was another issue. The development of an autonomous, emotionally independent individual was thought to come from being a bottle-fed baby. Bottle-feeding employs a scientifically prepared formula which guarantees more complete nutrition, and the amount of milk the child consumes can be easily estab-

FIGURE 9.15 *Big Baby.* John B. Watson (1878–1958) taught that children should never be coddled or kissed and should be taught to do everything for themselves. Otherwise baby might take over the home. Photo, Grancel Fitz, 1938. Keith de Lellis Gallery, New York.

lished. Intake from the breast, on the other hand, is difficult to determine. The breast, which had been viewed as a source of nurturance for toddlers and infants was thus repudiated.[112] Until the 1990s it was generally assumed that it was illegal to breast-feed in public.[113]

In his popular *Psychological Care of Infant and Child*, John Watson warned against excessive mother love. Young children should never be cuddled, seldom kissed, and never be allowed to sit on your lap. A handshake will do.[114] Petting and cuddling rob the child of "the opportunity for conquering the world."[115] Under the guise of "affection" most mothers displace their unsatisfied sexual longings onto their children. Therefore, mothers "love their children to death."[116] Indulging children with love during infancy, Watson claimed, results in invalidism—adults who constantly complain of aches and pains.[117] Children should be taught to do almost everything for themselves as quickly as possible.[118] The general rule was to keep baby on a tight leash and a totalitarian schedule. The less contact between the baby and the mother the better. In Watson's era, some editors dropped the word "mother" for the more emotionally neutral "parent."[119]

Psychiatrist Margaret A. Ribble warned that constricting clothes hinder emotional development in that they may prevent the infant from developing awareness of its body.[120] She pointed out that a mother's task is to make it possible for the infant to feel. "To the average mother . . . bathing and grooming are simply hygienic processes to be performed consciously and thoroughly."[121] "These activities, however, contribute to a child's development of reflexes and sense of touch."[122]

Dr. Benjamin Spock instructed mothers to love their children, rejecting child-rearing recommendations advanced by Watson. At least until the age of three, children needed the love and care of their mothers. In *The Common Sense Book of Baby and Child Care*, Dr. Spock instructed parents to touch the arms or legs to find out if the child is cold. He encouraged parents "not to take too seriously all that neighbors say." The way the individual child feels should determine if he or she needs more or less clothing. The bodies of children, who are too warmly dressed, lose the ability to adapt to change and these children are more likely to get chilled.[123]

Toys

In the first part of the century advertisements for children's toys focused on the ideas that toys make children happy, result in self-education, and give mother a rest.[124] *Parents Magazine*, which began publishing in 1920, was committed to a better life for children through wise consumption by mothers dedicated to the improvement of their maternal role.[125] *Parents* popularized the view that buying toys makes children happy and demonstrates maternal love, but making children happy is not enough for upward social mobility. Articles published in the magazine introduced mothers to lifestyles of the wealthy and those higher in social rank. They proceeded from the belief that mothers will attempt to emulate the actions and spirit of the well-to-do; they will pattern their consumption according to the behavior, tastes and styles of their betters.[126] Emulating one's "betters" can take place only when people believe that social mobility is a likely possibility, it has been suggested.[127]

Advertising in the 1920s was directed to the adults. A Playschool ad adopted the slogan, "Learning while playing." It offered toys that consisted of small desks, typewriters, and chalkboards, claiming that "a child is educating himself at home through his play just as surely as he is being educated at school."[128] Manufacturers promised parents that educational toys "speed the child's education."[129] Playschool insisted that its toys provide valuable benefits for "mental stimulation, coordination of mind and muscle, and general sense of training."[130] The advertisements assumed that parents want their children to get ahead in the world, and certain kinds of toys would assure success.[131]

In the 1940s and 1950s there were new assertions regarding toys. Transogram claimed that children's toys were "tools to express their creative-

FIGURE 9.16 Older Scout teaches younger scout. Older children are encouraged to learn skills, such as tying various kinds of knots. Here the older Boy Scout teaches the younger Cub Scout; both are serious about their task. Norman Rockwell, *A Guiding Hand*, 1946. Boy Scout Calendar.

ness."[132] Playschool contended that a creative environment can raise a preschooler IQ by as much as twenty points. It promised that the toys they made would help create children who were creative, imaginative, and inquisitive.[133] The toys children played with were simple, and boys and girls aged eight years and older joined the Scouts and learned a variety of skills, including tying knots (see Fig. 9.16).

To conclude, as in the past, quality of dress and standards of appearance separated and distinguished the social classes. Being a nation of immigrants, the United States needed common standards, and in fact a set of standards emerged. The consumption of children' clothes was dependent on parents, whose concern was that their children should meet societal standards. The children's clothes reflected an identity that the clothing industry, the schools, and public health professionals helped to support.

Notes

1. The United States Public Health Service, in the hope of improving children's health, had been conducting household surveys on pellagra, diet, housing, and

illnesses, as well as providing medical services to all school children since 1915. It also sought to prevent malnutrition, dental disease, and tuberculosis. These activities, together with water and sewage control, prenatal care, vaccination and neonatal care, resulted in a decline in death rate of children and infants, making possible a change in boy's attire. In 1900, 24 children aged one to fourteen died for every 1000 born. In 1918, the ratio was 18 per 1000 born. By 1930 it was 8 children per 1000 born.

Moreover, World War I had revealed a shocking absence of loyalty to the nation's military effort by foreign-born citizens.

Aimed at children and adults, educational programs were established by the Americanization movement and classes held in the public schools. Stanley Coben (1973) "The First Years of Modern America: 1918–1933," in William E. Leuchtenburg, ed., *The Unfinished Century, America Since 1900.* Boston: Little, Brown and Company, pp. 260–261, 287.

2. Viviana A. Zelizer, (1985) *Pricing the Priceless Child.* New York: Basic Books, pp. 60–61. Zelizer uses wrongful death awards, adoption records, and insurance markets to demonstrate the diffusion of the child as an emotional asset rather than an economic one. See chapter 1 in Zelizer.

3. The Child Labor Law, which went into effect in April 1918, provided that a tax of ten percent be imposed on the earnings of companies employing children under fourteen years old. Those employing children, who were between fourteen and sixteen and working more than eight hours a day, were similarly taxed. Child labor had been reduced by 40 percent.

4. Diane Ravitch, (1974)*The Great School Wars: New York 1805–1973: A History of the Public Schools as Battlefield of Social Change.* New York: Basic Books, p. 168. Historian Christopher Lasch argued that the removal of children from the labor market was an effort to remove children from family influence, especially the influence of the immigrant family. Public policy sought to place the young under the influence of state and school. This policy led to children's alienation from the home. It marked the beginning of the end of the family as a "haven in a heartless world." Christopher Lasch, (1977) *Haven in a Heartless World.* New York: Basic Books, p. 13.

5. On November 16, 1919, the Internal Revenue Bureau reported that child labor in the United States had decreased by 40 percent since the child labor provisions went into effect in April 1918. Widespread compliance reflected a belief that the Supreme Court will uphold the law. In *Chronicles of the 20th Century.* (1987) Mount Kisco, N.Y.: Chronicle Publications p. 257

6. Zelizer, op. cit., pp. 73–75, 112.

7. *The Children's Costume Royal,* 1921. Styles: #1334, #1335, #1398 # 1339.

8. Linda Martin, (1978) *The Way We Wore: Fashion Illustration of Children's Wear, 1870–1970.* New York: Charles Scribner's Sons, p. 10.

9. Ibid.

10. Hilde Jaffe, (1972) *Childrenswear Design.* New York: Fairchild Publishers, p. 5.

11. George Bush and Parry London, (1960) "On the Disappearance of Knickers: Hypothesis for Functional Analysis of the Psychology of Clothing," *Journal of Social Psychology* 51, pp. 359–366.

12. Reported in *The Infants' Department*, which later became *Earnshaw's*. "Setting the Stage for *Earnshaw's* Debut," *Earnshaw's*, Nov. 1996, p. 79.

13. Ibid.

14. Norman Margolis, (1968) "The New Fashion Awareness," *Earnshaw's*, May, p. 148.

15. Patricia A. Farrell, "The Good Old Days of Children's Fashions," *Earnshaw's*, August, p. 100.

16. Farrell, op. cit., p. 101.

17. Patricia A. Farrell, (1977) "Fashion for the Jazz Babies," *Earnshaw's*, September, p. 75, p. 101.

18. Farrell, op. cit., p. 101.

19. Patricia A. Farrell, (1967) op. cit., p. 99.

20. Feltman Bros. Inc., (1931) "New Fall Innovations for Tiny Folks," *Earnshaw's*, July, p. 755.

21. Ibid.

22. C. E. A. Winslow, (1952) *Men and Epidemics*. Princeton, N.J.: Princeton University Press.

23. Virginia Briton, (1975) "Stretching the Clothing Dollar," in *Family Economics Review*, Consumer and Food Economics Institute, Agricultural Research Service, U. S. Department of Agriculture, Fall, pp. 3–7. See also Barbara Schreier, (1995) *Becoming American Women: Clothing and Jewish American Experience, 1880–1920*. Chicago: Chicago Historical Society, p. 94.

24. The right of a married woman to work was an issue that women had fought for. Their attempt to get work was interpreted as taking jobs away from men who might be heads of household. During the Depression the majority of the states (26 out of 48) had laws prohibiting the employment of married women. Among other large institutions the majority of the nation's public schools enforced rules on not hiring married women. David Halberstam, (1993) *The Fifties*. New York: Villard Books, pp. 588–589.

25. Mending and altering children's clothes were often necessary. "Boys' blouses that have grown shabby around the collar and cuffs be may cut down to a semi-low neck and short sleeves and used for play particularly during the summer. Girls' school dresses can be cut in the same way making play dresses."

"Dresses may be lengthened by inserting a band above the hem and a band may be put in above the belt line." *Singer Sewing Machine Manual*. (1927) New York: Singer Sewing Machine Company, p. 33.

26. Even young single women were allowed to sign their own contract for a down payment of $5 for a $100 machine. Repayments consisted of one, two or three dollars per month. Each purchaser was given a book of coupons, and when the payments were made every month the coupon was pasted in the appropriate space. Judith Hennessee and Joan Nicholson, (1972) "The Song of the Shirt," *Ms. Magazine*, October, pp. 65–70.

27. *Singer Sewing Machine Manual*, op. cit., p. 26

28. Ibid.

29. *How to Make Children's Clothes the Modern Singer Way*, op. cit., p. 34.

30. *Singer Sewing Machine Manual*, op. cit., pp. 26–28.

31. "A Million Dollar Service *Free*," (1935) *Earnshaw's*, February, pp. 32–33.

32. In the December 1928 issue of the *Infant's Department*, a trade journal that began publishing in 1917, later named *Earnshaw's*.

33. "Raising the Average," *Earnshaw's*, December, 1928, p. 1797.

34. Ibid.

35. "Child Health Institute, Store Promotion Feature," (1931) *Earnshaw's*, June, p. 705.

36. "The Infants' and Children's Department," *Earnshaw's* 15, March, 1931, p. 333.

37. Flora Krauch, (1935) "Self Help! Self Help!" *Earnshaw's*, May, p. 42.

38. Ibid.

39. Florence E. Young, (1938) *Clothing the Child*. New York: McGraw Hill, p. 41.

40. Young, op. cit., p. 71.

41. Young, op. cit., p. 72. Other characteristics of a well-dressed child: attentiveness, mental alertness, intellectual curiosity, originality, foresight, industry, persistence, and accuracy.
A twelve-year-old girl, Bobby-Ann can be evaluated in terms of what kind of a person she is on the basis of her clothing. pp. 50–52 ; 58.

42. Margaret Story, (1924) *How To Dress Well*. New York: Funk and Wagnalls. Described in Young, op. cit., p. 78.

43. Ellen Herman, (1995) *The Romance of American Psychology*. Berkeley: University of California Press, p. 5.

44. Ravitch, op. cit., p. 182. Ravitch notes that the New York public school system influenced public education in other communities.

45. Farrell, op. cit., p. 101.

46. Ravitch, op. cit., p. 230.

47. Ravitch, op. cit., p. 234.

48. In his study of homesickness, Zwingman observed that a basic reaction to isolation and unfamiliarity may be hostility, outward aggression, and suicide. The appropriate style clothing for new immigrants acquired a prophylactic dimension, in that it helped to bridge the past and the present and direct the focus on the future. Charles A. A. Zwingmann, (1959) *"Heimweh" or Nostalgic Reaction: A Conceptual Analysis and Interpretation of A Medico-Psychological Phenomenon*. A Dissertation Submitted to the School of Education and the Committee on Graduate Study of Stanford University, pp. 323–324.

49. Ravitch, op. cit., p. 234.

50. Ravitch, op. cit., p. 235.

51. Ibid.

52. Ibid.

53. Trip Gabriel, (1996) "Oh Jane, See How Popular We Are," The *New York Times*, Oct. 3. A review of two museum shows, and a recently published book, *Growing up with Dick and Jane*.

54. Ibid.

55. William S. Gray and May Hill Arbuthnot, (1946–1947 edition) *Our New Friends*. Basic Readers Curriculum Foundation Program. New York: Scott, Foresman and Company.

56. Fred Davis, (1979) in *Yearning for Yesterday: A Sociology of Nostalgia,* argues that discontinuity in identity may lead to feelings of nostalgia evident in the pop-

ularity of the Dick and Jane Stories, and the fact that copies of the books, particularly the years 1940, 1946, 1951 and 1956, have become collectors' items. New York: Free Press.

57. Oscar and Mary F. Handlin, op. cit., (1971) *Facing Life: Youth and the Family in American History*. Boston: Little, Brown, p. 167.

58. Handlin, op. cit., p. 164.

59. In the obituary for Headmistress Jean Fair Mitchell. *New York Times*. August 6, 1998.

60. Handlin, op. cit., pp. 164–165.

61. Uniform appearance had always been used to create a sense of connectedness and allegiance to the group. See Nathan Joseph, (1986) *Uniforms and Nonuniforms: Communicating Through Clothing*. Westport, Conn.: Greenwood Press.

62. Edwin Hardin Sutherland, (1937) *The Professional Thief: By a Professional Thief*. Chicago: The University of Chicago Press.

63. Norman Margolis, (1968) "The New Fashion Awareness," *Earnshaw's*, May, p. 140.

64. Ibid.

65. They did. Sweaters with a shawl collar to keep warm in the chilly movie houses, leather buttons, heavy stitching, and leggings fastened with zippers— these elements of dress were both functional and fashionable. Patricia A. Farrell, op. cit., p. 99.

66. According to Baltzell, the schools that qualified were the following: In New England, the Episcopalian schools were St. Paul's, St. Mark's, Groton, St. George's, and Kent. The nondenominational schools were Exeter, Andover, Taft, Hotchkiss, Choate, Middlesex, and Dearfield. In the Middle and Southern States the acceptable schools were Lawrenceville, Hill, Episcopal High School, and Woodbury Forest.

Girls who hoped to move into the proper social circles also had to attend schools that carried the greatest social authority. E. Digby Baltzell, (1958) *Philadelphia Gentlemen*. Glencoe, Ill. The Free Press, p. 293.

67. Baltzell, op. cit., p. 306.

68. Elizabeth Ewing, (1977) *History of Children's Costume*. New York: Charles Scribner's Sons, p. 146.

69. Patricia A. Farrell, (1967) "The Good Old Days of Children's Fashions." *Earnshaw's*, August, pp. 98–103.

70. Farrell, op. cit., p. 100.

71. Margaret Jackson, (1936) *What they Wore, A History of Children's Dress*. London: G. Allen and Unwin, pp. 130–131.

72. *Godey's Lady's Book*, (1884) Philadelphia: J. H. Houlenbeek and Company.

73. M. Jackson, op. cit., pp. 130–131.

74. Earnshaw's (1996).

75. Children's Bureau of the United States Department of Labor, (1933) *Infant Care*. Publication no. 8. Washington, D.C.: United States Government Printing Office.

76. Jackson, op. cit., p. 129.

77. Young, op. cit., p. 39.

78. Martin, op. cit., p. 151.

79. John B. Watson, (1928) *Psychological Care of Infant and Child.* New York: W. W. Norton, pp. 42, 92–93.

80. Watson, op. cit., p. 93

81. Watson, op. cit., p. 94.

82. Children's Bureau of the United States Department of Labor, (1933) *Infant Care.* Publication No. 8. Washington, D.C.: United States Government Printing Office, p. 28.

83. Ewing, op. cit., p. 141.

84. *Earnshaw's,* Feb. 1936, p. 70.

85. Ibid.

86. *Earnshaw's,* (1996) p. 80.

87. Ibid.

88. Helen Goodman, (1989) *The Art of Rose O'Neill.* Catalogue for exhibition, Brandywine River Museum, Chadds Ford, Pa.

89. *Earnshaw's.*

90. Singer Sewing Machine Company, (1927) *How to Make Children's Clothes the Modern Way.* pp. 20, 23.

91. "Story Book Fashions, at John Taylor's Proves Smash Hit," *Earnshaw's,* July 1931, p. 826.

92. Jaffe, op. cit., p. 47.

93. Ewing, op. cit., p. 146.

94. William De Mille, (1980) "Mickey Versus Popeye," in Gerald Peary and Danny Peary, eds., *The American Animated Cartoon: A Critical Anthology.* New York: E. P. Dutton, p. 241.

95. Comic Artist, (1931) "We See by the Funny Papers," in *Earnshaw's,* June, p. 709.

96. De Mille, op. cit., p. 242.

97. *Earnshaw's,* April 1935, p. 56.

98. Hilde Jaffe, (1972) *Children's Wear Design.* New York: Fairchild Publications, p. 27.

99. Antonia Fraser, (1966) *A History of Toys.* London: Delacorte Press, p. 207.

100. *Earnshaw's,* June 1935, p. 58.

101. *Earnshaw's,* May 1935, p. 18.

102. *Earnshaw's,* April 1937, p. 62.

103. These short, simple, colorful, and pretty dresses have acquired the nick name "baby dresses." Many older girls refused to wear them. Personal communication from former children's wear designer Hilde Jaffe.

104. Personal communication from former children's wear designer Hilde Jaffe.

105. *The Girls' and Teens' Merchandiser: A National Trade Magazine for the Girls' and Teens' Industry,* April 1946, front page. The publication of the magazine began in New York City on February 12, 1946.

106. George Bush and Perry London, (1960)"On the Disappearance of the Knickers: Hypothesis for Functional Analysis of the Psychology of Clothing," *Journal of Social Psychology* 51, pp. 359–366.

107. Martin, op. cit., p. 151.

108. Bush and London, op. cit., p. 264.

109. Bush and London, op. cit., p. 364.

110. After the Hitler-Stalin pact, signed August 23, 1939, Congress passed a conscription law, which was approved September 6, 1940. Pictures of the outfits were portrayed in *Earnshaw's*, p. 85.

111. Jerome Kagan, Richard B. Kearsley, and Philip R. Zelazo (1978). *Infancy: Its Place in Human Development*. Cambridge, Mass.: Harvard University Press, pp. 23–27.

112. The Prado museum in Madrid has a large number of paintings where milk drips from the Madonna's breast to the mouth of a bishop, who is kneeling to receive the gift. In Picasso's "La Fuente" (1921), the fountain and the woman are one.

113. In the 1990s women campaigned and sued for the right to feed their babies in public. *New York Times*, March 4, 1993. *New York Times*, February 14, 1997.

114. Watson, op. cit., p. 81.

115. Watson, op. cit., p. 80.

116. Watson, op. cit., p. 69.

117. Watson, op. cit., p. 76.

118. Ann Douglas, (1978) *Feminization of American Culture*. New York: Alfred A. Knopf, p. 43.

119. Douglas, op. cit., p. 44.

120. Margaret A. Ribble (1943) *The Rights of Infants: Early Psychological Needs and Their Satisfaction*. New York: Columbia University Press, p. 56.

121. Ibid.

122. Ibid.

123. Benjamin Spock, (1946) *The Common Sense Book of Baby and Child Care*. New York: Hawthorne Books, p. 162.

124. Mary Lynn Stevens Heininger, (1984) "Children, Childhood, and Change in America, 1820–1920," in Heininger, et al., *A Century of Childhood*. Rochester, New York: The Margaret Woodbury Strong Museum, p. 30.

125. Ellen Seiter, (1993) *Sold Separately: Children and Parents in Consumer Culture*. New Brunswick, N.J.: Rutgers University Press, p. 52.

126. Veblen wrote, "The standard of expenditure which commonly guides our efforts is not the average, ordinary expenditure already achieved; it is an ideal of consumption that lies just beyond our reach, or to reach which requires some strain. The motive is emulation—the stimulus of an invidious comparison which prompts us to outdo those with whom we are in the habit of classing ourself." Thorstein Veblen (1899/1957) *The Theory of the Leisure Class*. New York: Modern Library, p. 103.

127. N. McKendrick, (1982) "Commercialization and the Economy," in N. McKendrick, J. Brewer, and J. Plumb, *The Birth of Consumer Society: The Commercialization of Eighteenth Century England*. Bloomington, Ind.: Indiana University Press, p. 20.

128. Seiter, op. cit., p. 68.

129. Ibid.

130. Ibid.

131. Seiter, op. cit., p. 64.

132. Seiter, op. cit., p. 70.

133. Seiter, op. cit., p. 71.

10

Conformity and Social Mobility: Children's Clothes Between 1950 and 1965

By 1950 it had become clear that clothes that impede an infant's movement are inimical to societal expectations of active participation in social life. Infants were no longer bound by their underwear and could move their arms and legs freely. Special outfits were designed for children between two and five, and the distinction between the sexes was minimal. Garments for toddlers allowed them to romp around unfettered. The style of clothes that the preschool child wore became more relaxed. Boys, whatever the age, wore some kind of pants.

Clothes for children older than six continued to be governed by expectations for gender distinction. Boys' and girls' attire followed the standards established in the nineteenth century. New styles for boys were based on heroic-mythical images, cowboys, for example. Many urban middle-class boys were expected to wear a white shirt, some form of a jacket, short pants for the younger boy, long pants for the older one, and sometimes a tie.[1]

Girls' attire was a much simplified version of late nineteenth century Paris fashion, seen, for example, in Monet's *Femmes au Jardin* (1866–1867) and reinvented as the New Look after World War II by Christian Dior.[2] It consisted of a tight-fitting bodice, narrow waist, and a full skirt that was rounded at the hips.[3] Full and frilly girls' attire echoed adult fashion.

Children's attire was thus guided by scripts that identified expectations for gender role behavior. Girls were to become wives and homemakers, and boys were to participate actively in the public sphere. Boys were to enter the armed services and later become breadwinners.[4]

Mothers, school policies, and teachers enforced these standards. Before a child left home for school in the morning a mother would usually check if her child was clean, neat, and properly dressed.[5] Mothers often judged

FIGURE 10.1
Checkup. Different
style dresses, each
of which recalls the
smock and pinafore
of nineteenth-
century England.
Together with the
above-the-knee
hemline and
hairband that keeps
the hair in place,
these styles speak
of childhood as
"childish," a period
of doing
unimportant things.
The girls also wear
sneakers (Keds?).
Norman Rockwell,
original oil painting
for The Saturday
Evening Post,
September 7, 1957.

FIGURE 10.2 Smocked dress. Smocked
dresses for girls two to ten were popular in
England in the second half of the
nineteenth century. Instructions for
construction were offered in *Waldon's
Practical Smocking*, 1984. Photo, Greg
Kitchen.

their own competence by how well their children looked. Most of the time they were responsible for buying the clothes their children wore.

In school teachers insisted that girls wear skirts.[6] Girls wearing slacks were prevented from entering the classroom, dining room, or library. It was unthinkable that boys wear dresses except when required by a role in a play.[7]

Perhaps the "paint-by-number" game symbolized the expectation for conformity that characterized children's clothes during this period. The paint-by-number set was the most popular hobby in the United States, with predicted sales of 200 million before the end of 1954.[8] It was "a fad so contagious that it amounted to national mania."[9] The endeavor entailed re-creating a well-known masterpiece, a Van Gogh, for example, by filling in the spaces on a printed canvas board. Each space bore a number corresponding to one of twenty or so capsules of ready-mixed oil paint supplied with the kit. The execution required no thought beyond conforming to the established boundaries and the use of the paint from the designated jar.[10] Because recreating the paintings looked like a complicated task that was difficult to perform, its completion engendered a sense of pride, observed an inventor of other hobby kits, Leu Glasser.[11]

In 1953, the paint-by-numbers kits were advertised on television by "America's favorite family," the smiling Ozzie, Harriet, David, and Rick Nelson. In the television advertisement David's clothes (born 1936) portray the tenet of "fixity." Everything is in place. Holding a paint brush, David is wearing a white, long-sleeved shirt, white sweater, and white long pants. Visually they merge and convey a unified whole.[12] Younger brother Rick's clothes (born 1940) portray nonchalance, an easy-going casualness. Rick is also holding a paint brush. He is wearing short sleeves and his shirt is hanging loose to just above the waistline. His pants seem crumpled. Since Ozzie Nelson was known for his careful attention to every detail on the program, Rick's appearance suggests that younger children enjoyed leeway in self-restraint.[13]

Gender distinctions were enforced by television programming, too. In *The Adventures of Ozzie and Harriet*, longest running sitcom on television (from 1952 to 1966), it was difficult to tell where reality ended and the show began because the Nelsons were a real family and they were shown in believable activities.[14] Father and sons tossed a ball on the front lawn, while Harriet was looking on smiling. All four are in the kitchen admiring a fish the boys caught; Ozzie, Harriet, and the boys are in the kitchen sharing a birthday cake the mother has made.

The Nelson's house had a fully equipped kitchen, like that of the other sitcom mothers, where they appeared to make and serve meals "without so much as mussing their aprons."[15] Ozzie and Harriet's ranch house was in Memphis on Audobon Drive, near Graceland, the house Elvis Presley bought to demonstrate that he had achieved success.[16]

Television commercials used women to advertise cars. Putting a woman behind the wheel justified the purchase of "extras" such as power steering and power brakes. In a make-believe TV interview with "Roving Reporter" Bob Lamont, a perky housewife chirped, "I drive just as well as my husband in our new Olds." "You certainly look lovely after a whole day of driving around town," he cooed, suggesting that the task of driving was not particularly demanding.[17] She was depicted wearing a hat with a veil, gloves, and a crisp print shirtwaist. Character June Cleaver wore such an outfit to PTA meetings.[18]

Women were to drive their children where they needed to go. In one of the segments of *Father Knows Best* the father, Jim Anderson, teaches his wife Margaret how to drive. This was the only segment on which the two were depicted having a fight.[19]

The Nuclear Family

Cultural ideals regarding individual success, production, and consumption were dependent upon the nuclear family in the 1950s. Prior to the Civil War, industrialization, production, and consumption exchanges involved households. Households were the central locale of economic activity. Education also took place in the home, and the parents were the principal, authoritative interpreters of the world for their children. The parents generally possessed the skills that children knew they needed to get on in the world. Except for orphans, the young had few, if any, alternatives to parental counsel. Access to clothes, toys, and education depended on blood and marriage links.

Modern industrial society required that the extended family abandon its productive functions and widen kin ties. By the beginning of the twentieth century, the shift of production out of the household and into factories and workshops, together with the rise of markets, enabled households to buy more of the goods and services required for daily life. Increasingly the nuclear family's energies came to be directed toward meeting its own needs rather than fulfilling obligations to an expansive array of kin. By the 1920s, skills learned from parents were no longer the only skills or the most important skills needed to get ahead in the world. With the development of factories, schools, and advertising, children became aware before their parents that interaction in modern society is impersonal and goal directed.[20]

Extended family ties were rekindled during the Great Depression. Sociologist Glen Elder observed that economic insecurity and upheaval in the home characterized the Depression. In the early 1930s to the mid-

FIGURE 10.3 *Walking to Church*. Middle-class respectability here consists of clothes that clearly identify gender, head covered by a hat, hands gloved, hemlines below the knees, solid colors. The nuclear family members proudly carry Bibles. Norman Rockwell, original oil painting for *The Saturday Evening Post*, April 4, 1953.

1940s, there was little opportunity for social mobility and America's class structure had changed little.[21] Fathers lost their jobs, forcing hundreds-of-thousands of women to work as maids to support their families (woman as breadwinner). Many felt the shift in family life and gender roles as profoundly "alien" to the American dream.[22] The norms of mutual obligation and aid that characterized the extended family were revived. Most people experienced dependency on members of the family as stultifying and oppressive.[23] To escape family obligations they turned to marriage and suburbia.

Television sitcoms projected the nuclear family and its suburban domesticity as a mark of upward mobility.[24] Suburban homes pictured in magazine advertisements depicted family and recreation rooms big enough to accommodate train sets and to provide a place to sit for everyone in the family when watching television or listening to the radio.[25] The suburban house became the embodiment of an egalitarian relationship between husband and wife. Discarded were formality and the traditional representations of separate spheres for men and women, kitchen, den and sewing room. The new ideals became "livability," "comfort," and "convenience."[26] There were separate children's bedrooms to be filled with toys.[27] Driveways, broad sidewalks, and sparse traffic provided safe places for bicycling and roller skating.

The nuclear family became an indicator of middle-class status.[28] A house in the suburbs was a way of lessening exposure to crime, crowds, and pollution, and in general to problems associated with the urbanization based on industrialization. The ability to commute to work from one's private house, which would have a garden and a workshop, had been a vision of utopia in the United States since the nineteenth century.[29] It was seen as a way of securing refuge from life in the city, which Americans experienced as "inimical to childhood joy, unnaturally paced, polluted, and just too crowded."[30]

Public opinion polls found that in America a single-family house in an attractive congenial community was thought to represent achievement of "the dream of happiness."[31] The 1950s was the first time that a wholehearted effort was made to create a home that would fulfill virtually all the personal needs of all its members, suggested historian Elaine Tyler May.[32]

Societal Reproduction

At the end of World War II social mobility was mostly available to men. Women were "evicted" from the work place. Woman's place became the home; her role, wife and mother.[33] The nation's maternity wards were filled with babies in the years between 1946 and 1964. Most of the increase in the birthrate came from early and near-universal marriage and childbearing (over 90 percent).[34] When respondents to a 1955 marriage study were asked what they thought they had sacrificed by marrying and raising a family the overwhelming majority of them replied, "Nothing." Less than 10 percent of Americans believed that an unmarried person could be happy.[35] Americans consistently told pollsters that home and family were the well-springs of their happiness and self-esteem.[36] Women who did go to work were housewives whose low-paying jobs helped ends meet.[37]

Maternal employment was viewed as having a negative impact on cognitive development of children under the age of six. Children were seen as social capital to which stay-at-home mothers contributed.[38] Few middle-class mothers with children under six were in the work force.[39]

In story after story women's magazines extolled motherhood and domesticity.[40] *McCall's* characterized life in the suburban family by what it called "togetherness."[41] Togetherness legitimated the new postwar suburban family, in which occasionally daddy changed diapers, helped with the shopping, and took charge of the kids on Saturday and Sunday afternoons.[42] Unhindered by kinship ties, the society of the 1950s offered an opportunity for social mobility.

Child-Rearing

Children were appreciated in the 1950s. Anthropologist Margaret Mead observed that judging by the standards of most other societies, American middle-class children were given an extraordinary amount of attention. Their needs, wishes, and performances were regarded as central and worthy of adult attention.[43] Relationships were personal.[44]

Parent-child closeness was accompanied by apprehension about the possibility of losing parental love and social rejection. The middle-class child was induced to behave well, noted Harold C. Lyon in *Learning to Feel–Feeling to Learn*.[45] Parents shifted away from the customary parental strategies that threatened punishment—"If you do X, I will hurt you." They directed their child-rearing practices toward enabling children to care about parental feelings. A parent was much more likely to say, "If you do X, you will hurt me." Obedience came because conformity to the parents' wishes was implicitly expected.[46] Parents taught their children to take "the other person into consideration," observed Melvin Kohn.[47]

Child-rearing practices at home centered on emotional nurturance, observed Talcott Parsons and other sociologists.[48] In school, however, children became more knowledgeable about the need for self-reliance, competition, and entrepreneurship.

Believing that education is the key to the society's future, Americans directed community resources towards the education of children. Ninety percent of all public school tax bills were approved by voters in the 1950s.[49]

Continuity of Basic Style

The clothing shortages that had plagued the country during World War II had disappeared in 1950. Most Americans, however, were still dressing in clothes made from natural fibers, which needed ironing and wrinkled

FIGURE 10.4 "Riegel Flanelettes." Family life. *Earnshaw's*, By permission.
Photo, Greg Kitchen.

badly in the heat. Business and professional men always wore coats and
ties in public and never (save when playing tennis) appeared on the
street wearing shorts.[50]

An advertisement by the Riegel Company (see Fig. 10.4) promoting a
new fabric called "flannelettes," uses the nuclear family ideal to promote
its pajamas. The ad is titled: "Family life in the '50s." It depicts the son
and daughter in their pajamas engaged in a pillow fight. They are making a racket. Stepping in to quiet the commotion is the mother, who is
wearing a robe from the same fabric. The father is behind her. He, too, is
wearing pajamas made out of the same fabric his children are wearing.[51]

The styles children wore to school and to parties were, for the most
part, merely updated versions of older styles and still echoed traditional
gender roles. Play attire that boys were wearing recalled the Western
theme. The pants, however, had rolled-back cuffs and an elasticized

waist. The style was practical. The cuff allowed for a later growth in height.[52] The pants were worn with a variety of tops. Girls wore full and frilly dresses and sweater twin sets that echoed adult women's fashions.

Increased demand for clothes led to rising prices, forcing retailers to look for substitutes for natural fibers. They soon began using fibers invented or improved during World War II. Acrylic, for example, made from a chemical compound called acrylonitrile, was developed in 1950. The garments produced were still in the traditional mold.[53] The man-made fiber companies offered engineers and scientists data on handling every aspect of their brand of fibers, from yarn production to cutting, sewing, and even to dry-cleaning and laundering procedures, in order to encourage manufacturers to use the new products.

Perma-press and drip-dry fabrics made the ironing chore almost obsolete. Girls could wear the full-skirted dress with four crinolines without worrying about the starch giving out. Baby panties could sport rows and rows of nylon lace, allowing maternal pride but requiring no maternal effort.[54] Many of these synthetics, however, smelled or didn't "breathe," and some even caught fire.

The skeleton suit was transformed into a one-piece coverall for infants. Feet and snaps were added and stretch fabric was used. It was easy to put on, comfortable to wear, and easy to open for changing the diaper.[55]

This new garment, called "Wear-a-Blanket," was based on a Dr. Denton suit (see Fig. 10.5), which originated in 1865, where booties were attached to a union suit to help prevent a cold. The cover fabric was often ineffectual and couldn't keep the child warm when he or she threw off the blanket.[56] The new version, made of a new combination of fabrics, such as wool and rayon or wool with cotton, kept children warm at night. It came in sizes up to six and in pink or blue. It had a high collar, cuffs, full-length zipper down the back for ease in using the toilet, and a fly front for boys.[57]

Snowsuits for small children (nine months to four years) and storm coats for boys or girls were made out of water-repellent fabrics created during the war by DuPont. Under the headline "Doctor Says—Keep Them Warm and Dry," for the Fall-Winter season of 1950, "Play Town Togs" offered "improved" versions of older styles in raincoats, flannel dressing gowns, wool jackets, knit suits, and cotton overalls for boys and girls.[58]

Grant Knitting Mills offered swimwear and knitwear in sizes for children from "infancy to sixteen." It used a mixture of several new fabrics: cotton-nylon-lastex, for example, or satin and nylon combinations for swimwear. Knitwear was made out of the "finest zephyr yarns . . . in the newest Spring shades." Also advertised were sweaters made out of combed cotton and nylon. First produced by the DuPont Laboratories in 1938, nylon was named after the cities where it was hoped the fabric

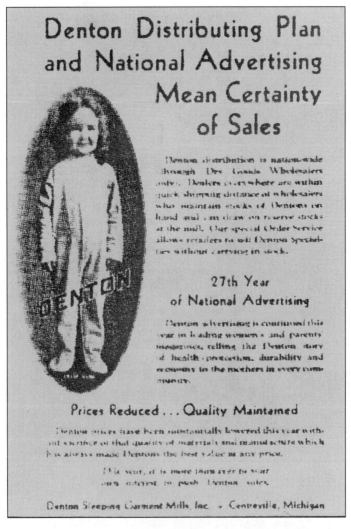

FIGURE 10.5   Dr. Denton Sleeping Garment. Updated from 1909. *Earnshaw's,* 1953. By permission. Photo, Greg Kitchen.

would sell, New York and London, observed Michael Tambini.[59] Nylon, fine, strong, and elastic, was thought to be an ideal substitute for rayon or silk.

Sneakers, also known as, "sneaks," "sand shoes," and "croquet sandals," had been updated and adapted to modern needs after the turn of the century, with Keds in 1916, and Converse "All Stars" in 1917.[60] Their

FIGURE 10.6   Boys' playwear. *Earnshaw's*, 1953. By
permission. Photo, Greg Kitchen.

original style was maintained for over fifty years.[61] The only change that
took place in 1950 was adding ventilating eyelets on the sides of the
sneaker. The shoes still consisted of canvas uppers to which rubber soles
were bonded.

In 1868, the new rubber-soled shoes, costing six dollars, were too expensive for the general public to buy. They did, however, become the preferred shoe for aristocratic lawn games. In *Female Life in Prison*, published
in England in 1862, the word "sneaks" refers to prison night guards, who
wore rubber shoes in order to creep by the women at Brixton prison. In
1870, American etymologist James Greenwood associated sneaks with

cat burglars or "sneak thieves."[62] The word "sneaker" was first used in England in 1875.[63]

By 1897 Sears Roebuck Catalogue had begun listing factory-made rubber-sole shoes for only sixty cents a pair. Seventeen years later, U. S. Rubber introduced Keds (named from a combination of the words "kids" (the target audience) and "ped" (Latin for foot).[64] In the 1920s and the 1930s traction was added to soles and companies advertised different shoes for different sports, as well as distinct models for boys and girls.[65]

Sneakers became the shoe of choice as families flocked to the suburbs and had leisure to mow the grass and play sports. Thirty-five million pairs of sneakers were sold in 1952, *The New Yorker* reported. Sales grew to 130 million pairs in 1961, and in 1962 to over 150 million pairs. After dress codes were relaxed in the 1960s and sneakers could be worn to school, children had at least two pairs, one for daily wear and one for gym. This resulted in sales of 600 million pairs annually.[66]

Competition between leather shoe manufacturers and sneaker producers launched the phenomenon of endowing sneakers with "pseudoscientific enhancements." "U.S. Keds" highlighted the "shock-proof arch cushion." On television when a clown named Kedso asked children why they wore Keds, they answered, "So that I can run faster and jump further."[67] The P.F. Flyers, on the other hand, "provided Posture Foundation."[68] In 1961 Disney's film *The Absent-Minded Professor* gave voice to the hope that the right shoes could transform also-rans into champions.

The girls' dress market consisted of fitted dresses—either a fitted bodice with above-the-knee full skirt, or fitted with a dropped waist, to usually one inch above the hipline, and the princess style. The fullness of the skirt was sometimes contrasted with slacks called "Slim Jims," which were cut slim and tapered to a tight-fitting ankle. A rounded collar called a "pie plate" was the collar of the 1950s. It was made in every size. The 1950s girls' clothes were in styles that had met the Papal decree on modesty.[69] The arms were covered and the slip made sure that the body remained concealed even if the shirt slipped out.

Boys' suits continued to be in adult style. The March 20, 1950, issue of *Life* advertised two different styles of boys' suits by a company called Twigs. The headline says: "Stunning Young Garments Styled Like Daddy's." The suits were available in sizes two to seven. One was an all-wool Eton jacket with a wide white collar and tie. The outfit included short pants in a "harmonizing" color. The second was of wool and rayon and consisted of a striped wool blazer with contrasting trousers.[70] The colors in boys' wardrobes were subdued, like those of their fathers. They were loden green, chocolate brown, navy, and charcoal gray.[71]

It seems that only manufacturers who produced good quality clothes put their names on the garments. A manufacturer's name on a garment generally meant that the clothes were reliable. The thinking was that a manufacturer who put his name on something was selling not only his product but his self-respect. Buyers were thus encouraged to stay with brand-name merchandise. Regal, Tam-O-Shanter, Turtle Bay, Cinderella, and Health-Tex were some of the better known brands.[72]

Status Symbols

Prosperity characterized the 1950s.[73] Despite the affluence, there was little innovation in clothing styles. *Fortune* magazine noted that Americans were earning enough so that the number of families moving into the middle-class (earning more than $5,000 annually after taxes) was 1.1 million a year. By the end of 1956 there were 16.6 million such families in the country. By 1959 half the families in the United States would be middle-class families, *Fortune* predicted.[74] Americans had jobs, 53 million in a total population of 150,697,131.[75] Unemployment was less than 2 percent. Americans had money ($140 million in liquid savings). The unparalleled prosperity was accompanied by the availability of "wonder drugs," such as streptomycin and penicillin, the growth of science and technology, and a decrease in the infant mortality rate.[76] The passage of the GI Bill of Rights in 1944 helped millions of Americans acquire education and work skills as well as housing.[77]

Anxiety and uncertainty about the future, however, encouraged clothes that indicated achievement: status symbols. The need to ward off feelings of anxiety and insecurity led to the pursuit of status symbols, suggested Vance Packard in *The Status Seekers*.[78] As Thorstein Veblen suggested, apparel is always in evidence and its cost can be gathered at a glance.[79] Rather than desiring a change in the basic style of dress, manufacturers and consumers were motivated by fear to focus on constructing status symbols, elements of dress suggesting economic success.[80]

Ornaments and accessories are the finishing touch that can make an ensemble exquisite or reduce it to frumpy, dull, and dowdy expression, advised Marian L. Davis in *Visual Design in Dress*.[81] "When price is the primary consideration" ornamentation is kept to a minimum or eliminated altogether, observed children's wear designer Hilde Jaffe.[82] Embroidery, ribbons, and bows were used to ornament outfits. Smocking, which entailed the use of embroidery stitches to hold gathered cloth in even folds, was extolled.[83]

Trimmings were another way of putting one's affluence in evidence. The full skirt gave designers a multitude of choices for trim, from French poodle appliqués to brightly sequined butterflies. Pockets decorated with buttons and lace would form a row and extend completely around the skirt.[84] Another way of varying a garment once its basic shape was

FIGURE 10.7 Girls' playwear. Status symbols. *Earnshaw's,* 1950s. By permission. Photo, Greg Kitchen.

determined was to repeat it in different fabrics and apply different trimmings. A dress, for example, cut in gingham might be trimmed with eyelet. When it was cut in velveteen it was ornamented with lace; in organdy it was trimmed with embroidery. Sweaters were decorated with sequins, seed pearls, or tiny appliqués.

Collars were also a means of ornamenting dresses, blouses, jackets, and coats.[85] The collar frames the face and draws attention to it. A large variety of collars became available in the 1950s for girls between the ages of four and twelve. Collars stood high on the neck or lay flat on the shoulders. Some were big, like a bertha, a cape-like collar generally made of lace popular in the second half of the nineteenth century, or small, like a mandarin, a standing collar attached to a close-fitting neckline.[86] A detachable fur collar could be worn with a variety of outfits. Complementing the silhouette theme could be a headband style of hat made in white bunny fur, sequined felt or velvet.

Shopping in the more expensive department stores, such as Saks Fifth Avenue, Marshal Field, or Neiman Marcus, and in some specialty stores was also prestigious. The clothes were reputed to have professional styling and good quality cloth.

In boys' apparel the quality of the fabric and the fit were important indicators of affluence. The influence came from adult male attire; climate and local custom also influenced status symbols for boys' attire, a fur or velvet collar, for example, according to a 1959 advertisement by Modes D'Enfant.[87] Infant wear also saw the introduction of status symbols: French fly-front pants for little boys and can-can crinoline dresses for girls.[88]

The wide-spread use of status symbols reflected the fact that America had become a more urban nation and the urban character of the environment provided a larger and broader audience to which people felt they must show off their success. The census bureau reported that nearly two-thirds of the population lived in a universe different from the world of farms, small towns, and modest-sized cities—places where neighbors knew each other.[89]

Toys

Many of the toys children played with were unisex. Alone or with their friends girls and boys frolicked with the hula hoop, jumped rope, played with paint-by-the-numbers sets, yo-yo's, jacks, and pick-up sticks, and rode tricycles and bicycles, and went roller skating. Magazines and advertisements for toys, however, focused on gender differences.

Parent's Magazine informed their readers that a child's age, sex, level of development, and natural inclination must always be kept in mind when considering purchasing a toy.[90] "A toy too advanced may be frustrating"[91] to a child, they warned. Magazine columns and feature articles set out to convince mothers that by merely providing the right toys, they would find that wonders would be accomplished. A toy would enable a child to achieve, make progress, compete, and get ahead.[92]

Girls usually played with dolls or stuffed animals and often in a space different from the one that boys used. On a Saturday afternoon in the 1950s, a popular pastime among girls was cutting out paper dolls. Sitting on the floor, with blunt-tipped scissors, girls cut carefully around the tabs, arguing with their best friend over who got the bridal gown and who was stuck with the pedal-pusher outfit.[93] Once the doll was dressed in a strapless evening gown, or a revealing swimsuit, the most popular outfits in the 1950s, the doll was placed on a freestanding little platform and admired, enabling little girls to tell stories and spin fantasies.[94]

FIGURE 10.8 Mimi Jordan from West Hartford, Conn., in a hula-hoop contest. November 5, 1958. UPI.

Women's magazines encouraged the practice. A paper doll Betsy Mc-Call, a cute little girl of about six, was launched on the pages of *McCall's Magazine* in May 1951.[95] The doll was presented in her underwear accompanied by "occasion-appropriate" outfits. "Betsy McCall Goes to a Wedding," for example, is accompanied by several different kinds of dresses appropriate for wearing at a wedding. Betsy McCall was the only paper-doll character in a major magazine who lasted into the 1970s.[96]

Dolls came in the image of movie stars, such as June Allyson, Natalie Wood, Grace Kelly, and Rock Hudson, as well as TV personalities Ozzie and Harriet, Lucille Ball, Desi Arnaz, and the Mouseketeers. Jackie and Caroline Kennedy were dolls, as was Tricia Nixon.[97] A three-dimensional

Barbie doll appeared in 1959, a perforated punch-out doll with plasticized clothes.

Advertisements reinforced gender distinctions by suggesting that girls were physically less capable. An advertisement for Legos, for example, showed a boy stretched on the floor building a wide-sprawling structure, and another standing on the highest rung of a ladder completing a towering structure. The girls in the ad (sisters?) are seated passively on the floor watching, or building a simple one-level structure.[98]

Ads portraying children with their parents further supported gender differences by showing fathers with their sons and mothers with their daughters. Father and son are often depicted working on a project together. In advertisements for train sets, father and son are playing with a model train, using the switches. Mother and daughter are seated outside the train's perimeter, depicted as an appreciative audience.[99]

"Just Like Mother's," girls' play was a miniature version of their mothers' domestic work. Girls' toys were miniature replicas of vacuum cleaners, ovens, strollers, shopping carts, kitchen sets, and doll houses. Advertisements for the appliances describe them in terms of stylishness and "smartness."[100] Advertisements often portray mother and daughter side by side competing rather collaborating with each other.[101] Through the 1960s advertisements for girls' toys revolved around childcare, cooking, cleaning, and shopping.[102]

Advertisers for the *Book of Knowledge*, on the other hand, suggested that books may be more important than toys, and books were available to girls as well as boys. In 1956, the caption of an arty close-up of an upside-down doll says, "Will your gift last a day or a lifetime?" The question was repeated in 1957 with a picture of a boy unwrapping a new football. Addressed to parents, an advertisement from 1961 suggests that the decision to buy an encyclopedia instead of a toy is a parental declaration of independence from children's wishes. The ad says, "Let Santa give them what they want, you give what they need."[103] Toys are depicted abandoned under the tree. A boy six or so is sitting in his pajamas reading the encyclopedia, ignoring the toy train nearby.[104]

Leisure

Leisure became a mass phenomenon in the United States, and *Fortune* proclaimed it to be a boost to consumption.[105] *Business Week* observed, "Never have so many people had so much time on their hands—with pay—as today in the United States. That means two day weekends, a three week annual vacation, daily lunch and coffee breaks and early retirement on pension."[106] It was also a boost to community life, which revolved around schools, churches, and other local institutions.[107] New and

FIGURE 10.9 Girls' leisure playwear. *Earnshaw's*, 1950s. By permission. Photo, Greg Kitchen.

informal playwear was developed for girls. Pedal-pushers with three-quarter dolman sleeve tops (deep cut under the arm, adding fullness to the armbust area), and Jamaica shorts were practical for the lifestyle of the suburban family.[108]

What made shopping for clothes easy in the postwar period was the fact that shopping centers followed the consumer to the suburbs, making shopping in the suburban mall easy and fun. For suburbanites, shopping in the big city could be time-consuming, expensive, and a chore. The mall, however, provided off-the-street parking and no dress requirements. Mothers and children could go shopping in shorts, slacks, or in whatever they were wearing.[109]

Manufacturers and retailers, moreover, enticed shoppers by offering new ways of paying: buying on the installment plan, with layaway, and through the use of credit. In 1955 there were a thousand malls in the country. By 1956 there were sixteen hundred, and by 1962 there were

FIGURE 10.10   Boys are reading *Three Dimension Comics* with the aid of special glasses, which give the images depth. August 28, 1953. UPI/Corbis.

over five thousand, covering about forty-six thousand acres across America. Leisure made it easier to shop. Mothers, however, often bought new clothes only for the first two born, and passed them down to those born later. There were also hand-me-downs from other relatives, which children often felt embarrassed or uncomfortable wearing. They believed the clothes didn't fit right—sometimes hand-me-downs did fit and at other times they didn't. Reasonable prices at the mall made it possible to get children the clothes they wanted. They could now skate in style; in a full skirt that was short, fancy panties, and ornaments, such as poodles or hearts. Boys' jackets acquired cardigan styling.[110]

Colors became brighter after 1957, as if to counteract the darkness induced by the political scene. The colors were given the names of refreshing fruits: watermelon, lime, lemon, peach, and pineapple.[111] Also offering a lighter touch were Bermuda shorts, pedal pushers, and Capri pants in these mellow colors.

FIGURE 10.11   The Lone Ranger.
Heroic male figure. *Earnshaw's*, 1950s.
By permission. Photo, Greg Kitchen.

Peer Culture

Most children left home in the morning and spent the day with other children their own age. School, television, toys, and comic books encouraged interaction with same-sex peers. Children could spend the whole day in the gender-specific community of their peers.

After school, wearing the appropriate costume (to play Batman, for example, in addition to the cape, a cowl and gauntlets were also required), children talked about the abilities of the characters they were imitating. Hopalong Cassidy and The Lone Ranger were among the favored charac-

FIGURE 10.12   Davy Crockett. His outfit, as worn by the star of Disney's film, Fess Parker, became very popular in the 1950s. *Earnshaw's*, 1950s. By permission. Photo, Greg Kitchen.

ters. They made the Western look popular among boys. Roy Rogers's embroidered shirts were worn with tight jeans, a cowboy hat, and lasso.[112]

Buffalo Bob Smith, a singing piano player who created *The Howdy Doody Show*, was on NBC for much of the 1950s. Mr. Smith was a big man and almost always wore a fringed cowboy outfit. His puppet, called Howdy Doody, wore jeans, a bandanna, and a checked shirt. The third character on the show was Clarabell the Clown, who said not a word but hopped around honking a horn or spraying Buffalo Bob with a bottle of seltzer. *Howdy Doody* was so popular that people gathered in the streets in front of appliance store windows to watch it.[113] TV was still a novelty in the 1950s.

An enormous boost to the advertising business was the legend of frontiersman Davy Crockett who fell at the Alamo. The story was dramatized by Walt Disney in a one-hour TV show in 1955. His natural rustic manner of dress was celebrated. Three-hundred million worth of fake coonskin caps, Davy Crockett T-shirts, dolls, and toys were sold.[114]

Upset by the spread of consumption, critics argued that "runaway consumerism" was undermining what they considered "traditional Ameri-

FIGURE 10.13 Four
African-American
children. Boy's attire
is different from that
of the girl, who
wears a plaid dress.
1965. Moebes;
Jack G. Courtesy
of Corbis.

can values."[115] What people were buying, critics claimed, was not so
much about what they needed in their lives, but about what they needed
to consume in order to impress or keep up with their neighbors.[116]

Consumption by the lower classes has often met with a hostile reaction, argued Albert O. Hirschman.[117] Those of inferior rank threaten the
upper-class sense of themselves and the social order. In the eighteenth
and nineteenth centuries, and even earlier, liberty to consume was perceived as a threat that the visible gap between the rich and the poor
would be obliterated.[118]

Appliqués and prints of cartoon characters and imaginary heroes
emerged in a social context where the ties that used to bind the child to the
larger family had weakened. The wearing of such costumes or the playing
with such toys with one's friends may have helped children feel less alone
and afraid. Wearing these costumes and playing with these toys may have
been a reflection of a desire to be a part of a community, to share in the
magical qualities of the "caped crusaders" (Superman and Batman), for example. These characters emerged in the 1930s and with minor updating
continued to be relevant to children through the early 1960s[119] and later.

FIGURE 10.14
Superman. Heroic male
figure. *Earnshaw's,*
1950s. By permission.
Photo, Greg Kitchen.

A collective search for security may have underlain the continuity of familiar styles of dress. America faced the future with apprehension, the Nearings observed.[120] People stayed within boundaries that were safe. McCarthy's allegations, which began in February of 1950, ended after the Army-McCarthy hearings in 1954,[121] but they continued to have an impact on politics well into the 1960s.[122]

The Korean War, the Cold War, and the threat of nuclear war, were also a source of apprehension, the Handlins argued. They suggested that American society feared the future and nurtured the caution of old age. The newly elected President Eisenhower (1953–1961) may have been concerned, too. Five days before his inauguration, staring out the window of his hotel room in New York, he swiveled around and said to evangelist Billy Graham, "America has to have a religious revival."[123] As a military man, he knew that in times of stress prayer offers comfort and support.

Ike's first year in office saw music by Bill Haley, Richy Valens, Elvis Presley, and Chuck Berry soar in popularity, but Les Paul and Mary Ford's "Vaya con Dios" (Go with God) and Frankie Lane's "I Believe" were also among the ten top hits. The threat of communist domination loomed large. In 1954 Congress voted to add the phrase "under God" to the pledge of allegiance and in the following year made "In God We Trust" mandatory on all U.S. currency.[124]

At sixty-three years of age, Dwight D. Eisenhower was then the oldest man ever elected president and was slow to make decisions. The Eisenhower presidency was described by journalist Murray Kempton as, "The great tortoise upon whose back the country sat for eight years."[125] Like President Eisenhower, the clothes children wore offered a sense of security and comfort.

There was little important change in children's clothes even after the election of John F. Kennedy in 1960. In the White House, the two Kennedy children were conventionally dressed, although with elegance and grace. Two aspects of their dress caught public attention: matching sister and brother coats, and the haircut John-John wore, which was current in England.[126]

Notes

1. "Real Western Wear" offered by Sears Roebuck in its catalogue appeared to be restrictive. The outfits consisted of a short-sleeve knitted shirt, long pants designed with a narrow waist, a snug seat, tapered legs, and turned-up cuffs. Linda Martin, (1978) *The Way We Wore: Fashion Illustrations of Children's Wear 1870–1970.* New York: Charles Scribner's Sons, p. 174. Real cowboy clothes were tight to avoid snags and to aid in riding.

2. Valerie Steele, (1988) *Paris Fashion.* New York: Oxford University Press, pp. 124–125.

3. Martin, op. cit., pp. 170–174.

4. James T. Patterson, (1997) *Grand Expectations.* New York: Oxford University Press, p. 374. Girls' dresses had a natural waistline and the hips were emphasized. The jacket and tie that boys wore distanced the self and one's feelings from the environment. See Ruth P. Rubinstein (1995) *Dress Codes: Meaning and Messages in American Culture.* Boulder, Colo.: Westview.

5. It is a scene common in movies and television programs of the period.

6. Arlene Skolnick, (1991) *Embattled Paradise: The American Family in An Age of Uncertainty.* New York: Basic Books, p. 72.

7. Cross-dressing as an addiction is attributed to the prohibition of playing with dressing in female clothes during childhood. An important diversion among the Ivy League educated political elite at the Bohemian Club in California is getting dressed in female attire; it is considered a degenerate activity by religious conservatives.

8. Ann Karal Marling, (1994) *As Seen on TV, The Visual Culture of Everyday Life in the 1950s.* Cambridge, Mass.: Harvard University Press, p. 59.

9. Ibid.

10. Ibid.

11. Ibid. It did, however, require precision and manual dexterity.

12. Marling, op. cit. p. 50.

13. Ibid.

14. Skolnik, op. cit., p. 52.

15. Marling, op. cit., p. 217.

16. Marling, op. cit., p. 194.

17. Quoted in Marling, op. cit., p. 156.

18. Ibid.

19. Marling, op. cit., p. 129.

20. Jan E. Dizard and Howard Gadlin, (1990) *The Minimal Family.* Amherst: University of Massachusetts Press, p. 69.

21. Glen Elder, (1974) *Children of the Great Depression.* Chicago: University of Chicago Press. See also, Patterson, op. cit., p. 11

22. Elder, op. cit.

23. Stephanie Coontz, (1992) *The Way We Never Were.* New York: Basic Books, p. 26.

24. David Halberstam, (1993) *The Fifties.* New York: Villard Books, p. ix; Patterson notes that 10 percent of the families in the United States had television sets in 1950 (op. cit., p. 10).

25. Ellen Seiter, (1993) *Sold Separately: Children and Parents in Consumer Culture.* New Brunswick, N.J.: Rutgers University Press, pp. 15–16.

26. Clifford Clark, (1986) *The American Family Home 1800–1960.* Chapel Hill: University of North Carolina Press pp. 209, 216.

27. Seiter, op. cit., p. 16.

28. Stephanie Chains, in Coontz, op. cit., p. 26.

29. John R. Stilgoe, (1988) *Borderland: Origins of the American Suburb, 1820–1939.* New Haven, Conn.: Yale University Press, p. 2.

30. Stilgoe, op. cit., p. 132.

31. Stilgoe, op. cit., p. 2.

32. Elaine Tyler May, (1988) *Homeward Bound: American Families in the Cold War Era.* New York: Basic Books, p. 11.

33. Halberstam, op. cit., p. 586.

34. In 1950, 55.4 percent of children were born to white married women between the ages of fifteen and nineteen; 33.3 percent to mothers between the ages of twenty and twenty-four.

Among African Americans, 30.8 percent of children were born to mothers between the ages of fifteen and nineteen, and 28.9 percent to those between the ages of twenty and twenty-four. In *Historical Statistics, Bicentennial Edition,* Vol. 1 op. cit. p. 54. Charles F. Westoff, (1986) "Fertility in the United States," *Science,* p. 234. In the peak year of 1957, 4.3 million babies were born, but by 1965 the birthrate had declined to below 3.8 million.

35. Chains, in Coontz, op. cit., p. 25.

36. Ibid.
37. Richard A. Easterlin, (1980) *Birth and Fortune: The Impact of Numbers on Personal Welfare.* Chicago: University of Chicago Press.
In 1970, the percentage of married women (with children under age six) who worked year round and full time was 9.6 percent. Source: *Bureau of Labor Statistics, Monthly Labor Review,* June 1994.
38. For example, Thomas S. Achenbach and Craig Edelbrock, (1981) *Behavioral Problems and Competencies Reported by Parents of Normal and Disturbed Children Aged Four Through Sixteen.* Monographs of the Society for Research in Child Development, serial no. 188. Chicago: University of Chicago Press.
39. Skolnick, op. cit., p. 65.
40. Patterson, op. cit., p. 362.
41. *McCall's,* April, 1954, Easter issue.
42. Marling, op. cit., p. 96.
43. Attributed to Margaret Mead by Elizabeth Ewing (1977) in *History of Children's Costume.* New York: Charles Scribner's Sons, p. 14.
44. D. F. Alwin, (1988) "From Obedience to Autonomy: Changes in Traits Desired in Children, 1924–1978," *Public Opinion Quarterly* 52, pp. 33–52.
45. Harold C. Lyon Jr. (1971) *Learning to Feel-Feeling to Learn.* Charles E. Merrill Publishing Company, pp. xii-xiii.
46. Dizard and Gadlin, op, cit., p. 76.
47. Melvin Kohn, (1959) "Social Class and Parental Values," *American Journal of Sociology* 64, p. 351.
48. Talcott Parsons and Robert Bales, (1955) *Family Socialization and Interaction.* Glencoe, Ill.: The Free Press.
49. Chains, op. cit., p. 24.
50. Patterson, op. cit., p. 11.
51. *Earnshaw's,* November, 1996 p. 86.
52. Ibid.
53. Hilde Jaffe, (1972) *Childrenswear Design.* New York: Fairchild Publications, p. 59.
54. "Fashion in the 50's: Wooing the Preteen Princess," *Earnshaw's,* September 1977, p. 93.
55. Designed by inventor Walter Airs. Ewing, op. cit., pp. 172–173.
56. *Earnshaw's,* November 1996, p. 79.
57. *Earnshaw's,* January 1950, p. 187.
58. *Earnshaw's,* January 1950 p. 186.
59. Michael Tambini, (1996) *The Look of the Century.* Cooper Hewitt, National Design Museum, p. 138.
60. Tom Vanderbilt, (1998) *The Sneaker Book: Anatomy of An Industry and an Icon.* New York: The New Press, p. 9.
61. Laurie Lawlor, (1996) *Where Will This Shoe Take You?* New York: Walker and Company, p. 109.
62. Vanderbilt, op. cit., p. 9.
63. Colin McDowell (1989) *Shoes, Fashion and Fantasy.* New York: Rizzoli.
64. Lawlor, op. cit., p. 108.
65. Vanderbilt, op. cit., pp. 10–11.
66. Vanderbilt, op. cit., p. 13.

67. Vanderbilt, op. cit., p. 14.

68. Ibid.

69. "Morality and Good Taste in Apparel," (1955) *America*, 93, July 2, p. 342.

70. *Earnshaw's*, January 1950.

71. *Earnshaw's*. August 1977, p. 112.

72. An editorial by *Earnshaw's* editor Thomas W. Hudson. January 1970, p. 35.

73. See Joseph C. Goulden, (1976) *The Best Years*. New York: Athenaeum, p. 6; see also Patterson, op. cit., pp. 68–69.

74. David Halberstam, (1993) *The Fifties*. New York: Villard Books, p. 587.

75. *Bicentennial Edition of Historical Statistics of U.S., Colonial Times to 1970*. Part 1. September, 1975. Washington, D. C.: U.S. Department of Commerce, Bureau of Census.

76. Goulden, op. cit., p. 6.

77. Patterson, op. cit., pp. 68–69.

78. Vance Packard, (1959) *Status Seekers*. New York: David McKay, pp. 128–130.

79. Veblen, op. cit., p. 119

80. Packard, op. cit., p. 7.

81. Marian L. Davis, (1996) *Visual Design in Dress*. Upper Saddle River, N.J.: Simon and Schuster, p. 123.

82. Jaffe, op. cit., p. 73.

83. Jaffe, op. cit., p. 65.

84. *Earnshaw's*. September 1977 p. 93.

85. Jaffe, op. cit., p. 126.

86. Jaffe, op. cit., pp. 87, 126–136.

87. An advertisement in *Life* in 1959, replicated in *Earnshaw's*, November 1996, p. 87.

88. "Fashion in the 50's," *Earnshaw's*, September 1977, p. 93.

89. Patterson, op. cit.

90. Ibid.

91. Quoted in Seiter, op. cit., p. 67.

92. Seiter, op. cit., p. 94.

93. Susan Jonas and Marilyn Nissenson, (1994) *Going Going Gone: Vanishing Americana*. San Francisco: Chronicle Books, pp. 106-107.

94. Ibid.

95. *Earnshaw's*, Oct. 1988 pp. 117–118.

96. Jonas and Nissenson, op. cit., p. 107.

97. Ibid.

98. Seiter, op. cit., pp. 72, 73.

99. Seiter, op. cit., pp. 84–85.

100. Seiter, op. cit., p.75.

101. Seiter, op. cit., p. 78.

102. Seiter, op. cit., pp. 78, 80.

103. Seiter, op. cit., p. 64.

104. Ibid.

105. Marling, op. cit., p. 52.

106. "The Leisured Masses," *Business Week*, Sept. 12, 1953, pp. 142, 145.

107. Patterson, op. cit., p. 340.

108. *Earnshaw's*, November 1996, pp. 86–87.

109. Robert B. Medvin, (1962) "Think Wild; Think Big; Think Different," *Earnshaw's*, January, pp. 64–65

110. Martin, op. cit., pp. 170–173.

111. The new colors may have come from the attempt by the automobile industry to turn cars into fashion items, with a new color scheme and new style every year.

112. *Earnshaw's*, September 1977, p. 87.

113. Richard Severo's obituary for Buffalo Bob Smith in *The New York Times*, Friday, July 31, 1998.

114. Patterson, op. cit., p. 353.

115. C. Wright Mills, (1951) *White Collar*. New York: Oxford University Press, p. xv.

116. Halberstam, op. cit., p. 506.

117. Albert O. Hirschman, (1982) *Shifting Involvements, Private Interest and Public Action*. Princeton, N.J.: Princeton University Press, pp. 53–57.

118. Hirschman, op. cit., p. 56.

119. Joe Desris (1994) *DC Comics*. New York: Abbeville Publishing Group, pp. 6–8.

120. The Nearings claimed that one of the reasons for fearing to take a risk is that public discussion was throttled through efforts by the oligarchy to establish and maintain conformity of thought, action, and association through a balanced pattern of economic and social pressures. Helen and Scott Nearing, (1955) *USA Today*. Harborside, Maine: Social Science Institute.

121. McCarthyism left an impact at least on the politics of the country through the Johnson administration. Thomas A. Bailey and David M. Kennedy, (1988) *The American Pageant: A History of the Republic*. Lexington, Mass.: D. C. Heath, p. 843.

122. David F. Trask, (1973) "The Imperial Republic: America in World War Politics, 1945 To Present," in William E. Leuchtenburg, ed., *The Unfinished Century: America Since 1900*. Boston: Little Brown, pp. 575–669.

123. Handlin, op. cit., p. 257.

124. Leuchtenburg, op. cit., pp. 745–746.

125. Murray Kempton (1967) " The Underestimation of Dwight D. Eisenhower," *Esquire*, Sept.

126. *Earnshaw's*, August 1967, p. 103.

11

Challenging Gender Boundaries: Children's Clothes Between 1965 and 1980

The culture of the 1960s was symbolized by Rock'n Roll, observed cultural historian Morris Dickstein.[1] Rock is music that made you want to dance, Dickstein suggested.[2] Its "hallmarks were energy and intensity."[3] Other forces full of energy and intensity that moved American society beyond traditional standards and personal restraint were the civil rights movement,[4] the sexual revolution, the counterculture and the birth control pill.[5] The power of these movements affected the production and consumption of children's clothes in two ways: the development of specifically children's fashion and the diffusion of clothes that normally belong in the outside region to frontstage performance.

Child-Rearing

The approach to child development promulgated by Dr. Spock had deepened to include some of the ideas about child development suggested by thinkers as diverse as John Dewey and Piaget. These ideas freed parents from being punitive, setting the stage for parent-child interaction that involved caring and nurturing.

The basic idea was that children learn through experience. Hence, children need an environment where they can pose questions. Making mistakes is also essential for learning and so is getting involved in conflict situations.

Disposable diapers eased the burden of changing diapers. Advances in the textile industry led to a leakproof paper and plastic diaper. The old-fashioned cotton rectangle was slowly replaced. The likelihood of diaper rash and discomfort decreased. Social opposition to disposable diapers was dropped after it was found that disposable diapers took much less space in a landfill than had originally been feared.[6]

The prominent Harvard pediatrician T. Berry Brazelton recommended that parents let their children decide when they wanted to become diaper-free, that is, toilet trained. Since children in disposable diapers don't feel as much wetness, would toilet training come later? Would infancy last longer? At the same time, infants' attire during this period acquired a new and liberated attitude. Pant dresses, denims, calicos, madras, and "everything ethnic was showing up on the tiniest tots."[7] Two contradictory imperatives had come to affect infants: Grow up more slowly and grow up faster.

The Emergence of Fashion[8]

In 1966, advancements in chemistry led to new fibers and fabric blends that required new joining techniques instead of sewing.[9] They offered an opportunity for styles that took this new approach into account. The development of these new styles also took into account the idea that activity and physical mobility are basic to American culture. New silhouettes emerged, and they challenged the convention that girls act demure.

Production proceeded from the idea that in children there is practically no difference between waist and hip measurements and the waist is barely defined until puberty. Also, the new approach recognized that children's tummies protrude, that the torso, arms and legs are predominantly tubular, and that clothes must be easy to get into and out of. Also of concern was the fact that children's bodies grow, and therefore the style must be able to accommodate change (raglan sleeves, for example).[10] Moreover, designers recognized that children like clothes in bright colors and that they also like garments that are ornamented.

Girls' Fashions

To advertise the potential of Orlon, in 1967 DuPont created a set of five dresses characterized by what the company called a "Wandering Waist." The likeness of a waistline appears in three different places: high on the body, empire; dropped waist, one inch above the hipline; and the third, somewhere in between, but avoiding the natural waistline.[11] The traditional dress for girls was a fitted dress whose waistline cut the body in half. It acted as an anchor. The waist was fitted on a model with darts and required careful refinement to fit. Cutting and assembling the different parts of the dress was labor-intensive, time consuming, and costly. When they used fabrics developed through chemistry, on the other hand, lami-

FIGURE 11.1 Laminated fabrics and the "Wandering Waist" dress. *Earnshaw's*, December 1967. By permission. Photo, Greg Kitchen.

nates for example, designers made it a point to overlook the natural waistline, simplifying production and cutting costs.

A laminated fabric entailed bonding two different fabrics, one as a "face" (the outside of the cloth) and one as a backing, which are then fused together by heat or adhesive. It is like fashioning a sandwich. A thin fabric might be fused with foam, giving it the appearance of extra weight and a more expensive appearance.[12] An A-line silhouette dress

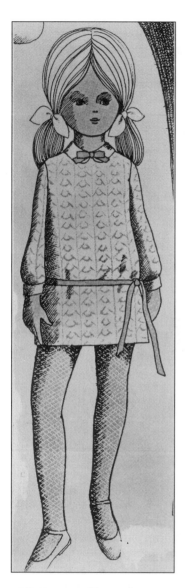

FIGURE 11.2   Laminated fabrics and the "Wandering Waist" dress. *Earnshaw's,* December 1967. By permission. Photo, Greg Kitchen.

FIGURE 11.3   Laminated fabrics and the "Wandering Waist" dress. *Earnshaw's,* December 1967. By permission. Photo, Greg Kitchen.

FIGURE 11.4 Stretch nylon tops and tights. Jumper in wide-wale corduroy. Sears Roebuck Catalogue, 1967. By permission. Photo, Greg Kitchen.

made of laminated fabrics or knits without a fitted waistline proved to be popular among girls.[13]

Another invention by DuPont was stretch yarns. The garments that emerged were easy to wear, relatively low in cost, and easy to maintain. They allowed even greater freedom of movement.[14] Stretch nylon was fashioned into body-hugging outfits. Slacks, tops, and bodysuits were soft and stretched with movement. Slacks and tops came in different colors and could be matched and mixed according to the wearer's taste. Clothing made out of stretch fabrics required little maintenance.[15] After a wash the garments went right back to their original shape.[16] Outfits of stretch fabrics helped to enable little girls to do somersaults and splits, to jump up and down and do cartwheels.

For the back-to-school crowd two categories of clothes emerged. The first was for customers for whom updated styles were appropriate. They had a budget and were price conscious. The second category of clothes was for customers interested in fashion, the latest desired appearance.[17]

FIGURE 11.5
Sweater dressing.
Earnshaw's, June
1970. By
permission.
Photo, Greg
Kitchen.

Manufacturers and retailers spoke of the lack of clear new style trends. Dress houses sat awaiting buyers, and buyers were refusing to commit themselves until they saw their customers' reaction. No one knew how mothers would react to the new fashion. Anxiety enveloped the industry.[18]

In May 1967, exhibitors showed silhouettes that followed the "flare of the tent or the closeness of the skimmie." Also accepted were the jumper, the pant dress, and the dropped waist with the pleated skirt.[19] The girls' market quickly adopted fashion.

Girls were no longer demure. Moreover, girls' fashionable attire violated the biblical injunction that girls refrain from wearing male-style dress. Long pants were worn by girls of all ages. Other male-style dress adopted by girls were Nehru and safari suits. A safari suit shown by Dior and adopted in the United States featured a regimental jacket, loop-flapped patch pockets, and a gilded link-chain belt. It gently shaped the body.[20] In Dallas, striped sailcloth brief culottes with a modish necktie were shown at the Texas Fashion Creators Association Dallas Press Week.[21] The outfit was sighted two months later on city streets.[22]

Corduroy had been a coarse fabric used for overalls or knickers and worn mostly by men and boys.[23] The Crompton-Richmond Company[24] created a new type of corduroy where different textures and colors could be realized. Cotton was blended with synthetic fibers and rayon was added for luster. Polyesters made the fabric crease-retaining (durable press) and wrinkle and dirt resistant. Garments made out of the new corduroy needed no starching or ironing and came at a reasonable cost.[25]

The clothing industry began a concerted effort in May 1966, to turn corduroy into a fashion fabric. Leading American couture designers were convinced to use the new corduroy in their high-priced ready-to-wear lines. Corduroy was described as produced in "breezy floral designs, lush wide wales or thick and thins that look like cut velvet. . . ."[26] Colors could be deep, pastel, or bright, and the printing of color could be achieved. Colors could be stone-blue, faded blue, burgundy, whiskey, rust, and bottle green. The new corduroy was easy to care for and was successfully adapted to the babies', toddlers', and girls' market.[27]

Reports on what was being exhibited and what was selling, published in August 1967 and October of 1968, revealed that the phenomenon of fashion affected mostly girls' attire and that it evolved around violating norms of modesty, exposing large portions of the body.[28] In Texas in the summer of 1967, hems were short. Girls wore the pantdresses and culottes forbidden during school hours. Miniskirts and pantdresses "would have been unthinkable in this section of the country earlier," a reporter observed.[29] They also wore bikinis to the beach or pool.[30]

In 1968, the back-to-school promotions by chain stores handling standard clothing items offered pants—long, short, and knickers.[31] Also popular were jeans and permanent-press shirts, now considered "a classic style of dress" for girls.[32] Best-sellers were dresses with the "wandering" waistline, a Nehru-style dress along with medallions and matching beads, [33] a canvas dress in striped cotton and flared silhouette accented by a Mao collar,[34] and dresses where swatches were cut out from the most provocative areas. Other fashionable items were hooded knit striped tops and Bermuda shorts, colorful separates, patterned tights, and stockings in black or in bright sun colors.[35]

Girls' fashions included "body-baring cut-outs, midriff ties, stretch pants, Indian inspired prints and borders, along with elasticized peasant tops."[36] By the late 1960s, dresses were replaced by slacks, and pantsuits made out of polyester were designed for every occasion.[37] In the realm of girls' clothes, fashion came to reside alongside traditional styles.

Girls' fashionable attire was the same throughout the country, observed Betty Sperling, director of Gaychild Ltd, a firm specializing in children's clothes in England. The uniformity she found in different parts of the country was such that, "The whole lot of merchandise could have been produced by one manufacturer."[38] In 1967 "the only difference between Dallas and California was the mart."[39]

In 1968 the leather look, a style suggesting empowerment and traditionally worn by young men, was reported to be "the most" popular style in the United States. Girls bought skirts, jumpers, jackets, coats, and even dresses in suedes and in the new imitation leathers.[40] In May 1970 the French designer Courreges introduced a highly structured "space age" image, a haute couture design for girls. It consisted of an A-line silhouette and was inspired by Mondrian paintings, with their bold, dramatic contrasts of primary colors. High, round necklines; short, tight fitting sleeves; and a loose, straight, hanging body. To complement the short hemline "go-go" boots were introduced in vinyl. These could be manufactured cheaply, allowing the wearer a different pair of highly colored boots to complement every dress.[41]

A large variety of clothes characterized the 1971 children's wear market. According to Cleo Paturis, writing in *Earnshaw's*, back-to-school dresses were "beautifully designed and in exciting prints." There were long sleeves and short ones. Dresses were short and skirts mini, but midi skirts were also being offered. Sweater knit dresses were trimmed with all kinds of hardware, and so were vests, jackets, and skirts made of crinkly vinyl. There were suedes with lots of fringe and modified bell-bottom pants came in denim and in menswear stripes.[42] Responding to mothers seeking pants for their daughters, the industry created a pants dress made in polyester doubleknit "in blazing tri-color combinations."[43] The wearing of fashion spread throughout the country.

Fashionable attire made it possible for girls to choose an identity they wanted and to be free to act accordingly. Girls could act demurely or dance and engage in other physical activity if they wished. Girls' fashions supported the attempt to negotiate a less prescribed character to girls' participation in social life. Ads showed girls in roller skates and wearing boxing gloves and sneakers.[44]

Boys' Fashions

The industry initially resisted the push to introduce the fashion process, the periodic change in desired style of appearance, into the boys' apparel market. The February 1968 issue of Earnshaw's reported an industry-wide effort to support traditional style of clothes for boys. The theme they decided on was, "He Wears the Country Look." The colors sug-

FIGURE 11.6   Zipper
dressing. *Earnshaw's,*
1971. By permission.
Photo, Greg Kitchen.

gested were earthy browns, burnished golds, earthy greens, and wood-
land russets. To promote the look, fabric swatches were distributed by
the industry.[45]

Best and Company's vice president for sales promotion complained that
members of the industry had a narrow vision of boys' attire. He observed
that in the many meetings he had attended with boys' wear buyers and
management, time after time the topics were, "should the trousers be
slims—should they be beltless—how many colors of khaki does it come
in—are we covered in checks, plaids and solids."[46] "We have to stop neg-

ative thinking, if we keep saying our customers won't buy contemporary fashion—they won't—how can they if you don't sell it."[47]

Designer of men's and boys clothing John Weitz suggested that instead of manufacturers and retailers deciding on what boys should wear, children should be consulted on what they would like to wear.[48]

Reflecting on the supposed hopelessness of introducing the fashion process into the boys' apparel market, Patricia A. Farrell asked: "Could a boy in 3 to 7 range be a fashion leader? He is cute and small and just starting school and he is not as yet hampered by the business world and its slowly grinding mills of fashion acceptance."[49] "Brave New Fall Fashion," declared Patricia A. Farrell in June 1968, in the pages of *Earnshaw's*. The new fashion campaign was designed to turn the industry from "a sawed-off follower to a trend-setting leader."[50]

Young designers in London, however, with their Mod and Carnaby Street Designs, challenged the manufacturing of the boys' clothing industry in the United States and introduced a "close to the body fit" style of dress.[51] Earlier, in 1962, British designer Mary Quant had been commissioned by J.C. Penney Inc. to design four collections a year for America's teenagers to be marketed throughout the retail chain's 1700 stores. Her style sense, the angular shaped silhouette, and the new colors she used influenced the average American. Her clothes laid the groundwork for what *Earnshaw's* called "the British invasion."[52]

The Beatles discouraged the industry's resistance to fashion. In addition to the fashion set by their hair, which they wore long and then longer, the "Tom Jones" look was attributed to them. Fashion reporter Patricia A. Farrell characterized the look as that of "Buccaneers and Brigands."[53] It consisted of a shirt with a jabot or ascot and a squared-off double-breasted and high-collared jacket with a deeply notched lapel. Also fashionable was the guru look. It consisted of an overshirt with trumpet sleeves, often in brocade fabrics. The Nehru coats and suits, along with beads and medallions, lasted only one season and were considered the fashion bust of 1967.[54]

A "denim explosion" began in 1967 and became an important element of the back-to-school promotions for boys.[55] Indigo blue denim, the traditional jean, was the first to sell; the dress-up jean, and the jean-cut pants became important later.[56] By 1971, denim or the denim look went into coats, boots, and sportswear.

In the early 1970s the favorite color in the formerly sedate boys' wear market became purple. By the mid–70s there was a return to natural tones. Ecrus and creams showed up as grounds for florals and prints. The conventional suit became unconventional, as the look became free and liberated. The look was bright, sporty, and individualistic. The favorite

FIGURE 11.7
Hip-huggers,
bell-bottom
striped pants.
Earnshaw's,
March 1970.
By permission.
Photo, Greg
Kitchen.

fabrics in boys' suits were the polyester doubleknit in multi-colored seer-sucker stripes and tweed looks in shades of purple and plum. Silhouette lines were contoured, jackets nipped in at the waist, and pant legs were tapered to the knee with a gently flared bottom. A wide waist band was in.[57] The "poor boy" look was also popular. It consisted of frayed-bottom shorts, bleached-out denims, union shirts, and work shirts.[58]

In the late 1960s and early 1970s jeans came in new colors—black, new greens, powder, and wheat. Jeans were worn at the hips with turtlenecks

FIGURE 11.8
Boys' fashionable
suits. Anchored
to the waistline,
the suits have
flared pants legs.
Earnshaw's, 1971.
By permission.
Photo, Greg
Kitchen.

and mock-turtle shirts. A new favorite combined traditional attire with fashion—a double-breasted jacket worn over a turtle or mock-turtle shirt.[59]

Boys' trousers were anchored to the hips and worn with big belts,[60] and the legs had some kind of a flare. Fashionable attire for boys included bell-bottoms. Bell-bottoms had been worn by college students dancing the Charleston in the 1920s.[61]

Mothers encouraged their sons to wear what was in fashion. It had been assumed that a mother's interest in fashion would decrease in proportion to the number of children living at home. A 1970 study found that mothers with four or more children at home were as interested in their children wearing fashionable clothes as mothers with one or two children.[62] A mother often chose for her children a fashion similar to what she was wearing. Manufacturers realized that a new fashion had to appeal to the fashion-conscious mother.[63] She expected her child to wear clothes in the latest style, texture, and color.[64]

The availability of discount retail merchants who sold fashionable attire at a lower cost [65] made it easier on mothers to buy fashionable attire: polyester pants suits, brocade vests, and tunic suits. Discounters saw their volume and profits rise.[66]

Critical of mothers imposing their ideas regarding color and style was French designer Emanuel Ungaro who warned that when a mother buys clothes according to what she would like her child to wear, she destroys the image of "child." "What would be magnificent," he suggested, "would be if children could buy their own clothes."[67]

Lagging sales in traditional attire, suits, for example, forced many manufacturers to close their doors. Some were unable to adapt to the rise of fashion; some were unable to keep up with the increased pace of competition; and some were unable to deal with the slowing down of the economy.[68] Some shifted to "non-suiting," spurning the heavy basic structure that characterized adult male attire. They chose "a lighter attitude and a relaxed style of dressing," instead.[69] Rather than the traditional wool, they used polyester doubleknit. A bright and sporty look coordinated sportswear, knitwear, and leisure dressing, all at lower prices.[70]

Clothes from the Outside Region

Bankruptcies, recession, unemployment, inflation, and oil shortages by the mid-seventies created anxiety in the children's wear industry. Bewildered, manufacturers and retailers searched for guidelines on how to proceed.[71] One of the major manufacturers of children's clothes, the Rosenau Company, the company that in 1935 produced Shirley Temple dresses,[72] had ignored the signs that the market for girls' dresses was changing. The company called Cinderella Clothing Industries continued to produce dresses fitted at the waist and ornamented with white pinafores. The company declined in the late 1960s, and in 1971 reported a loss of $1 million. By 1973 the loss had climbed to $4.5 million.[73] The owners of the company sought protection under Title Eleven of the Federal Bankruptcy Law. The firm then rejected the traditional way of dressing girls, concluding that "staying close to the consumer was essential." Watching for trends became the new way, which meant watching consumers' choices.[74]

The names of American children's clothes designers were usually unknown. Clothes they designed carried the name of the manufacturer. Three of such designers were interviewed by *Earnshaw's* to find out in which direction they intended to proceed. The courses they took affected the path of the children's wear market.

"Design Superstar" Peter Goldfarb, a designer for the Strechini line, argued for children's fashion. New styles should depend on the designer's vision. The designer knows "what is right," and should believe and fight for it.[75] He explained that in Europe most children don't have much say about what they are wearing and what they will wear. Even in England children's fashion isn't a force. Children in England have neither the money nor a lifestyle in which fashion matters. Children wear uniforms to school. After school they wear the outfit kids have been wearing for the past twenty-five years, crewneck sweater and tweed jacket.

According to Goldfarb, the French understand the body and know how clothes should fit. French children, however, dress in the fashion look of the moment. When they shop they see the same style is in all the stores; even the color range will be the same. In the United States you can't dictate fashion, the country is too diverse.[76]

In many places in the United States adults put clothes on without planning or worrying about what goes with what. Children in the United States, however, should have the opportunity to develop taste. They should find out what looks good on them, what they like, and what they don't, and then have freedom to dress "their" way.[77] Only with knowledge comes real choice, designer Goldfarb concluded.

The sportswear designer for *Charlie's Girls*, Erika Elias, said that she intended to design clothes for the "anti-fashion" market. Whatever the industry thought the trend was, she'd design the opposite. Instead of jeans, the harsh, tough looks that were fashionable, she would design "soft fuzzy things."[78]

Ann Webster was the third person interviewed. She had designed dresses for Tiny Town, but had resigned from the company to create a new manufacturing company able to switch production to whatever consumers demanded whenever they demanded it.[79]

Wished-for Identity

The back-to-nature movement reflected the desire for a simpler life. It consisted of styles reminiscent of the "good old days" of living on the farm, of ethnic and country-style clothes. For toddlers the style emphasized handcrafted looks. Checks, florals, and gingham were the favorite patterns. They evoked a sense of homespun nostalgia.[80]

For older children the theme was interpreted into two distinct looks. Tiered skirts, flounces, peasant braid, gingham, calico, pioneer necks, and fringes alluded to small towns and rural areas.[81] In 1978, new fabrics, imitating the nineteenth-century soft brushed challis and flannel, led to the updating of the grandmother look, a long dress in subdued heathered colorations. It was designed to reflect a quaint and old-fashioned mood.[82]

FIGURE 11.9   Andrea English, two years old. Sitting in the sun, she is wearing a Quaker-style bonnet and big sunglasses. June 14, 1977, UPI.

The counterpart for boys was a rugged, functional attire reminiscent of frontier life in the Old West. The look was casual, inspired by life on the prairies, mountains, and plains of the American frontier.[83]

Another expression of the desire for the simple life took the form of fabrics that reflected democracy and honesty: denim and patchwork. Denim was interpreted in shirtwaist dresses. Patchwork and denim jumpers were popular for the younger girls. The "poor boy" look was also popular among girls. Some children wore frayed bottom shorts or bleached-out denims with work shirts to school.[84]

Desired Association

The industry responded to the sports-minded child who demanded the look "of real sports" but with high styling. Participating in sports was one way children in American society could learn the skills they might need in adult life.[85] Watching a game is a means of experiencing the game without actually participating in it. Veblen called it vicarious consumption. By the end of the 1970s there were as many sportswear looks as there were sports. One of the favorite shirts was a printed tank-top shirt with baseball, golf, or tennis players screened across the top.[86]

Special stores and departments developed to sell specialized clothes. The world of sports was represented by stores or departments such as the NFL's Lil Pro, National Hockey League, and, for baseball, Major Leagues. There were even three styles of sweaters (cardigan, long sleeves, pullover and vest) for sizes two–four and four–seven, that featured authentic NFL team insignia and team colors and stripes.[87]

"Being With It"

Other children responded to whimsical appliqués designed to amuse or delight the preschooler. The appliqués consisted of animals adapted from cartoon characters Bugs Bunny and Donald Duck, pigs, and other farm animals. They were placed on pockets, aprons, and sleeves. Unlike the 1930s appliqués, which were hand-made, embroidered, and conceived to enhance parental status, the 1970s appliqués were machine-made but designed to appeal to children's personal taste. The giant sunflower that covered the whole dress took the place of an intricate floral design.[88]

There were also stores that specialized in licensed merchandise. Neil Armstrong, the first man to set foot on the moon in 1969, was represented by a space suit.[89] T-shirts, sweatshirts, and pajamas carried portrayals of storybook and cartoon characters, such as Superman, Snoopy, and Charlie Brown.[90] One of the popular characters was the nearsighted, gravel-voiced Quincy Magoo, who was returned to TV in a series of half-hour animated shows called *Great Americans*.

Keeping Warm

An embargo by the Arab oil-producing nations, imposed late in October 1973, resulted in an industry-initiated drive to keep warm. A T-shirt and jeans were no longer sufficient for a child attending school in the winter. This became particularly relevant when the cold weather continued in 1976 and 1977 and thermostats had to be turned down to fifty-five or sixty degrees. Keeping warm was essential. The layered look became the fashion. Several layers of close-fitting clothing were warmer than one heavy garment. Layers can be peeled off if the temperature changes. A cowl neck that converts into a hood, a bateau neckline, a wide neckline that extends to the tip of the shoulders became the new desired appearance. A sweater-dress with a mid-knee sweater rib hem coordinated with leg warmers was fashionable. Another style was a shirt made of fine gauge cotton with a cowl or turtle neck, worn under the sweater dress. [91]

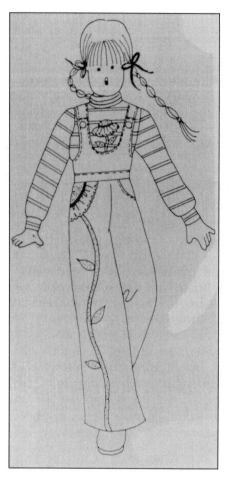

FIGURE 11.11 Superhero—
Superman. Superhero shops opened
in boys' departments throughout
the country, offering popular images
from the past. *Earnshaw's*, August
1975. By permission. Photo, Greg
Kitchen.

FIGURE 11.10 Bell-bottom
overalls and a long-sleeved T-shirt.
Ornamented with a flower. *Earnshaw's*,
August 1975. By permission. Photo,
Greg Kitchen.

Some traditional styles were redesigned for cold weather dressing. The
traditional skirt could be replaced by a split skirt or the gaucho and
teamed with a vest and a print shirt. Bulky hooded sweaters, warm overalls, pants, knit shirts, and blousons were also helpful.[92] The children's
wear industry met the challenge by creating interesting styles to please
mothers and children.

FIGURE 11.12 Mr. Magoo. Although scarcely a superhero, Mr. Magoo was definitely another of the popular images from the past. *Earnshaw's*, August 1975. By permission. Photo, Greg Kitchen.

FIGURE 11.13 Mickey Mouse. Another of the popular images from the past. *Earnshaw's*, August 1975. By permission. Photo, Greg Kitchen.

Gatekeepers

By the 1970s it became clear that teachers were trying to pressure students to return to wearing traditional styles of dress. Girls in a simple neat dress and boys in a jacket, shirt, and tie were rewarded. Teachers became gatekeepers.

Early in the school year students could tell who the teacher favored. It was usually "girls who dressed like cute little girls,"[93] and boys who were polite and wore a jacket, trousers, shirt and tie. Teachers called on these children frequently, giving them "guided questions that lead to correct answers," observed psychologist Dr. Joyce Brothers.[94] This help was likely to lead students to have high expectations of themselves and to expect and get high achievement, Dr. Brothers observed.[95]

Girls who didn't fit the "cute" image "suffered a lot." But they learned to deal with it, students reported. "It didn't stop me from being who I was or who I am," reported several.[96]

FIGURE 11.14   Toddle Tyke, an outfit designed for warmth and style. The overalls have wide legs and a logo that says, "Conserve Fuel." *Earnshaw's,* September 1977. By permission. Photo, Greg Kitchen.

A child's appearance also affected peer response. Children who dressed "differently" were often subject to cruel teasing by their peers, Dr. Brothers offered. Parents can help a child avoid embarrassment that will affect the child's sense of well-being and result in a negative impact on the child's self-esteem, which may translate to poor academic achievement.[97] It is important that parents find out what the other children are wearing, Dr. Brothers suggested. By finding out how the other children are dressing and dressing the child accordingly, parents were likely to prevent future emotional and behavioral problems, Dr. Brothers advised, encouraging conformity to peer culture. This conformity is particularly important for a school function such as a party, where the dress may be formal, a jacket and tie, or informal, jeans and T-shirt.[98]

Toys

Reflecting the struggle for racial equality in the 1970s, the television program *Sesame Street* created an association between racial integration and educational value, which advertisers used to their advantage.[99] Toys for preschool children began to include black children in their target market. The makers of preschool-age toys were also more likely than other manufacturers to use black and white children together in their general market advertising.

In the mid–1960s, Mattel began manufacturing African American Barbies. But not until the 1980s did the company develop a multiracial series of dolls.[100] The toys advertised as "active centers" occasionally included a black or an asian child. The toy's purpose was to encourage children to be physically involved in the fun. A "Busy Center" structure, for example, could engage several children at the same time. It offered, at least, nine activities appropriate for several age groups. One advertisement showed a nine-month-old to a three-and-a-half-year-old playing together, crawling, sliding, climbing, playing with all kinds of colorful objects and even making music. The advertisement also showed a merry-go-round with three children, one of whom was black; each provided power to make the toy revolve.[101]

It would be simple to attribute the change in children's clothes to advances in the chemical and textile industries of the kind that had boosted the boom of the 1950s, since these industries did continue to push for ever greater technological innovation. Moreover, poverty as measured by the government declined from an estimated 22 percent of the population in 1960 to 12 percent in 1969. Prosperity made it possible to consume clothes. However, it was the freedom to use the body in dance and sports that provided the styles and impetus for change. These styles, moreover, allowed parents and children to claim a particular socio-cultural identity.

Wearing fashionable attire in the late 1960s and 1970s reflected the desire for social expression that was less gender-oriented and restrictive, offering a relief from the pain of discrimination and repression. Fashion thus acted to maintain social order by siphoning off feelings of discontent, as Blumer suggested it could.[102] At the same time, by making possible inter-gender and inter-class discourse, children's clothes helped to negotiate social and cultural change.

Notes

1. Morris Dickstein (1977) *Gates of Eden*. New York: Basic Books, p. 185.

2. Dickstein, op. cit., p. 210.

3. Dickstein, op. cit., p. 185.

4. James T. Patterson, (1997) *Grand Expectations*. New York: Oxford University Press, p. 788.

5. Beth Bailey (1994) "Sexual Revolution(s)," in David Farber, ed., *Sixties: From History to Memory*. Chapel Hill: University of North Carolina Press.

6. Constance L. Hays, (1997) "In the Diaper Wars, Cloth Has Just About Folded," *New York Times*. February 9.

7. *Earnshaw's*, November 1996, p. 89.

8. After 1966, columns began appearing in *Earnshaw's* under such titles as "Brave New Fall Fashion," "Fashion Beat," "Fashion Notes," or "Knit Fashions." Earlier, stories about fashion for children had been given such names as "The Children's Style Show," "Children's Spring Show" and "Style-Rightness." *Earnshaw's*, August 1923, pp. 1310–1311.

9. *Earnshaw's*, December 1967, pp. 34–35.

10. Hilde Jaffe and Rose Rosa, (1990) *Childrenswear Design*. 2nd ed. New York: Fairchild Publications, p. 146.

11. *Earnshaw's*, May, 1967 pp. 27–29.

In 1963 and earlier a manufacturer would sometimes offer a dress without the traditional waistline. But this remained an individual attempt.

12. *Earnshaw's*, December 1967, p. 34.

13. Alice Guppy, (1978) *Children's Clothes 1939–1970, The Advent of Fashion*. Poole, U.K.: Blanford Press, pp. 236–237.

14. The uses for stretch fabrics have grown beyond dance and exercise clothes. In the 1990s they are being used in the design of elegant shoes.

15. Patricia A. Farrell, (1968) "It's Beginning to Look a Lot Like Easter," *Earnshaw's*, January, p. 63.

16. Advertisement by Joseph Horne Co. in *Earnshaw's*, July, 1968, p. 26.

17. Reported by Mel Courtney from Joske's of Texas. *Earnshaw's*, July 1968, p. 28.

18. Farrell, *Earnshaw's*, January 1968. pp. 60–66.

19. "Cross Country," a column in the May 1967 issue of *Earnshaw's*, p. 150.

20. "Fashion Beat," *Earnshaw's*, April 1967, p. 19.

21. Ibid.

22. Patricia A. Farrell, (1968) "It's Beginning to Look A Lot Like Easter," *Earnshaw's*, January, p. 61. This new fashion was seen on the streets despite the fact that Southerners from North Carolina and Texas have claimed that they have no need to pursue fashion.

23. Corduroy was a pile fabric developed in eighteenth-century England. It was made out of cotton in colors considered dreary and described as "wearable neutrals and earthy darks" by fashion coordinator for Montgomery Ward, Rita A. Perna, (1966),"What's Happened to Corduroy?" *Earnshaw's*, April, p. 67.

24. It is the oldest cotton textile mill in the United States. In May 1967 it celebrated its 160th birthday.

25. Perna, op. cit., pp. 66–68.

26. John S. Thompson, (1967) "'67 Fashions Turn to Surface Interest," *Earnshaw's*, May, p. 50.

27. *Earnshaw's*, April 1966, p. 69.

28. Margaret M. Clayton, "Charlotte Report," *Earnshaw's*, August 1967, pp. 150–151.

29. "Cross Country," a column in the May 1967 issue of *Earnshaw's*. Some natives of southern states like Texas and the Carolinas maintain that in the South the emphasis is on traditional style, because fashionable attire is really for those who have to impress others. The well-to-do are known and don't have impress anyone, themselves included.

30. The rumor is that bikinis were named after Bikini Beach, the beach in Japan on which the atom bomb was exploded.

31. In the Judeo-Christian tradition cross-sex dressing is prohibited.

32. *Earnshaw's*, October 1968, pp. 8, 65, 68, 69.

33. Ibid.

34. "Fashion Beat," *Earnshaw's*, 1968, p. 34.

35. *Earnshaw's*, August 1967, p. 103.

36. *Earnshaw's: Special 80th Anniversary Issue.* November 1996, p. 89.

37. *Earnshaw's*, September 1977, p. 113.

38. Patricia A. Farrell, (1967) "The Lady from "Cool," *Earnshaw's*, December, p. 37.

39. Farrell, op. cit., pp. 36–37.

40. *Earnshaw's*, October 1968, p. 8.

41. *Earnshaw's*, September 1977, p. 113.

42. Cleo Paturis, (1970) "Preteen Scene," *Earnshaw's*, May, p. 47.

43. *Earnshaw's*, September 1977, p. 105.

44. "Knockout Knits, The Smashing Turnouts," *Earnshaw's*, May 1971, p. 78.

45. "Fashion Beat," *Earnshaw's*, February 1968.

46. Norman Margolis, (1968) "The New Fashion Awareness," *Earnshaw's*, May, pp. 148, 149.

47. Margolis, op. cit., p. 149.

48. John Weitz, (1968) "Fashion Through the Designer," *Earnshaw's*, May, pp. 142–146.

49. Patricia A. Farrell, "Brave New Fall Fashions," (1968) *Earnshaw's*, June, pp. 40–45.

50. Ibid.

51. *Earnshaw's*, May 1967, p. 50.

52. "Fashion in the 60's: The British Are Coming!" *Earnshaw's*, September 1977, pp. 99, 113.

53. Farrell, (1968) "Brave New Fall Fashions," *Earnshaw's*, June, pp. 40–41.

54. *Earnshaw's*, September 1977, p. 113.

55. "Denim Still a Super Star," *Earnshaw's*, October 1971, p. 50.

56. *Earnshaw's*, July 1968, p. 25.

57. *Earnshaw's*, September 1977, p. 105.

58. Ibid.

59. *Earnshaw's*, October 1968, p. 68.

60. *Earnshaw's*, April 1966, p. 56.

61. O. E. Schoeffler and William Gale, (1973) *Esquire's Encyclopedia of 20th-Century Men's Fashions*. New York: McGraw Hill, p. 91. For adults trousers with flared legs were cut long and wide around the hem to accommodate platform shoes and made hips and thighs look extra slim.

62. Donna L. Bonaker, (1971) "Fashion and Children," *Earnshaw's*, April, pp. 54–55.

63. Bonaker, op. cit., p. 55.

64. Leonore Bloom, (1971) "Boys Wear in a Dress Down Groove," *Earnshaw's*, January, pp. 42–44.

65. There are five categories of retailers: chains, department stores, specialty stores, discounters, others.

66. Miller-Wohl, Arlans Department Stores, Giant Stores, Topps, and G. E. M., for example. They later failed. *Earnshaw's*, September 1977, p. 106.

67. Helen R. Albert, (1967) "Emanuel Ungaro: An Interview," *Earnshaw's*, November, pp. 54–55.

68. Regal, Tam-O-Shanter, Turtle Bay, and Hop-Scotch, among others. *Earnshaw's*, January 1970, p. 35.

69. *Earnshaw's*, August 1972, p. 38.

70. Bloom, op cit., pp. 42–44.

71. Birth rate was found insignificant to the children's clothing industry because parents tended to buy new clothes for the first and second born only. They passed these down to those born later.

72. *Earnshaw's*, June 1935, p. 58.

73. Frank Santillo, (1978) "The Saga of Cinderella: Bringing a dying firm back to life," *Earnshaw's*, July, p. 34.

74. Ibid.

75. *Earnshaw's*, May 1972, p. 72.

76. Ibid.

77. Ibid.

78. *Earnshaw's*, May 1972, pp. 72–73.

79. *Earnshaw's*, May 1972, pp. 74–75.

80. *Earnshaw's*, September 1977, p. 105.

81. "The Liberated Look of the Un-Fashions," *Earnshaw's*, September, 1977, p. 105.

82. Lynn Kelly, (1978) "Celebration of American Classics," *Earnshaw's*, March, p. 63.

83. Ibid.

84. Kelly, op. cit., p. 105.

85. Sociologist George Herbert Mead (1931) had suggested that when playing varsity, children are socialized to the skills they would need as adults. They learn to give and take, to be ready to take different roles, and to win and to lose.

86. *Earnshaw's*, September 1977, p. 116.

87. *Earnshaw's*, August 1975, p. 40.

88. "Pure Fantasia," *Earnshaw's*, September 1977, p. 64.

89. The space program, set in motion by President Kennedy in 1961, made it possible for the astronaut Neil Armstrong to be the first man to set foot on the moon on July 20, 1969.

90. *Earnshaw's*, August 1975, p. 40.

91. *Earnshaw's*, April 1977, p. 90.

92. *Earnshaw's*, April 1977, p. 91.

93. Mary Ryan, Fall 1989, "My Personal Style," a term paper. With permission. Fashion Institute of Technology.

94. Dr. Joyce Brothers, (1979) "How Clothes Form a Child's Self Image," *Earnshaw's*, November 1979, p. 49.

95. Brothers, op. cit., p. 49.

96. Students taking the course "Clothing and Society" at the Fashion Institute of Technology in New York City.

97. Ibid.

98. Brothers, op. cit., pp. 48–49, 111.

99. Ellen Seiter, (1993) *Sold Separately: Children and Parents in Consumer Culture.* New Brunswick, N.J.: Rutgers University Press, p. 88.

100. Ibid.

101. Seiter, op. cit., pp. 88–89.

102. Herbert Blumer, "Social Movements," (1951) in Sanford M. Lyman, ed., (1995) *Social Movements.* New York: New York University Press, p. 81.

12

Themes of Success and Delight: Children's Clothes in the 1980s and 1990s

In the 1980s children began challenging clothing dependency. Until the 1980s, adults bought or made the clothes their children were expected to wear. Adults were the customers and children were the consumers. Except for objecting vehemently to wearing a particular garment, children, for the most part, merely influenced parental clothing choices. Retailers and merchants, such as Sears, K Mart, J.C. Penney, and Lands-End, directed their advertising to parents, particularly through back-to-school promotions. The thought was that the description and depiction of the clothes would make it easier for parents to discuss the clothes with their children, in particular children's preferences as to product and brand.[1] Merchandisers hoped that shopping for back-to-school clothes at home would be an informed process during which children could influence parental choices.[2] As the 1980s progressed, however, children in the United States were increasingly able to choose and purchase their own clothes.[3] Children became both customers and consumers.[4]

Children as Customers

Beginning in 1985 children in large numbers began buying their own clothes.[5] Most of the money children used came from the allowances parents were giving their children. Parents gave an allowance even to a child whose age was only four.[6] It was estimated that 55 percent of households gave their children an allowance each week, and this allowance amounted to 50 percent of the income received by children four to twelve.[7] Another 15 percent of children's income came from gifts of money "as needed," and these gifts were tied to various occasions and to the performance of household chores. Grandparents and other relatives were a source of income for 5 percent of the sample, while 12 percent came from part-time work outside the home. Work such as baby-sitting, yard work for neighbors, picking up aluminum cans, and delivering newspapers was a source of income for children from low-income families and single-parent households.

The average weekly income for a four-year-old child in 1984 was $1.08. Expenditures amounted to about $0.49 and savings were $0.59. For the twelve-year-old child the figures in 1984 were income $5.49, expenditures $5.26, and savings $0.23. In 1989 the average weekly income for a four-year-old child was $1.78, expenditures $0.83, and savings $0.95. For the twelve-year-old, income in 1989 rose to $9.83; expenditures to $6.90, and savings to $2.93.[8] In 1984 children received $6 billion and spent $4.2 billion; in 1989 they received $8.6 billion in income and spent over $6 billion.[9]

Parents obviously realized that children need more money as they grow older, and they increased the allowance with each year. Children used the money to buy and to save and appeared to be enthusiastic about taking charge of their finances.[10]

Economic recession and stagnation in the early 1980s made it difficult for many families to live on one paycheck (see Fig. 12.1). Many mothers had to go to work. Also joining the labor force were single mothers and women in dual-career marriages. Holding jobs and keeping house gave women little time to shop. Working mothers and divorced fathers who wanted to please their children gave the children money and the autonomy to select their own clothes. Divorced fathers often felt guilty and often showed their love by "spoiling" their kids, giving them permission to buy what they wanted.[11] Mothers reported that they were happy they had the money and could please their children.[12]

According to the parents interviewed in one study, they gave their children an allowance to help them learn to manage money and to get accustomed to getting things they need for themselves.[13] Some parents viewed their children's choosing their own clothes as taking a part in the real world—a learning experience.[14] Children's income was discretionary, and they could spend their money on almost anything they wished.[15] Parents or an older sibling accompanied the child to the store, but children often decided on what clothes they wanted to wear and bought them.[16]

After mid-decade, as children had more income and more parents acceded to a child's request for particular clothing, it became possible for the child to choose the clothes that were relevant for him or her. Friendships facilitate adjustment to school life.[17] Children who choose their own clothes are likely to select the clothes that would strengthen friendship ties. Baggier garments, or a particular ice hockey jersey, for exam-

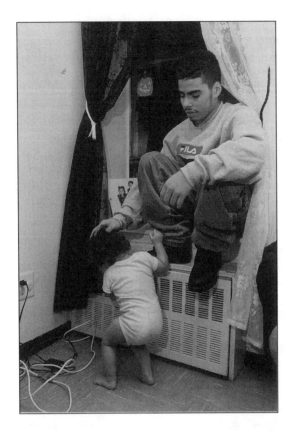

FIGURE 12.1   With the
mother at work, the father,
Herbert Carrasquillo, is
staying at home with his
daughter. The child is
wearing a disposable
diaper. November 17,
1996. Photo, Norman
Leno/NYT.

ple, can enable children to feel and show that they are a part of the
group.

In 1989 spending on clothes amounted to 11.5 percent of children's expenditure.[18] By 1992, children were spending almost $700 million a year
of their own money on their clothes.[19] Children's money, by then, from
allowance (53 percent), household tasks (15 percent) and gifts from parents (15 percent), was really the parents' money being spent by children.

Nationwide in 1989 there were around 7 million (18.5 percent) of children ages four to twelve identified by McNeal as overprivileged because
they averaged "receiving, saving, and spending twice that of children
overall."[20] Nevertheless, none of them thought that the amount of money
they were receiving was enough. At least 77 percent of these children
came from a dual-career marriage, with 78 percent employed in the professions (accounting, architecture, teaching).[21]

By 1992 the "overprivileged" children knew more and did more as
consumers than their counterparts in the 1950s, who were penny-candy
purchasers, McNeal reported.[22] Children became "benefit seekers," able

to justify or rationalize what they wanted to purchase. Children believed that it would be easier to convince their parents to obtain an item if it was free or low-cost. A premium offer that stated "Free with two proofs of purchase" was often interpreted as, "Mom can't complain or refuse if it is free."[23] This was also true for anything that offered an educational benefit. They would say, "You want me to learn, don't you?"[24] Children were able to strike out on their own, assured that the parent would be there for support and they would not be left in the lurch.

As more working mothers acquired economic resources, they shared these resources with their children. *Wall Street Journal* reporter Ellen Graham described it in a different way. She suggested that parents were too busy working. Increasingly, she said, they have been relinquishing their responsibility for their youngsters.[25] Therefore, as the title of her article puts it, "As Kids Gain Power of the Purse, Marketing Takes an Aim at Them."[26] A request for a desired garment or accessory that is granted increases feelings of goodwill within the household. Moreover, enabling a child to buy his or her clothes successfully may slowly erode emotional dependency and increase the chances that the child will develop as a more independent being.[27]

Themes in Children's Clothes

The array of children's clothes that became available in the 1980s fell into two categories. One consisted of styles that in the adult world symbolized success, that is, clothes that are fashionable or sports-inspired.

The second category of children's clothes emanated from the child's realm and evoked delight. It consisted of plush fabrics that are soft in color and appearance, and clothes ornamented in appliqués of animals, flowers, or cartoon characters. These "success" and "delight" groupings of dress helped dislodge age, gender, and class from their position as the most significant categories of children's wear.

Themes of Success

Unisex

The unisex image emanated from new research about sources of gender identity. Families had become smaller; "Children are often spared all the household chores in the interest of concentrating on their education, outside activities and social life."[28] Small families are much more likely to have children of the same sex. Growing up in a house with siblings of one sex is a different experience from growing up in a family with sib

FIGURE 12.2   This preppie style for the school child consists of buttoned-down Oxford shirt with sleeves peeking from under the sleeves of the blazer, plaid tie, and khaki pants. *Earnshaw's,* February 1995. By permission. Photo, Greg Kitchen.

lings of the opposite sex, sociologist Orville Brim suggested. He found that siblings of the opposite sex were more likely to have cross-sex personality traits. For example, a girl with a brother was more likely to have "high masculinity traits," such as ambition or competitiveness, than a girl whose sibling is another girl. Similarly, the boy whose sibling is a sister is somewhat more likely to show "high femininity traits," such as "affectionateness" or obedience.[29]

Designers, who had once produced clothes only for teens and adults like Calvin Klein, Donna Karan, and Nicole Miller, started offering styles that both boys and girls could wear. They also created adult-style clothes in children's sizes.[30]

The preppy image

The preppy life-style choice consisted of the "preppy look" and the "athletic style." They were offered by the industry in 1980 and described as life-style choices. The preppy look consisted of both formal and less formal attire, depending on the fabrics and styles used: tweeds with corduroys, suede vests with khaki trousers, woven flannel plaids, heavy fisherman knits, tassled loafers, crewneck shetland sweaters, Oxford cloth shirts with button-down collars.[31]

Gant, for example, produced a full line of clothes tailored for the "serious student attending school," aimed at ages eight to twelve. The clothes were "designed to send tomorrow's leaders to the head of the class in style."[32] Gant produced a full line of clothes, traditional in style: pants, suits, sport coats, tops, even activewear—swimwear and a jogging suit. Gant tops were done in "cut and sew" woven fabric, Oxford cloth, button-down collars, and a box pleat in the back. Shirts were in solids, stripes, or plaids. There were also knit tops called Ruggers. They consisted of a heavyweight knit body in bold Rugby stripes contrasted with a woven white collar and rubber buttons. The shirt evoked images of British colonial life.[33]

The Izod shirt with its alligator emblem was a Lacoste-like knit, which because of its simple lines conveyed elegance. It acquired a reputation for quality and for representing the taste level of students in Ivy League schools.[34] It advertised to children eight to fourteen. The look consisted of classic lines and colors that were clear, clean, and bright.[35] The shirt was advertised as worn on sunny golf courses, on country club tennis courts, and to fraternity rush parties.[36] The shirt was worn by boys who aspired to social mobility themselves, or whose mothers did. To other mothers the outfit meant "comfortable fashion conformity."[37]

Rather than elegance, a tough, active look characterized the athletic line, which was worn to school and to after-school activities. It consisted of a V-neck sweater in red or royal blue with gray, with a natural shoulder and loose-fitting, so that it was characterized as having an "easy American shape." It was teamed with training pants, sweatpants which were elasticized at the ankle and updated with piping or quilting. The classic sweatshirt in gray came in zip-front jacket styles.[38] The jock image was supported by clothes for the rugged outdoors. These consisted of work pants or painter's jeans with vests of denim, corduroy, or suede, lined or quilted. Jeans, activewear, and dress clothes were updated and offered in classic, simple lines.[39]

Outfits for girls also developed around the "preppy look" and the "athletic style." The preppy look for girls consisted of sweaters and skirts. The athletic look was represented in racing stripes added to fleeced sweaters, knit coordinates of tops and bottoms, pants and skirts in plaids, corduroys, and jeans. Shirtdresses and dresses were likely to extend just below knee-length.

Active Wear

In 1982, manufacturers merely added "pieces" to the "preppy look" and the "athletic style," creating a greater coordination within a category. The

FIGURE 12.3 Boy's rugged outdoor wear. Layered T-shirt, sweatshirt, and cut-off vest. *Earnshaw's,* February 1995. By permission. Photo, Greg Kitchen.

new pieces were expected to balance with what consumers had bought the year before.[40] In the process the industry shifted its emphasis to the active-wear category of clothing.

A mix of new fabrications was added to the active wear category and production was refined to create a bridge between play wear and a more dressy category of preppy attire. A ski jacket was structured in such a way that it could be worn over a suit and tie and enable a child to attend church. "Traditional silhouettes" were updated, "freshened up" through the use of fabric and color. Raglan sleeves in a jacket allowed sweatshirts to be worn underneath.

Fleece was polished and turned into an important fabric in active wear. The soft sensual look of the fabric was contrasted with hardware snaps and twill taping in the collar to create a striking and masculine look. Vests layered with fleece could be worn over sweaters, creating a feeling of warmth and a comfortable environment.[41]

Girls were given a choice. Two basic styles were offered to them. One was called the "romantic look." It consisted of country-style attire:

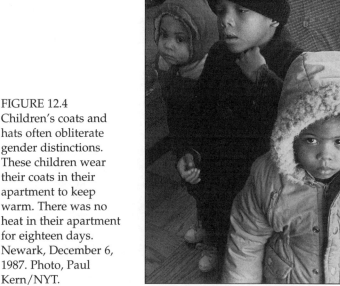

FIGURE 12.4
Children's coats and
hats often obliterate
gender distinctions.
These children wear
their coats in their
apartment to keep
warm. There was no
heat in their apartment
for eighteen days.
Newark, December 6,
1987. Photo, Paul
Kern/NYT.

mixed prints with embroidered lace, pull-on skirt with a ruffled shirt to
match. The romantic look idealized women in their traditional roles: as
dancers, entertainers, and homemakers. The second "look" consisted of
novelty bottoms and tops that created a rugged outdoors look.[42] It suggested that physical challenge and adventure attract contemporary
young women.

Detail on the "bottoms" shaped and defined the look; there was quilting, and seaming, rivets, snaps, and zippers. There was also a variety in
new pant lengths: short and long knickers, minisplits, cropped, Capri,
and jog pants with quilted leg patches. There were oversized pockets,
cargo pockets, pockets on pockets; there were suspenders, and side-seam
treatments with gussets or pleats running all or part of the way down the
leg. Trims were of suede and leather in piping or patches. Some "tops"
came in sweater knits, fleece, and velour. Some had quilted shoulders, or
yokes that provided the same effect. The new color scheme was stained-
glass brights, and jewel tones.[43] The same style garment in a different
fabric and color made it possible for a girl to individualize her appearance yet remain true to a feminine or a rugged ideal.

Designer Image

In the early 1980s the stage design for a fashion show was symbolically significant. Giant Raggedy Ann and Andy dolls were used to set the stage for the Children's Fashion Show at the Chicago Apparel Mart. The familiar characters suggested that the new collection would present updated styles. *Earnshaw's* reported that buyers seemed to be comfortable with the idea that the back-to-school "new fashions being shown" were in fact updated styles.[44]

Since children older than six were making their own clothing choices, producing clothes for children older than six may be courting financial ruin, designers suggested.[45] Referring to the French expression "the more things change the more they stay the same"(*plus ça change, plus c'est la même chose*), eight designers of girl's wear submitted that there would be little change in girls' attire in the 1980s.[46] According to them, girls' clothes should continue to reflect self in age and gender roles. They rejected "cutting down" adult women's fashions to create fashionable attire for girls. They claimed that the method didn't work because of problems with fit, movement, and eye appeal; "a child is a child is a child and should look like a child," they asserted.[47]

Designers also claimed that they were no longer arbiters of taste but "reflectors of it." In fact, every designer's line consists of two major elements, styles that reflect the designer's vision or point of view, and styles that reflect the country's current attitude or mood.[48] In the latest Ralph Lauren collection for children, instead of styling them according to his point of view, which mimics British aristocracy, he had created a line characterized by "pretty detailing and fresh innocence." His customers were asking for such an image.[49]

Self in a Social Role[50]

Parents who have special agendas for their children that involve play-acting an adult role require adult-style dress. That style of dress is usually not open to negotiation, because clothing and behavior have to conform to official rules established by those in authority. For children competing in beauty pageants, to take one example, mimicking adult appearance and behavior is required. A typical competition includes a wide range of children, from infants as young as three months old to teenagers. In one such event infant boys were dressed in a red cummerbunds over the diaper and infant girls appeared "in earrings and real leather shoes."[51] Some parents had coached their children hoping that they would win a modeling contract. Others, however, were hoping that the experience would give the child a competitive edge in school.[52] A

FIGURE 12.5 JonBenet
Ramsey in a pageant
costume, 1996. Photo,
Dave Sarten/NYT.

third-grade teacher, the mother of an eight-month-old daughter who
"was wearing gold earrings in her pierced ears," summed it up by saying
that public appearance at this pre-verbal stage would help her daughter
develop the poise she would need later for adult performance.[53]

With 3,000 beauty pageants a year in the United States, the children's
pageant business was a $1 billion-a-year industry with 100,000 contestants
under the age of fourteen. In December 1997, the number of participants in
the New York City version of the Prince and Princess pageant declined by
about a half (from 135 participants in 1996). The decline was attributed to
the murder of the six-year-old JonBenet Ramsey.[54] In the public's mind the
murder was somehow related to the extravagant and sexy, adult-style
make-up she wore in competing in beauty pageants (see Fig. 12.5).

The contests are popular in areas of the country where educational opportunities for women are less available, the South for example. Hundreds of pageants are held each year and contestants often "try" in several areas throughout the country. They come flanked by their fans and
other adults forming networks of information and support;[55] it is a sub-
culture focused on beauty.

Playing in Little League baseball is an activity that involves both play
and work. Participating in the game is intrinsically rewarding. The activity is oriented towards developing the skills needed in adult male society.
To function effectively in the corporation, a successful employee must be

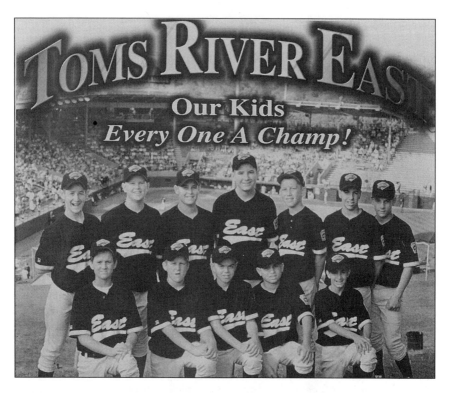

FIGURE 12.6   Tom's River Little League won the 1998 World Series
Championship. Courtesy Tom Gannon.

adept at exchanges that require give and take, be able to work with others, be ready to take on different roles, and be able to win and lose without too much emotional upheaval. Little League is one form of preadolescent "play" that is directed by adults, and it often includes parental
involvement.[56]

Instead of just playing softball, preadolescents in Little League baseball
are able to play baseball with the trappings of the adult world. The
promise of playing on a regular team, like adults, with real uniforms, a
brand new ball for each game, and bats that were light enough for them to
swing, started Little League baseball. Officially that beginning took place
in 1942, in Williamsport, Pennsylvania, with the construction of a baseball
diamond with fences, scoreboards, and bleachers.[57] Within six years
enough leagues had been established so that a national tournament could
be held. The 1948 tournament was called a World Series.[58] Despite criticism
by professionals, who argued that highly competitive sports harmed
preadolescent development, freedom from income tax and support by cor-

porate giants, such as Alcoa, Burlington Industries, Reynold's Aluminum, and U.S. Rubber, helped nurture it, and Little League baseball became a big business.[59] In 1983 Little League Baseball League, Inc., reported assets of over $10.2 million and total expenses of $3.9 million. In 1983 there were about seven thousand Little Leagues with over forty-eight thousand teams. There were well over half a million Little Leaguers.[60]

Heroic Image

In the mid–1980s, the image-making techniques used to promote the U.S. manned space program in the 1960s, voluntary hero-making mechanisms, adulation, and technojargon,[61] were adopted by manufacturers and retailers to sell clothes with sports themes.[62] Initially they built their advertising on the ideals of success in competition and science.[63] Keds sneakers, for example, in 1986 were advertised as a sound shoe for kids, and sales in 1986 were about $60 million. Keds then announced that their sneakers had been technologically upgraded and now they were lighter and had better cushioning. By 1989, sales increased to $227 million.[64] By 1996 sales were $286 million.[65]

Publicity suggested that garments worn by "Celebrity Athletes" were imbued with special powers. Athletes chosen to promote articles of dress had to be more than proficient on the field and their demeanor off the field had to be admirable. The marketing vehicle for the National Football League in 1995, for example, was Junior Seau, a star linebacker for the San Diego Chargers. He was chosen to represent the sport because, as a teammate put it, "off the field he looked cool."[66] He walked around in baggy shorts, sandals, and a tank top "no matter what the temperature was." His appearance suggested he did not need symbols of wealth and that he had triumphed over the powers of nature and was impervious to the cold.[67] His choice of dress, moreover, reflected personal autonomy, a quality considered cool among the young. Since most basketball shoe consumers do not play basketball, basketball shoes obviously have an appeal beyond their functional attributes.[68]

A nationally televised commercial showed Michael Jordan leaping towards the basket to the accompaniment of a jet engine. The outline of a leaping Jordan became an icon known as "the Jump Man," the logo recognized as Nike's swoosh.[69] In its first year the Air Jordan line accounted for $130 million of Nike's sales.

In his 1993 book *Shaq Attack*, Shaquille O'Neal, a basketball star, remarked, "It's funny, when I was just starting to play ball, kids didn't think much about shoes." From Jordan on, the creation of a persona with readily identifiable characteristics became important to shoe companies.[70] Publicity increased sales.

FIGURE 12.7 The street look. Popular media eclecticism, all in baggy over-size. *Earnshaw's*, February 1995. By permission. Photo, Greg Kitchen.

Across the industry basketball shoes acquired new cachet and companies increased the range of shoes available. They also introduced gadgets such as velcro straps, plastic clamps, and pumps. They also stepped up promotional efforts informally, on a street hoops level. By 1984 Nike and others were sponsoring summer basketball camps, building brand loyalty from the ground up, using kids as "all knowing." Children were used as "pawns" in the marketing of success.[71] Critic Michael Eric Tyson wrote that the sneaker symbolized "the ingenious manner" in which the dynamism of African-American cool, hip, and chic culture was integrated into the American cultural landscape.[72]

A Bond with Sports

Logo active wear emerged as a way of showing support for a team. Alex Kotlowitz told of a group of six kids accused of stealing a bike, who were sitting on the marble bench in the lobby of Juvenile Court House in Chicago. While their mothers were waiting anxiously, five of the boys were ribbing the one called Lafayette for his T-shirt, which "hailed the Detroit Pistons as the NBA champions."[73] Though they were members of the same gang they aligned themselves with different teams. Lafayette's T-shirt identified the team he would be cheering.

FIGURE 12.8
Swimsuits in the 1990s
often have logos or
symbols. Play clothes
are inadequate for
admission to the
swimming pool at
Astoria Park in Queens,
July 4, 1990. Photo,
Fred Conrad/NYT.

A sports uniform made it possible for children to take on three distinct roles: a team player, a fan cheering on a team, and a buddy to one's father if the uniform was for the same team the father rooted for. Members of the sports teams thought that wearing a team uniform was an efficient means of recruiting future fans.

In August 1991, P. F. Flyers announced that four out of the ten new styles of shoes they had developed for children are "actual basic adult styles scaled down for children."[74] The most popular outfit among boys of all ages for school and for play continued to be a flannel shirt or a T-shirt, with a pair of jeans or shorts and a light weatherproof jacket. By 1995, sportswear licensees produced children's apparel from jerseys down to socks that looked identical to those worn by adult athletes. What had been athletic and active-wear categories of dress had become further differentiated and specialized.[75]

Sport uniforms for children were now available in children's sizes, toddlers, four–seven and eight–twenty. They could be worn to play or to attend baseball, football, basketball, or hockey games.[76] There were also sweatsuits in hooded pullover style, windbreakers, screen-printed cotton T-shirts, sweaters, turtlenecks, denim jackets and jeans, and logo-intensive outerwear. The National Football League Properties saw itself as the official outfitter of "America's playgrounds." Mighty-Mac Sports, an official licensee of the NFL, NHL, MLB, and NBA, carried a collection of outerwear, activewear, playwear, and headwear for Rookie League, Jump Ball Club, and Touchdown Club. "Not Sleepwear, Teamwear," said an advertisement for a sweatshirt with the logo of the Dallas Cowboys.[77]

The NFL target for youth wear was divided into two main segments: parents purchasing the apparel for infant, toddler, and four–seven size; and the six to twelve-year-olds, 40 percent of whom had a say in what their parents would buy for them.[78]

Adult Image

In the 1990s school age kids were offered the opportunity to dress like Mom or Dad. The marketing of father-son and mother-daughter outfits was based on the idea that children like to dress like their parents because they need to identify with certain adults and to separate from certain others.[79]

Catalogs, magazines, and store windows displayed father and son and mother and daughter outfits.[80] Father and son were in formal attire, a jacket and a tie, or casual attire, khaki pants, shirt, and windproof jacket.

Some mother and daughter outfits replicated adult women's fashion described by the industry as displaying "fashion-rightness." In the early 1990s girls as young as eight years of age were wearing leather. Some were depicted in a black dress, black jacket, and boots. Another fashionable look was wearing elements of male dress such as pants, shirts, and suspenders. (See Fig. 12.9.)

The variety of clothes and styles available for casual occasions was extensive. In whatever the style, the silhouette was relaxed and loose-fitting, making getting dressed easy. Some had a scalloped neckline, drop-waist, long or short, in floral or stripes. The clothes were simple and cheerful.[81]

Themes of Delight

The Cute

In general, elements of dress and styles of appearance that are appealing, yet unanticipated, call attention to the person, imbuing him or her with special allure. In adults the impact is called "the charm of the unexpected."[82] In the same way, clothes that are appealing and unexpected

FIGURE 12.9   A little girl wears a Blue Knights costume similar to her father's at a Hell's Angels outing, August 12, 1996. Photo, Jim Estrin/NYT.

call the child to the attention of the observer and imbue the child's appearance with the charm called "cuteness." For example, both children and adults are enchanted by the illustrations in Ludwig Bemelmans classic children story, *Madeline*. The twelve little girls look adorable in their unexpectedly neat school uniforms, particularly when they are portrayed marching "in two straight lines."[83] In the same way, a jean fabric with flourishes and ruffles is unexpected. The contrast is likely to elicit a response from the observer.[84] Popular decoration, such as dogs, cats, a deer, or a bear are unexpected and therefore draw attention to the child. These ornaments, moreover, often represent a young child's choice. Between eighteen and twenty-four months children are aware of animals, though they don't know the species.[85] An adult's smile is likely to be interpreted as approval of the child's choice.

Outfits designed in the style of adult occupational dress, such as sports uniforms, or fishing or mining attire, are usually cute (see Fig. 12.10). Also cute are oversized garments. They render the child vulnerable and in need of adult care. Adult-style everyday dress worn by young preschool children may also be cute (see Fig. 12.11).

In a *Newsweek* story (October 29, 1990) Barbara Kantrowitz reported about babyGap, which used the same colors and prints as grown-up Gap clothes; many babyGap styles looked like miniature versions of the big

FIGURE 12.10 Eleven-month-old David Rubinstein in simulated team sports attire. By permission. Photo, Kathryn Hall, 1997.

FIGURE 12.11 A toddler couple in the traditional preppie style: plaid jumper, plaid trousers with navy crested blazer. Adapted for toddlers. *Earnshaw's*, February 1995. By permission. Photo, Greg Kitchen.

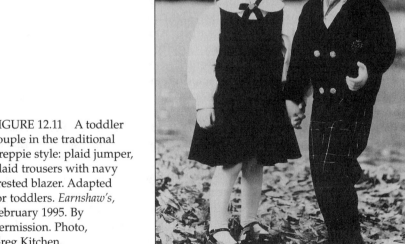

kids' clothes. The unexpected style could elicit an emotional response, encouraging feelings of affection and perhaps resulting in a hug.

Advertised as "cute" by Oshkosh B'Gosh was the "Unisex" style. The clothes were loose-fitting, colorful, and gender-nonspecific.[86] Being decorative and gender-nonspecific caught the observer's attention.[87]

In 1991 designers who had been trained as artists introduced unexpected imagery, playful food prints of hamburgers, hot dogs, sundaes, and frisky monkeys, on the clothes they made.[88] Instead of pastels the outfits came in arresting colors: black, orange, red, cobalt, and muted shades of earth, clay, and sand.[89] The unexpected imagery rendered the child wearing the garment cute. These designers limited the clothes they made to children up to the age of six, the period when parents still choose the child's clothes.[90] After the age of six, children begin to attend school, and parental preferences, they believed, were less likely to prevail. Moreover, the "cute" image may not have worked on the older child. Clothes that are cute increase the chances that adults would pay more than simple attention to the child.

The Cuddly

In the 1980s and 1990s lines of clothes for infants and young children included those soft in texture and design, highly tactile fabrics that encouraged cuddling. Infants' overall sets, creepers, jumpsuits, and beach towels were made of soft cotton and were often designed with suggestive symbols, hearts, kisses, and hug-me teddy-bears.

Clothes that are soft encourage touch, as a kitten's soft fur encourages petting. Infants respond to touch. The simple act of holding an infant's arms or legs or pressing on the abdomen is often enough to quiet an infant.[91] Being touched is one way through which the infant establishes social and emotional awareness. Transforming the child into a reasonable functioning adult requires emotional connectedness to a significant other.[92] Clothes that encourage cuddling help to move the child towards social connectedness,[93] and have the capacity of reaffirming children's affective value.[94]

Choosing an Attitude

An attitude refers to a posture, or a position of a figure, a bearing that indicates action or feelings.[95] Children in the 1980s were usually familiar with the attitude of a character appearing in cartoons, movies, comic strips, or special promotions. These characters were placed on garments through the process of licensing, the borrowing of someone else's name, or buying the consumer franchise to use the character on another product, allowing

FIGURE 12.12 A child in cute and cuddly clothing. The hat represents the likeness of a cat, an unexpected image that is cute. The outfit, made out of soft, plush fabric, looks cozy and likely to inspire a desire to hug the child. Photo, Kathryn Hall, 1998. By permission.

FIGURE 12.13 This child looks cute and cuddly because his hat represents the likeness of a bear. Since the hat is too big the image calls forth feelings of tenderness and warmth and the desire to cuddle. Photo, Kathryn Hall, 1998. By permission.

the manufacturer to reproduce it on apparel. These garments often please children because the character imbues the garment with special magical qualities attributed to the character, the Lion King, for example. Sometimes these characters evoke nostalgia for an earlier time and a simpler period.[96] Action, talk, or song by any of the characters may be imitated.

The Peanuts characters suggested that blundering was all right. The soft blanket that Linus carries around suggested that children sometimes needed comfort. Space-oriented characters, from shows such as *Star Trek* and *Star Wars*, wore weird uniforms and provided a sense of adventure. There were also 1930s and 1940s Buck Rogers and the Looney Tunes characters and the updated images of Mickey Mouse and Popeye, creating a landscape of characters who are familiar and fun. They appeared on suspenders, belts, and belt buckles. Popeye's punching fist with the resounding "Pow" also appeared on night shirts, pajamas, and T-shirts.[97]

A 1986 study by *Better Homes and Gardens* of the number of consumers who bought licensed apparel, attire with "the likeness of a cartoon, comic, toy or TV personality in the past year," found that 42.3 percent of the population purchased such merchandise; 13.7 percent bought it for their own children, and 18.2 percent purchased it as a gift.[98] Consumers purchased licensed merchandise in about even numbers for boys (59.2 percent) and for girls (59.8 percent). While 43 percent of consumers who purchased character apparel in the last year did so for a child up to the age of three, 61.5 percent purchased for the older child, four to seven years of age. Over 50 percent (57.5 percent) of the adult buyers bought them because they were cute; 62.6 percent bought them because the child requested it (the numbers include multiple responses). In this category of dress children influenced consumption over 50 percent of the time, and much of what was purchased consisted of sleepwear, shirts, socks/underwear (at 72.1 percent; 66.5 percent and 38.5 percent respectively).[99] At least 72 percent of the garments were such that they would normally not be seen by strangers and were therefore likely to be worn for personal reasons, be it comfort, support, or empowerment.

School Uniforms

Many adults view uniforms as a mode of oppression. Some children do too. Many others, mothers and children, view them with delight. Girls experience joy in their pleated plaid skirts, and they twirl and jump up and down, declaring their youthfulness and with much new energy around them. Uniforms free the child and adult from making decisions about what to buy and what to wear in the morning. Uniforms look neat and demand respect. A uniform may be seen as a prestigious garment and worn with pride. It sends a message of social connectedness.[100]

At P.S. 71 in the Bronx, New York, uniforms were merely suggested,[101] yet children from kindergarten through the sixth grade were happy about adopting and wearing the uniform. For students in poor neighborhoods the uniform indicates membership, belonging, community, continuity, equality, and social acceptance—all the reasons why children join gangs.[102] Uniforms mask poverty and social inequality.

About a year earlier, at a rally outside Jackie Robinson Academy, a Long Beach Public School in California where students wear uniforms, it was announced that preliminary evidence suggested that uniforms had had a positive effect on a learning environment, President Clinton noted.[103] Administrators and teachers claimed that student's attitudes and behavior changed once they wore uniforms; they now had higher self-esteem, were more serious about their work, were better behaved, had a higher attendance record, and took greater pride in their school.[104] What was missing from the reports was evidence about learning.

Cities with a large number of minority children, such as Dallas and Miami, began requiring students to wear uniforms.[105] Mandatory uniform policy dictates what students should wear, restricting children's freedom of choice. While uniforms may bring order to the classroom through controlling anger, violence, and drug-related activities, they also reduce a child's ability to make choices from which he or she may learn. Since uniforms are mass-produced, their fit may be poor, and at least some of the teachers will be less than supportive of students wearing ill-fitting clothes.

A growing number of students across the country like wearing uniforms. They report that, "It makes getting dressed in the morning a lot easier."[106] Many retailers have joined in launching a school uniform catalog for back-to-school sales. These feature oxford tailored shirts, khaki chinos, and navy blazers, Ivy league schools' style of dress.[107]

Cultural Literacy

In schools where uniforms have always been required, parochial schools, for example, the dress code is a challenge. William Hamilton, writing for the *New York Times*, reported that students and former students who are now adults have revealed that uniforms encouraged them to find ways to bend and stretch the rules with their own sartorial statement. In subtle and not such subtle ways they managed to get around the rules. There are ways of dressing according to the code, yet not being in uniform. "Everybody finds their own different way to get around the rules" reported a fifteen-year-old tenth-grader at the Convent of the Sacred Heart School in Manhattan. Skirts were rolled up, navy pants acquired a droop, or were baggy. Shoes "became" boots, had big heels that were sometimes clunky, or were made out of suede. The aim is to transform the school uniform (white blouse and navy skirt or slacks for girls, white shirt and navy pants for boys) into a personal fashion statement.[108]

Public schools are rich and complex universes in which children can cull friends and information beyond that which they can gather at home. Clothing styles in the 1990s offer variety. Dresses worn to school may be formal, informal, preppy, hippie, "white-bread" (meaning boring), heavy-metal, or leather. These styles are often associated with a point of view or with values that children have learned by hanging out with their peers. School children can, thus, examine the ideas and ideologies around them and reflect; indeed they must reflect, since the ideas and ideologies sometimes collide with one another.

Commitment to a style at one time doesn't preclude shedding it and trying another, searching for a "fit." A news report by Deborah Hoffman, in the *New York Times* (March 19, 1989), is an example.

Interviewed about accessories and style, Yvonne Everett, nine years old, of Miami is quoted: "Anything about surfing is far out, for big kids, but I can't relate to that yet." Her book bag, however, was decorated with the once-ubiquitous yellow happy face. "It was my idea to buy it," Yvonne said, "But Mommy said O.K. She said it always made her feel good, too."[109]

By embracing a particular style children participate in the process of self-differentiation and self-identification. The ability to choose is central to life in American society. One must make selections from among many offerings in books, games, courses, food, movies, friends, political ideas, and candidates. From toddlerhood to their teens, "Many children choose what they want to wear—and how, when and whether they will put them on," reports Nancy Kalish in "Clothes Wars."[110] Children seem to make choices just for the sake of making choices. Experimenting with clothes is an important way of experimenting with independence, and parents should not discourage it, points out clinical psychologist Debbie Webb Blackburn.[111]

Some parents may find it maddening—and sometimes embarrassing, so much so that they are tempted to hang a sign on the child's back that reads, "I DID NOT DRESS THIS CHILD."[112] Strong and stubborn preferences are not only normal but developmentally desirable. Preschoolers in American society also choose costumes and unusual clothes as they push towards self-expression. They may try several identities in their search for their own. Childcare specialists have become aware of children's developmental needs, which require time and openness to alternatives.

Some parents and childcare specialists argue that the United States is a success-oriented society. Children need to be pushed, prodded, and guided into starting everything early—making friends, attending school, and playing sports. Some parents depend on their children to relinquish infanthood early. They are expected to forgo large-size diapers. Many day-care centers require that a child be toilet-trained before being enrolled.[113]

In contrast, some parents and childcare specialists argue that children are being rushed into independence too soon. A child may not be ready to be toilet-trained, ask questions, or make friends.[114] Large-size disposable diapers preclude feces and urine running down their legs. Without this negative experience, however, some specialists believe the child will have little motivation to become toilet-trained. In somewhat the same way, school uniforms can be seen as giving children a chance to remain children, or as keeping them naive longer than necessary.[115]

Do these two contradictory approaches to child development reflect two distinct ideologies? It seems so. Does the current situation suggest that the "success" ideology, at least as applied to early childhood, may be in retreat? The result may be that childhood as a time of wonder, openness, spontaneity, creativity, innocence, and freedom from responsibility may once again last longer. Do cute and cuddly children's clothes, school uniforms, and children being toilet-trained at thirty months, rather than eighteen or twenty-four, foretell prolonging of childhood? Should childhood last longer?

Notes

1. James U. McNeal (1992) *Kids As Customers, A Handbook of Marketing to Children*. New York: Lexington Books, pp. 82–83.

2. McNeal, op. cit., p. 8.

3. Toy manufacturers used to rely on demonstrators to display the toy in department stores. Parents rather than children determined what would be bought. Toys "R" Us has changed this situation by making toys visible and accessible through the floor-to-ceiling display. Packaging gives children the feeling that the toy is virtually within grasp. Ellen Seiter, (1993) *Sold Separately: Children and Parents in Consumer Culture*. New Brunswick, N.J.: Rutgers University Press, p. 201.

Scarcity of employees at Toys "R" Us enhances the feeling that the child is a part of this environment. A visit to Toys "R" Us results in a great deal of frustration and dissonance for parents, as they battle for control over their children's consumer desires. Seiter, op. cit., p. 211.

4. McNeal, op. cit., p. 10.

5. Rather than merely influencing parental consumption, the child became a decisionmaker and sometimes a solo buyer after 1985. McNeal, op. cit., p. 6.

6. McNeal, op. cit., p. 28.

7. McNeal, op. cit., p. 26.

8. Ibid.

9. McNeal, op. cit., pp. 35–36.

10. McNeal, op. cit., p. 35.

11. Children are described as "spoiled and out of control" in "Kids These Days: What Americans Really Think About the Next Generation," a pamphlet published by *Public Agenda*, 6 East 39th Street, New York, New York, in 1998.

12. Mothers who did not have the money often bought clothes that were on sale, cheaper than the ones that were "hot," or fashionable among kids, those designated desirable by their peers.

13. McNeal, op. cit., p. 26.

14. McNeal, op. cit., pp. 77–79, reported a study of children's lives in Oakland, California, which found that the children of working mothers, especially daughters, increased somewhat their contribution to housework. See also pp. 142–144 in McNeal.

15. McNeal, op. cit., pp. 26–28, 34.

16. Toys "R" Us made easy access the basic principle underlying the course of mass-merchandising. Ellen Seiter, (1993) *Sold Separately: Children and Parents in Consumer Culture*. New Brunswick, N.J.: Rutgers University Press, pp. 205–206.

17. A. F. Newcomb and C. L. Bagwell, (1996) "The Developmental Significance of Children's Friendship Relations," in William M. Bukowski, Andrew F. Newcomb, and Willard W. Hartup, eds. (1996) *The Company They Keep: Friendship in Childhood and Adolescence*. Cambridge: Cambridge University Press, p. 303.

18. McNeal, op. cit., pp. 40–41.

19. McNeal, op. cit., p. 41.

20. McNeal, op. cit., p. 34.

21. McNeal, op. cit., p. 33.

22. McNeal, op. cit., pp. 16, 17.

23. McNeal, op. cit., p. 17.

24. Ibid.

25. Ellen Graham (1988) "As Kids Gain the Power of the Purse, Marketing Takes an Aim at Them," *Wall Street Journal*, Jan. 19, pp. 1, 8.

26. Ibid.

27. Jan E. Dizard and Howard Gadlin, (1990) *The Minimal Family*. Amherst: University of Massachusetts Press, p. 153.

28. James H. S. Bossard and Eleanor Stoker Boll. (1966) *The Sociology of Child Development*. New York: Harper and Row, pp. 39–40.

29. Orville G. Brim Jr. (1958) "Family Structure and Sex Role Learning by Children: A Further Analysis of Helen Koch's Data," *Sociometry* 21, pp. 1–15.

30. Companies like Esprit, Gap, Polo, Sassoon, and Gitano, for example. McNeal, op. cit., p. 41.

31. *Earnshaw's*, March 1980, pp. 98–99, 119.

32. From an advertisement in *Earnshaw's*, August 1983, p. 49.

33. *Earnshaw's*, March 1980, p. 129.

34. There is a difference between high-end status lines and the more basic commodity merchandise. High-end status lines, for example, Izod and Absorba, sold a garment from $25 and up, in contrast to the well-known brands of Health-tex and Baby Togs, which sold a similar item for around $15. *Earnshaw's*, June 1986, p. 87.

35. Patricia Van Olinda, (1980) "Boys' Wears' Three C's: Clean, Classic, Coordinated," *Earnshaw's*. October, pp. 68–69.

36. Izod JG, (1980) *Earnshaw's*, March, pp. 99.

37. Ibid.

38. "Boys' Wear 80: Jocks vs. Preppies," *Earnshaw's*, March 1980, pp. 107–109.

39. Patricia Van Olinda, (1980) "Boys' Wear's Three C's: Clean, Classic and Co-ordinated," *Earnshaw's*, October 1980, pp. 68–69.

40. Jane Glicksman, (1982) "The Separates Success Story," *Earnshaw's*, March, pp. 139–145.

41. Glicksman, op. cit., p. 139.

42. "BTS Magic: Color, Shape, Detailing," *Earnshaw's*, March 1982, pp. 180–185.

43. Ibid.

44. *Earnshaw's*, May 1986, pp. 68, 78–79.

45. Maureen Olin, (1980) "Girls' Wear in the 80s," *Earnshaw's*, March, pp. 105, 145.

46. Olin, op. cit., p. 145. The designers were Betty Adcock, Joanna DiBartolla, Ellie Fishman, Ruth Scharf, Joan Smick, Mary Sudjian, and Linda Wisener.

47. Ibid.

48. Ibid.

49. Ibid.

50. Sociologists distinguish between statuses *assigned* to the individual at birth, which in American society are central to one's identity—age and sex, for example, and statuses chosen by the individual, which are called *achieved* statuses. Clothes that reflect the self in a social role are clothes that reflect achieved statuses.

51. Douglas Martin, (1997) "Who's Fairest? For Tots, an Early Lesson," *The New York Times*, Oct. 19.

52. Ibid.

53. Ibid.

54. *New York Times*, "Week in Review," May 10, 1998.

55. Martin, op. cit.

56. Gary Alan Fine, (1987) *With the Boys, Little League Baseball and Preadolescent Culture*. Chicago: The University of Chicago Press, pp. 2–6.

57. Ibid.

58. Fine, op. cit., p. 7.

59. Fine, op. cit., p. 5.

60. Fine, op. cit., p. 4.

61. Michael L. Smith, (1983) "Selling the Moon, The U.S. Manned Space Program and the Triumph of Commodity Scientism," in Richard Whightman Fox and T. J. Jackson Lear, eds., *The Culture of Comsumption*. New York: Pantheon Books, pp. 175–209.

62. McNeal, op. cit., pp. 11–12.

63. Smith, op. cit., p. 177.

64. Tom Vanderbilt, (1998) *The Sneaker Book*. New York: The New Press, p. 31.

65. Vanderbilt, op. cit., pp. 22–23.

66. Vanessa Groce, "NFLP Kicks Off Fall '95 with Authentic Looks," *Earnshaw's*, February 1995, p. N6.

67. Ibid.

68. Vanderbilt, op. cit., p. 31.

69. Vanderbilt, op. cit., p. 29.

70. Vanderbilt, op. cit., pp. 30–31.

71. Vanderbilt, op. cit., p. 30.

72. Quoted in Vanderbilt, op. cit., p. 33.

73. Alex Kotlowitz, (1991) *There Are No Children Here. The Story of Two Boys Growing up in America.* New York: Doubleday, p. 270.

74. *Earnshaw's,* August 1991, p. 115.

75. Colin Campbell, (1987) *The Romantic Ethic and the Spirit of Modern Consumerism.* Oxford: Basil Blackwell, p. 203.

76. "The NFL Kids' Report 1995," *Earnshaw's,* February 1995, pp. N6–N42.

77. Ibid.

78. Groce, op. cit., p. N6.

79. McNeal, op. cit., p. 41.

80. Summer 1996, *J. C. Penney* and *Lands' End* catalogs, for example.

81. *Earnshaw's,* May 1992, p. 83.

82. Ruth P. Rubinstein, (1995) *Dress Codes: Meanings and Messages in American Culture.* Boulder, Colo.: Westview Press, p. 106.

83. Ludwig Bemelmans, (1939) *Madeline.* New York: Simon and Schuster.

84. Rebecca H. Holman and Suzanne E. Wiener, (1985) "Fashionability in Clothing: A Values and Life-Style Perspective," in Michael R. Solomon, ed., *The Psychology of Fashion.* Lexington, Mass.: D. C. Heath, Lexington Books, p. 87.

85. Frederick Elkin and Gerald Handel,(1989) *The Child and Society: The Process of Socialization.* New York: Random House, p. 53.

86. *Children's Business.* (1996) New York: Fairchild Publications, March.

87. *Earnshaw's,* July 1994, pp. 40–42.

88. Six designers were identified: David Brooks, Rhonda and Bruce Wall, Elan Bahk and Nikki Nicols, Cnoc Grafton, J. Morgan Puett. All work in New York and their clothes are for girls, boys, toddlers, and infants. Elaine Louie, (1991) "Hearts Are Cute. So Are Children. Must They Go Together?" *New York Times,* "Fashion," January 27.

89. Ibid.

90. Ibid.

91. T. B. Brazelton, (1969) *Infants and Mothers: Differences in Development.* New York: Dell.

92. H. F. Harlow and M. K. Harlow, (1962) "Social Deprivation in Monkeys," *Scientific American,* November, pp. 137–146.

93. In the past, mothers' clothing made their bodies not readily accessible or pleasant to infants. Starched collars and cuffs, aprons and corsets presented a barrier to the baby, marginalizing the mother's significance. M. D. Ainsworth, S. Blehar, M. C. Waters, E. and S. Wall (1979) *Patterns of Attachment.* New York: Halsted Press.

94. Viviana Zelizer, in *Pricing the Priceless Child* (1985), calls the process "sacralization" of the child. Children in American society have been invested with sentimental or religious meaning. New York: Basic Books, p. 11.

95. *The American Heritage Dictionary of the English Language,* Third Edition. New York: Houghton Mifflin, 1992, p. 463.

96. "The Business of Licensing," *Earnshaw's,* May 1986, pp. 40–41.

97. *Earnshaw's,* July 1980, pp. 43–44.

98. "Consumers Speak Out on Licensed Apparel," *Earnshaw's,* May 1986, pp. 44–48.

99. Ibid.

100. Nathan Joseph, (1986) *Uniforms and Nonuniforms: Communication Through Clothing*. Westport, Conn.: Greenwood Press, p. 75.

101. Jacques Steinberg, (1998) "Equality, Tyranny, Plaid, Navy? Schools Debate Plans for Uniforms," *New York Times*. February 11, pp. A1 and B 14.

Nancie L. Katz and Joanne Wasserman, (1998) "Dress for Success? Poll: Uniforms Are Wear It's At." *New York Times*, February 15, pp. 6–7.

102. The Educational Testing Service studied the impact of uniforms over a four-year period, 1988 to 1992, on the behavior of 1,300 high school students (from eighth through twelfth grade). The findings suggest that a set of "graduated penalties for bad behavior, from minor to severe" will have greater effect than uniforms. *Education Life*, Dec. 1998.

103. The district has fifty-six elementary schools and fourteen middle schools. Alison Mitchell, (1996) "Clinton will advise schools on uniforms," *New York Times*, Feb. 25.

104. Ibid. The district reported a 34 percent decrease in assault and battery since 1993, the year uniforms were instituted.

105. Michel Marriott, (1996) "Uniforms: Public Schools Stand up and Salute," *New York Times*, Feb. 4. "It's tragic when young people . . . wind up believing that it is all right to kill somebody for a pair of sneakers or jewelry or designer jackets," Mr. Clinton said, citing recent incidents of violence by teenagers. In his weekly address on the radio President Clinton declared, "If it means that teenagers will stop killing each other" and "if it means that school rooms will be more orderly, more disciplined," and that young people will learn to evaluate themselves "by what they are on the inside instead of what they are wearing on the outside, . . . then public schools should be able to require uniforms."

106. Stephanie Anderson Forest, (1997) "Dressed to Drill. School Uniforms are Hot—and Merchants are Cashing in." *Business Week*, September 8, p. 40.

107. Ibid.

108. William L. Hamilton, (1998) "Cracking the Dress Code: How a School Uniform Becomes a Fashion Statement," *New York Times*, February 19, p. B1.

109. Deborah Hofmann, (1989) "Children Make the 60s New Again," *New York Times*. March 19.

110. Nancy Kalish, (1998) "Clothes Wars," *Parenting*, March, p. 96.

111. In Nancy Kalish, op. cit., p. 96.

112. Marilise Flusser, *Party Shoes to School and Baseball Caps to Bed: The Parents' Guide to Understanding Kids, Clothes, and Independence*. Quoted in Kalish, op. cit., p. 96.

113. Erica Goode, (1999) "Two Experts Do Battle Over Potty Training," *New York Times*. January 12, pp. A1, A17.

114. Ibid.

115. By comparison to students who came from home to attend Harvard in the nineteenth and early twentieth century, boarding school graduates were naive "in the ways of the world" and slow in learning to make decisions. James McLachlan, (1970) *American Boarding Schools*. New York: Charles Scribner and Sons.

Conclusion

This study of children's clothing and of images of children in art was undertaken in order to examine Philippe Ariès's contention that children's clothes reflect the role children are expected to play in society. In particular, it sought to understand the current state of childhood in the United States, to find out if children are being absorbed into adult society, as they were in the Middle Ages. Is childhood disappearing?

The second goal of this study was to find out if a society's style in dressing its children is related to its cultural values. Do the clothes children wear represent social identities? Can patterns in the use of dress and style be identified? What forces underlie the production and consumption of children's clothes?

Until the 1960s in the United States, our findings suggest, children normally had little opportunity to make choices in dress. The production and consumption of children's clothes was governed by the societal definition of childhood and the role children were expected to play in family and society.

Childhood in medieval times was a period of transition that passed quickly and was quickly forgotten.[1] Children were expected to contribute as soon as possible whatever they could to the household's economic survival. Accordingly, they wore miniature adult attire.

In Renaissance Italy the children of the men who acquired power were expected to protect and uphold parental interests. Designated dynasts, children had little opportunity to reflect on their "legacy."[2]

Children's clothes in seventeenth-century Holland helped establish a new society, one informed by the confluence of Calvinist and humanist values, such as orderliness, cleanliness, and affection between parents and children. In art many of the paintings that include children show them dressed in gender-appropriate adult style.

Children in England and France between 1500 and 1800 were expected to reflect parental rank.[3] Middle and upper-middle-class boys passed "through a critically important *rite de passage* around the age of seven when they were shifted from the long frocks of their childhood into the breeches and sword-carrying attire of the adult world."[4] Play was denied special dress.

Children's clothes in nineteenth-century England were focused on the goal of creating the British Empire.[5] Plaids, sailor suits, sports-team clothes, school uniforms, and Boy Scout uniforms were designed to exhibit the loyalty the administration of the colonial bureaucracy required.

Until the Civil War there was little difference in the principles that underlay children's clothes in America and Europe. Boys were dressed in clothes similar to those of their fathers and girls in clothes similar to those of their mothers. Wearing adult-style dress meant that the child was a member of the family and would be contributing to the family's survival needs.

In the United States the clothes the children of the affluent wore after the Civil War helped to define, maintain, and support a new social class: the wealthy middle class.[6] Boys who attended boarding schools wore special attire that distinguished them from others. Those who stayed home could choose among a variety of suits: the Eton suit, Norfolk suit, sailor suit, Brownie suit, or the Lord Fauntleroy outfit, all costly and requiring wealth.

Moreover, children of the affluent had access to sports and special sports attire. The knickerbockers, tennis outfits, turtleneck shirts, and sweaters provided children with clothes that were functional and were also status symbols. They indicated access to wealth and gave the children entry to new realms of experience.

Children of the lower classes who sought to attain a higher social rank, like the boys in the Horatio Alger stories, had to adopt middle-class standards of dress. Untorn clothes and a neat and clean appearance became the ideals used to evaluate and judge children. Well into the twentieth century, in the cities and suburbs of the northeast, appropriate attire required age, sex, and social class marking. Decorum (self-restraint) was expected to prevail. Modified by regional attributes, these standards of dress became a national pattern.

As in the period between 1860 and 1918, in the 1950s affluence made it possible to participate in a particular type of sport and wear the appropriate style of dress, making exercise more enjoyable. Ice-skating, skiing and sunbathing, for example, were more fun when one was dressed in the appropriate clothes. Such attire had traditional goals. It showed off access to wealth. Even the tag from a ski lift attached to one's ski jacket zipper became a status symbol.

Since the late 1960s, standards concerning decorum, age, gender, and neatness have been ignored by styles that violated these precepts. Girls' fashionable dress was the first to negotiate a less stereotyped character to their participation in social life. With the disappearance of a waistline, the expectation that they would bear children disappeared from their appearance. In boys' attire elements suggesting self-restraint, such as a lack of color and ornament and body-denying style, were rejected. Rather than emblems of poverty and social decline, torn jeans and, later, unlaced shoes suggested that boys had acquired ideas and connections beyond those made possible by their families. Boys' style of dress in the late 1960s and the 1970s inspired the development of a more casual approach to social life. Unlike earlier times, in our current society no one set of goals animates the production of children's clothes. The choices available may seem bewildering and contradictory. They indicate, however, that children's clothes and childhood itself are informed by a variety of factors, which include parental values, economic and political forces, and the influence of a child's peers.

In the 1990s children's clothes seem to have been shaped by two distinct ideologies. One emphasizes clothes that symbolize achievement. Dressing children in such attire is not motivated simply by the idea that like creates like, that is, that just because a child is dressed in success-oriented clothes, he or she will necessarily succeed.[7] Dressing in this style has actually been believed to induce a child to develop the skills and attitudes that are needed for success.

Children dressed in clothes that encourage delight reflect the desire to make a child happy. Cute and cuddly clothes are pleasurable, helping the child experience the warmth, care, and affection parents feel towards the child. Internalizing these feelings may act to make a child less vulnerable and less dependent on adults for protection. This idea is based upon the belief that when something has been in contact with a person it can remain in contact even though physically absent.[8]

As the end of the twentieth century approaches, the array of options and choices of clothes available to children in the United States suggests that the boundaries of American culture are expansive, permeable, and amenable to change.[9] As for the question of whether childhood is disappearing as children are once more absorbed into the adult world, as some have suggested, the contemporary American world of flexible boundaries scarcely represents a return to Middle Ages. Moreover, even though there are some indications that children are growing up faster today than they were a few decades ago, these are outweighed by other signs of a deep appreciation of children and childhood.

Notes

1. Philippe Ariès, (1962) *Centuries of Childhood: A Social History of Family Life.* Trans. Robert Baldock. New York: Vintage Books, p. 34.

2. John F. Padgett and Christopher K. Ansel, (1993) "Robust Action and the Rise of the Medici 1400–1434," *American Journal of Sociology*, 98, pp. 1259–1319.

3. Monarchs Henry VII and Louis XI revived royal power in England and France, created state bureaucracies, and competed effectively with the Church for power. Mortimer Chambers, Raymond Grew, David Herlihy, Theodore K. Rabb, and Isser Wolloch, (1974) *The Western Experience*. New York: Alfred A. Knopf, pp. 584–585.

4. Lawrence Stone, (1977) *The Family, Sex, and Marriage in England, 1500–1800*. New York: Harper and Row, p. 409

5. The one-piece outfit, the skeleton suit worn by the young children in Otto Runge's painting *The Hülsenbeck Children* (1805–1806), represented the view that children were biological beings, elements of nature, related to animals, trees, and flowers, and as such, should be allowed physical freedom. The design of the garment also made provisions for physical growth.

6. Michael Hanagan, (1994) in "New Perspective on Class Formation: Culture, Reproduction, and Agency," *Social Science History* 18, pp. 77–93, emphasizes the importance of understanding identity formation in terms of self-conscious efforts to replicate and reproduce these ties through cultural objects. Among the wealthy middle-class private schools, clothes for recreational activities, and protective attire reproduce and support the new identity.

7. I am referring to "sympathetic magic," one of the categories of magical activity set by Frazer in his classic *The Golden Bough*.

8. "Contagious magic", the second category of magic suggested by Frazer.

9. This flexibility is in contrast to Europe, where cultural boundaries tend to be more fixed. Sameness, or uniformity in style, still characterizes the production of European children's clothes, and the focus has continued to be quality fabric and ornament, the needs of the upper class.

Selected Readings

Abelson, Elaine S. (1989) *When Ladies Go A-Thieving*. New York: Oxford University Press.

Achenbach, Thomas S., and Craig Edelbrock. (1981) *Behavioral Problems and Competencies Reported by Parents of Normal and Disturbed Children Aged Four through Sixteen*. Monographs of the Society for Research in Child Development, serial no. 188. Chicago: University of Chicago Press.

Adams, Laurie Schneider. (1994) *A History of Western Art*. Madison, Wis.: Brown and Benchmark.

Ahlstrom, Sydney E. (1973) *Religious History of the American People*. New York: Basic Books.

Alexander, Sidney. (1974) *Lions and Foxes: Men and Ideas of the Italian Renaissance*. New York: Macmillan.

Alwin, D. F. (1988) "From Obedience to Autonomy: Changes in Traits Desired in Children, 1924–1978." *Public Opinion Quarterly* 52, pp. 33–52.

Anderson, Olive. (1971) 'The Growth of Christian Militarism in Mid-Victorian Britain." *English Historical Review* 86, pp. 46–72.

Apple, Rima D. (1997) "Liberal Arts or Vocational Training? Home Economics Education for Girls," in Sarah Stage and Virginia B. Vincenti, eds., *Rethinking Home Economics, Women and the History of a Profession*. Ithaca, N.Y.: Cornell University Press.

Arnason, H. H. (1970) *History of Modern Art*. Third Edition. Revised and updated by Daniel Wheeler. Englewood Cliffs, N.J.: Prentice Hall and Harry N. Abrams.

Ariès, Philippe. (1962). *Centuries of Childhood: A Social History of Family Life*. Trans. Robert Baldock. New York: Vintage Books.

Bailey, Beth (1994) "Sexual Revolution(s)," in David Farber, ed., *Sixties: From History to Memory*. Chapel Hill: University of North Carolina Press.

Baker, Kevin. (1998) *The American Century*. New York: Alfred A. Knopf.

Baltzell, E. Digby. (1958) *Philadelphia Gentlemen*. Glencoe, Ill.: The Free Press.

Barasch, M.(1976) *Gestures of Despair in Medieval and Early Renaissance Art*. New York: New York University Press.

Barber, Bernard. (1973) "Family and Community Structure in Salem," in Michael Gordon, ed., *The American Family in Social Historical Perspective*. New York: St. Martin's Press.

Barenholtz, Bernard, and Inez McClintock. (1980) *American Antique Toys*. New York: Harry N. Abrams.

Baxandall, M. (1972) *Painting and Experience in Fifteenth Century Italy*. New York: Oxford University Press.

Baxandall, M. (1985) *Patterns of Intention: On the Historical Interpretation of Pictures.* New Haven, Conn.: Yale University Press.

Beisel, Nicola. (1997) *Imperiled Innocents, Anthony Comstock and Family Reproduction in Victorian America.* Princeton, N.J.: Princeton University Press.

Berger, Bennett M. (1960) *Working Class Suburb: A Study of Autoworkers in Suburbia.* Berkeley: University of California Press.

Blumer, Herbert. (1951) "Social Movements," in Sanford M. Lyman, ed., *Social Movements.* (1995). New York: New York University Press.

Boocock, Sarene Spence. (1976) "Children in Contemporary Society," in A. Skolnick, ed., *Rethinking Childhood.* Boston: Little Brown.

Braunstein, Phillipe. (1988) "Towards Intimacy: The Fourteenth and Fifteenth Centuries," in Georges Duby, ed., *A History of Private Life: Revelations of the Medieval World,* trans. Arthur Goldhammer. Cambridge, Mass.: the Belknap Press of Harvard University Press.

Briggs, Caroline. (1897) *Reminiscences and Letters.* Ed. G. S. Merriam. Boston : Houghton Mifflin.

Brink, Carol R. (1935) *Caddie Woodlawn.* New York: Macmillan.

Brion, Marcel. (1969) *The Medici: A Great Florentine Family.* New York: Crown Publishers.

Broun, Heywood, and Margaret Leach. (1927) *Anthony Comstock: Roundsman of the Lord.* New York: The Literary Guild of America.

Bukowski, William M., Andrew F. Newcomb, and Willard W. Hartup. (1996) *The Company They Keep: Friendship in Childhood and Adolescence.* Cambridge: Cambridge University Press.

Burckhardt, Jacob. (1860/1950) *The Civilization of the Renaissance in Italy.* New York: Phaidon Publishers.

Burnett, Frances Hodgson. (1886) *Little Lord Fauntleroy.* New York: Charles Scribner's Sons.

Callman, Ellen. (1979) "The Growing Threat to Marital Bliss as Seen in Fifteenth-Century Florentine Paintings." *Studies in Iconography* 9, pp. 73–92.

Carlyle, Thomas. (1836/1967) *Sartor Resartus.* London: A. M. Dent.

Carman, Harry J., Harold C. Syrett, and Bernard W. Wishy. (1960) *A History of the American People.* New York: Alfred A. Knopf.

Carter, Alison. (1992) *Underwear: The Fashion History.* New York: Drama Book Publishers.

Cawelti, John G. (1965) *Apostles of the Self-Made Man.* Chicago: The University of Chicago Press.

Chalfant, H. Paul, Robert E. Beckley, and C. Eddie Palmer. (1994) *Religion in Contemporary Society.* Itasca, Ill.: F. E. Peacock Publishers.

Chronicles of the 20th Century. (1987) Mount Kisco, N.Y.: Chronicle Publications.

Clay, George R. (1960) "Children of the Young Republic," *American Heritage,* April, pp. 46–53.

Coben, Stanley. (1973) "The First Years of Modern America: 1918–1933," in William E. Leuchtenburg, ed., *The Unfinished Century, America Since 1900.* Boston: Little, Brown and Company.

Coffin, Tristram, ed. (1990) *A Look At America's Children,* Dec. 1., Vol. 16, No. 22

Commager, Henry Steele, ed. (1968) *Documents of American History*. New York: Appleton-Century-Crofts.

Constantino, Maria. (1992) *Fashions of a Decade*. New York: Facts On File.

Coontz, Stephanie. (1992) *The Way We Never Were*. New York: Basic Books.

Couts, Joseph. (1850) *A Practical Guide for Tailor's Cutting-Room*. London: Blackie and Son.

Cranston, Maurice. (1966) *John Locke, A Biography*. London: Longman.

Davidson, Alexander. (1990) *Blazers, Badges and Boaters: A Pictorial History of School Uniform*. London: Scope Books.

Davie, Emily. (1954) *Profile of America: An Autobiography of the United States*. New York: Thomas Y. Crowell.

Davis, Marian L. (1996) *Visual Design in Dress*. Upper Saddle River, N.J.: Simon and Schuster

De Mille, William. (1980) "Mickey Versus Popeye," in Gerald Peary and Danny Peary, eds., *The American Animated Cartoon: A Critical Anthology*. New York: E. P. Dutton.

Degler, Carl N. (1980) *At Odds: Women and the Family in America from the Revolution to the Present*. New York: Oxford University Press.

Demos, John. (1973) "Infancy and Childhood in the Plymouth Colony", in M. Gordon, ed., *The American Family in Social-Historical Perspective*. New York: St. Martin's Press.

Desris, Joe. (1994) *DC Comics*. New York: Abbeville Publishing Group.

Dickens, Gerald. (1957) *The Dress of the British Sailor*. London: Her Majesty's Stationary Office.

Dickstein, Morris. (1977) *Gates of Eden*. New York: Basic Books.

DiMaggio, Paul. (1982) "Cultural Entrepreneurship in Nineteenth-Century Boston: Part I, The Creation of an Organizational Base for High Culture in America," *Media, Culture and Society* 4, pp. 33–35; and "Cultural Entrepreneurship in Nineteenth-Century Boston: Part II, The Classification and Framing of American Art," *Media, Culture and Society* 4, pp. 303–322.

Documents of English History 1832–1950. (1954) Ed. W. A. Barker, G. R. St. Aubyn, and R. L. Ollard. London: A. C. Black.

Documents of American History. (1968) Ed. Henry Steele Commager. New York: Appleton-Century Crofts.

Droste, Magdalena. (1990) *Bauhaus:1919–1933*. Berlin: Bauhaus-Archiv Museum für Gestaltung.

Duncan, Carol. (1973) "Happy Mothers and Other New Ideas in French Art," *Art Bulletin* 55, pp. 570–582.

Durantini, Mary Francis. (1979) *Studies in the Role and Function of the Child in Seventeenth Century Dutch Painting: An Iconographical Investigation*. Ann Arbor, Mich.: University Microfilms International.

Durkheim, Emile. (1893/1964) *The Division of Labor in Society*. New York: The Free Press.

Dyhouse, Carol. (1981) *Girls Growing up in Late Victorian and Edwardian England*. London: Routledge & Kegan Paul.

Dyson, Michael Eric (1993) *Reflecting Black: African American Cultural Criticism*. Minneapolis: University of Minnesota Press.

Earle, Alice Morse. (1903/1971) *Two Centuries of Costume in America, 1620–1820.* Rutland, Vt.: Tuttle.

Easterlin, Richard A. (1980) *Birth and Fortune: The Impact of Numbers on Personal Welfare.* Chicago: The University of Chicago Press.

Eckhardt, Roy A. (1958) *The Surge of Piety in America.* New York: Association Press.

Elder, Glen. (1974) *Children of the Great Depression.* Chicago: University of Chicago Press.

Elkin, Frederick, and Gerald Handel. (1989) *The Child and Society: The Process of Socialization.* New York: Random House.

Erickson, H. Erik (1962) *Young Man Luther.* New York: W. W. Norton.

———. (1959) *Identity and the Life Cycle.* New York: International Universities Press.

Ewing, Elizabeth. (1977) *History of Children's Costume.* New York: Charles Scribner's Sons.

Farrell, Patricia A. (1967) "The Good Old Days of Children's Fashions." *Earnshaw's,* August, pp. 98–103.

Ferguson, George. (1954/1977) *Signs and Symbols in Christian Art.* New York: Oxford University Press.

Fine, Gary Alan. (1987) *With the Boys, Little League Baseball and Preadolescent Culture.* Chicago: The University of Chicago Press.

Fitzgerald, Frances. (1987) *Cities on the Hill.* New York: Simon and Schuster.

Forbush, William Byron. (1901) *The Boy Problem.* Boston: Pilgrim Press.

Fox, Richard Wightman, and T.J. Jackson Lears, eds. (1983) *The Culture of Consumption.* New York: Pantheon Books.

Fraser, Antonia. (1966) *A History of Toys.* London: Delacorte Press.

Fraser, Steve, and Gary Gerstle, eds. (1989) *The Rise and Fall of the New Deal Order.* Princeton, N.J.: Princeton University Press.

Fried, Michael. (1980) *Absorption and Theatricality: Painting and the Beholder in the Age of Diderot.* Berkeley: University of California Press.

Friedan, Betty. (1963) *The Feminine Mystique.* New York: Dell.

Friedenberg, Edgar Z. (1960) *The Vanishing Adolescent.* Boston: Beacon Press.

Gans, Herbert. (1967) *The Levittowners: How People Live and Politics in Suburbia.* New York: Pantheon.

Geertz, Clifford. (1973) *The Interpretation of Cultures.* New York: Basic Books.

Gelis, Jacques. (1989) "The Child: From Anonymity to Individuality," in Roger Chartier, ed., *A History of Private Life.* General Editors, Philippe Ariès and Georges Duby. Trans. Arthur Goldhammer. Cambridge, Mass.: The Belknap Press of Harvard University Press.

Gernshein, Helmut. (1986) *A Concise History of Photography.* New York: Dover Publications.

Gilbert, John. (1986) *Another Chance, Post-War America 1945-1985.* Chicago: Dorsey Press.

Gillis, John R.(1973) "Conformity and Rebellion: Contrasting Styles of English and German Youth, 1900–33." *History of Education Quarterly.* Fall, pp. 251–252.

Goffman, Erving. (1959) *The Presentation of Self in Everyday Life.* Garden City, N.Y.: Doubleday.

Gombrich, E. H. (1972) "Action and Expression in Western Art," in Robert A. Hinde, ed., *Non-Verbal Communication*. New York: Cambridge University Press.

Goodman, Helen. (1989) *The Art of Rose O'Neill*. Catalogue of Exhibition, Brandywine River Museum, Chadds Ford, Pa.

Goulden, Joseph C. (1976) *The Best Years*. New York: Athenaeum.

Gray, William S., and May Hill Arbuthnot (1946–1947 edition) *Our New Friends*. Basic Readers Curriculum Foundation Program. New York: Scott, Foresman and Company.

Green, Arnold W. (1946) "The Middle Class Male Child and Neurosis," *American Sociological Review* (February).

Greenberg, Clement. (1961) "Avant-Garde and Kitsch," in Clement Greenberg, ed., *Art and Culture: Critical Essays*. Boston: Beacon Press.

Greven, Philip J. (1973) "Family Structure in Seventeenth-Century Andover, Massachusetts," in Michael Gordon, ed., *The American Family in Social-Historical Perspective*. New York: St. Martin's Press.

Griswold, Wendy. (1989) "A Methodological Framework for the Sociology of Culture." *Sociological Methodology* 17.

Gromort, Georges. (1922) *Italian Renaissance Architecture*. Trans. George F. Waters, Paris: A. Vincent.

Guarino, Guido A. (1971) *The Albertis of Florence: Leon Battista Alberti's Della Famiglia*. Lewisburg, Pa.: Bucknell University Press.

Gummere, Amelia Mott. (1968) *The Quaker: A Study in Costume*. New York: Benjamin Blom.

Jordan, Nina R. (1941) *American Costume Dolls: How to Make and Dress Them*. New York: Harcourt, Brace and Co.

Halberstam, David. (1993) *The Fifties*. New York: Villard Books.

Halbwachs, Maurice. (1980) *The Collective Memory*, trans. F. I. Ditter Jr. and V. Y. Ditter. New York: Harper and Row.

Hall, Courtney Robert. (1954) *History of American Industrial Science*. New York: Americana Library Publishers.

Hanagan, Michael P. (1989) *Nascent Proletarians: Class Formation in Post-Revolutionary France*. Oxford: Basil Blackwell.

_____. (1994) "New Perspective on Class Formation Culture, Reproduction, and Agency." *Social Science History* 18, pp. 77–93.

Handlin, Oscar, and Mary F. (1971) *Facing Life: Youth and the Family in American History*. Boston: Little, Brown.

Hartt, Frederick. (1969) *History of Italian Renaissance Art, Painting, Sculpture, and Architecture*. Englewood Cliffs, N.J.: Prentice-Hall and New York: Harry N. Abrams.

_____. (1993) *A History of Painting Sculpture Architecture*. Fourth Edition. Englewood Cliffs, N.J.: Prentice Hall and Harry N. Abrams.

Harvey, John. (1995) *Men in Black*. Chicago: University of Chicago Press.

Heininger, Mary Lynn Stevens, Karin Calvert, Barbara Finkelstein, Kathy Vandell, Ann Scott Macleod, and Harvey Green (1984) *A Century of Childhood: Children, Childhood, and Change in America, 1820–1920*. Rochester, N.Y.: The Margaret Woodbury Strong Museum.

Hennessee, Judith, and Joan Nicholson. (1972) "The Song of the Shirt." *Ms. Magazine*, October.

Herald, Jacqueline. (1981) *Renaissance Dress in Italy*. London: Bell & Hyman.

Herlihy, David. (1978)"Medieval Children," in *Essays on Medieval Civilization: The Walter Prescott Webb Memorial Lectures*. Austin: University of Texas Press.

Heskett, John. (1984) *Industrial Design*. New York: Thames and Hudson.

Hicks, J. S. (n.d.) *The Duchess Wore Blue*. Covent Garden [London]: Moss Brothers.

Hirsch, E. D. Jr. (1967) *Validity in Interpretation*. New Haven, Conn.: Yale University Press.

Hirschman, Albert O. (1982) *Shifting Involvements, Private Interest and Public Action*. Princeton, N.J.: Princeton University Press.

Hochschild, Arlie, with Anne Muchang. (1989) *The Second Shift*. New York: Viking Penguin.

Holman, Rebecca H., and Suzanne E. Wiener. (1985) "Fashionability in Clothing: A Values and Life-Style Perspective," in Michael R. Solomon, ed., *The Psychology of Fashion*. Lexington, Mass.: D. C. Heath, Lexington Books.

Jaffe, Hilde. (1972) *Childrenswear Design*. New York: Fairchild Publications.

Jaffe, Hilde, and Rose Rosa. (1990) *Childrenswear Design*. 2nd ed. New York: Fairchild Publications.

Jonas, Susan, and Marilyn Nissenson. (1994) *Going Going Gone: Vanishing Americana*. San Francisco: Chronicle Books.

Joseph, Nathan. (1986) *Uniforms and Nonuniforms: Communication Through Clothing*. New York: Greenwood Press.

Kagan, Jerome, Richard B. Kearsley, and Philip R. Zelazo. (1978) *Infancy: Its Place in Human Development*. Cambridge, Mass.: Harvard University Press.

Kempton, Murray. (1967) "The Underestimation of Dwight D. Eisenhower." *Esquire*, Sept., p. 68.

Kent, Francis William. (1977) *Household and Lineage in Renaissance Florence*. Princeton, N.J.: Princeton University Press.

Ketchum, William C. Jr. (1981) *Toys & Games*. New York: Cooper-Hewitt Museum, The Smithsonian Institution's National Museum of Design.

Kidwell, Claudia B., and Margaret C. Christman. (1974) "Suiting Everyone: The Democratization of Dress in America." Washington D.C.: United States Government Printing Office.

Kohn, Melvin. (1959) "Social Class and Parental Values." *American Journal of Sociology* 64, pp. 351–357.

Kotlowitz, Alex. (1991) *There Are No Children Here. The Story of Two Boys Growing up in America*. New York: Doubleday.

Lasch, Christopher. (1977) *Haven in a Heartless World*. New York: Basic Books.

_____. (1979) *The Culture of Narcissism*. New York: W. W. Norton.

_____. (1984) *The Minimal Self*. New York: W. W. Norton.

Lawlor, Laurie. (1996) *Where Will This Shoe Take You?* New York: Walker and Company.

Lawrence, Philip S. (n.d.) " The Health Record of the American People," *Health in America: 1776–1976*. U.S. Department of Health, Education, and Welfare; U.S. Public Health Service. Health Resource Administration. Washington D.C.: U.S. Government Printing Office, pp. 19–22.

Leach, Mark C. (1979) "Michelangelo Invenit, Joos Van Cleve Explicavit." *Studies in Iconography* 9.

Leslie, Eliza. (1864) *The Ladies' Guide to Politeness and Manners*. Philadelphia: T. B. Peterson.

Levine, Lawrence W. (1988) *Highbrow/Lowbrow: The Emergence of Cultural Hierarchy in America*. Cambridge, Mass.: Harvard University Press.

Levinson, Daniel J., with C. N. Darrow, E. B. Klein, M. H. Levinson, and B. McKee. (1978) *The Seasons of a Man's Life*. New York: Alfred A. Knopf.

Locke, John. (1690/1970) *Two Treatises of Civil Government*. New York: Dutton.

Locke, John. (1690/1979) *An Essay Concerning Human Understanding*. Oxford: Clarendon Press.

Logan, James. (1845-1847/1980) *The Clans of the Scottish Highlands*. London: Chancellor Press.

Longford, Elizabeth. (1956) *Queen Victoria: Born to Succeed*. New York: Harper and Row.

Lyon, Harold C. Jr. (1971) *Learning to Feel—Feeling to Learn*. New York: Charles E. Merrill Publishing Company.

Marcomb, David. (1985) *The Victorian Sailor*. Aylesbury, U.K.: Shire Publications.

Margolis, Norman. (1968) "The New Fashion Awareness." *Earnshaw's*, May.

Marling, Ann Karal. (1994) *As Seen on TV, The Visual Culture of Everyday Life in the 1950s*. Cambridge, Mass.: Harvard University Press.

Marrow, Alfred J. (1957) *Making Management Human*. New York: McGraw Hill Books.

Martin, Claude R. Jr. (1971–1972) "What Consumers of Fashion Want to Know." *Journal of Retailing* 47, pp. 65–71.

Martin, Linda. (1978) *The Way We Wore: Fashion Illustration of Children's Wear 1870–1970*. New York: Charles Scribner's Sons.

Mathiesen, Eske. (1982) "Libraries and Folk Art." *Art Libraries Journal* 6, pp. 5–11.

May, Elaine Tyler. (1988) *Homeward Bound: American Families in the Cold War Era*. New York: Basic Books.

May, W. E. (1966) *The Dress of Naval Officers*. London: Her Majesty's Stationery Office.

McClelland, Elisabeth. (1973/1904) *Historic Dress in America 1607–1870*. New York: Benjamin Blom.

McDowell, Colin. (1989) *Shoes, Fashion and Fantasy*. New York: Rizzoli.

McKendrick, N. (1982) "Commercialization and the Economy," in N. McKendrick, J. Brewer, and J. Plumb, *The Birth of Consumer Society: The Commercialization of Eighteenth Century England*. Bloomington: Indiana University Press.

McLachlan, James. (1970) *American Boarding Schools: A Historical Study*. New York: Charles Scribner's Sons.

McNeal, James U. (1992) *Kids As Customers, A Handbook of Marketing to Children*. New York: Lexington Books.

Melosh, Barbara (1991) *Engendering Culture*. Washington, D.C.: Smithsonian Institution Press.

Mills, C. Wright. (1951) *White Collar: The American Middle Classes*. New York: Oxford University Press.

———. (1956) *The Power Elite*. New York: Oxford University Press.

Mitchell, Susan. (1995) *Generations: Who They Are. How They Live. What They Think.* Ithaca, N.Y.: New Strategists Publications.

Monroe, Paul. (1940) *Founding of the American Public School System.* New York: Macmillan.

Montgomery, Florence M. (1984) *Textiles in America 1650–1870.* New York: W. W. Norton.

Moore, Doris Langley. (1953) *The Child in Fashion.* London: B. T. Batsford.

Naegele, Kaspar D. (1961) "Interaction: Roles and Collectivities," in Parsons Talcott, Edward Shils, Kaspar D. Naegele, and Jesse R. Pitts, eds. *Theories of Society: Foundations of Modern Sociological Theory.* Vol. 1. New York: The Free Press of Glencoe.

Nearing, Helen and Scott. (1955) *USA Today.* Harborside, Maine: Social Science Institute.

Newhall, Beaumont. (1982) *The History of Photography from 1839 the Present.* New York: Museum of Modern Art.

Newman, Katherine S. (1989) *Falling from Grace.* New York: Vintage.

North, Douglas C. (1966) *The Economic Growth of the United States 1790–1860.* New York: W. W. Norton.

Oakley, Ann. (1974) *Woman's Work: The Housewife, Past and Present.* New York: Vintage Books.

Pacey, Philip. (1984) "Family Art: Domestic and Eternal Bliss." *Journal of Popular Culture* 18, pp. 43–53.

Padgett, John F., and Christopher K. Ansel. (1993) "Robust Action and the Rise of the Medici, 1400–1434." *American Journal of Sociology* 98, pp. 1259–1319.

Panofsky, Erwin. (1939) *Studies in Iconology.* New York: Oxford University Press.

Paoletti, Jo B., and Carol L. Kregloh. (1989) "The Children's Department," in Claudia B. Kidwell and Valerie Steel, eds., *Men and Women Dressing the Part.* Washington D.C.: Smithsonian Institution.

Patterson, James T. (1994) *America's Struggle Against Poverty 1900–1994.* Cambridge, Mass.: Harvard University Press.

Philadelphia Museum of Art. (1978) *The Second Empire 1852–1870: Art In France Under Napoleon III.* Exhibition catalogue.

Pilgrim, Thomas (pseud. Arthur Morecamp). (1878) *The Live Boys; or Charlie and Nasho in Texas.* Boston: Lee and Shepard.

Pogrebin, Letty Cottin (1983) *Family Politics, Love and Power on an Intimate Frontier.* New York: McGraw-Hill.

Pope, Jesse Elizabeth. (1970/1905) *The Clothing Industry in New York.* New York: Burt Franklin.

Postman, Neil. (1982) *The Disappearance of Childhood.* New York: Laurel Books.

Ravitch, Diane. (1974) *The Great School Wars: New York 1805–1973: A History of the Public Schools as Battlefield of Social Change.* New York: Basic Books.

Reiss, David and Hoffman H. A. (1979) *The American Family: Dying or Developing?* New York: Plenum Press.

Remise, Jac, and Jean Fondin. (1967) *The Golden Age of Toys.* Greenwich, Conn.: International Book Society.

Ribble, Margaret A. (1943) *The Rights of Infants: Early Psychological Needs and Their Satisfaction.* New York: Columbia University Press.

Riesman, David.(1958) "The Suburban Sadness," in William Dorbiner, ed., *The Suburban Community*. New York.

Riis, Jacob (1892) *Children of the Poor*. New York: Doubleday.

Rodocanachi, E. (1922) *La Femme Italienne Avant, Pendant, Après, La Renaissance*. Paris: Librairie Hachette.

Rogers, Everett M., and F. Floyd Shoemaker. (1971) *Communication of Innovation*. New York: Free Press.

Roodenburg, Herman W. (19??) "The Autobiography of Isabella Moerloose: Sex, Childbearing and Popular Belief in Seventeenth Century Holland," *Journal of Social History*.

Rosenberg, Jakob. (1969) "Rembrandt in His Century," in Harold Spencer, ed., *Readings in Art History*. Vol. 2. New York: Charles Scribner and Sons.

Rosenberg, Jakob, and Seymour Slive. (1966) *Dutch Art and Architecture 1600 to 1800*. Baltimore, Md.: Penguin Books.

Rosenblum, Naomi. (1984) *The World History of Photography*. New York: Abbeville Press.

Rosenblum, Robert. (1984) *19th-Century Art*. New York: Harry N. Abrams.

Rousseau, Jean Jacques. (1945) *The Confessions of Jean Jacques Rousseau*. New York: The Modern Library.

Rowdon, Maurice. (1974) *Lorenzo the Magnificent*. Chicago: Henry Regnery.

Rubin, Gayle. (1975) "The Traffic in Women: Notes on the Political Economy of Sex," in Rayna R. Reiter, ed., *Toward An Anthropology of Women*. New York: Monthly Review Press.

Rubin, Leonard G. (1976) *The World of Fashion: An Introduction*. San Francisco: Canfield Press.

Rubinstein, Ruth P. (1994) *Dress Codes: Meanings and Messages in American Culture*. Boulder, Colo.: Westview Press.

Russell, John (1996) "Even The Victorians on the Wall Hang Looser." *New York Times*, December 15.

Savage, William W. (1979) *The Cowboy Hero: His Image in American History and Culture*. The University of Oklahoma Press: Norman.

Scarlet, James D.(1990) *Tartan: The Highland Textile*. London: Shepherd-Walwyn.

Schama, Simon. (1980) "Wives and Wantons: Versions of Womanhood in 17th-Century Dutch Art." *Oxford Art Journal*. April.

_____. (1988) *The Embarrassment of Riches*. Berkeley: University of California Press.

Schudson, Michael. (1984) *Advertising, The Uneasy Persuasion*. New York: Basic Books.

Segalen, Martine. (1996) "The Industrial Revolution: From Proletariat to Bourgeoisie," in *A History of the Family*, ed. Andre Burguiere, Christiane Klapisch-Zuber, Martin Segalen, Francoise Zonabend. Trans. Sarah Hanbury Tenison. Cambridge, Mass.: The Belknap Press of Harvard University Press.

Schoeffler, O. E., and William Gale. (1973) *Esquire's Encyclopedia of 20th Century Men's Fashions*. New York: McGraw-Hill.

Schreier, Barbara (1995) *Becoming American Women: Clothing and Jewish American Experience, 1880–1920*. Chicago: Chicago Historical Society.

Seiter, Ellen. (1993) *Sold Separately: Parents and Children in Consumer Culture*. New Brunswick, N.J.: Rutgers University Press.

Singer Sewing Machine Company. (1927) *How to Make Children's Clothes the Modern Way*. New York: Singer Sewing Machine Company.

Skolnick, Arlene. (1991) *Embattled Paradise*. New York: Basic Books.

Smith, Michael L. (1983) "Selling the Moon: The U.S. Manned Space Program and the Triumph of Commodity Scientism," in Richard Wightman Fox and T.J. Jackson Lears, eds., *The Culture of Consumption*. New York: Pantheon Books.

Snyder, James. (1989) *Medieval Art: Paintings—Sculpture—Architecture 4th–14th Century*. Englewood Cliffs, N.J.: Prentice Hall, and New York: Harry N. Abrams.

Sorenson, R. C. (1973) *Adolescent Sexuality in Contemporary America*. New York: World.

Spock, Benjamin. (1945) *Baby and Child Care*. New York: Hawthorne Books.

Springhall, John. (1971) "The Boy Scouts, Class and Militarism in Relation to British Youth Movements, 1903–1930." *International Review of Social History* 16 (part 2), pp. 125–158.

———. (1986) *Coming of Age: Adolescence in Britain 1860–1960*. Dublin: Gill and Macmillan.

Steele, Valerie. (1988) *Paris Fashion*. New York: Oxford.

Steinberg, Leo. (1996) *The Sexuality of Christ in Renaissance Art and in Modern Oblivion*. Chicago: University of Chicago Press.

Stilgoe, John R. (1988) *Borderland: Origins of the American Suburb, 1820–1939*. New Haven, Conn.: Yale University Press.

Stone, Lawrence (1968) "Literacy and Education in England 1640–1900." *Past and Present* 42, pp. 69–139.

———. (1977) *The Family, Sex, and Marriage in England, 1500–1800*. New York: Harper and Row.

Story, Margaret. (1924) *How To Dress Well*. New York: Funk and Wagnalls.

Strachey, Lytton. (1921) *Queen Victoria*. New York: Blue Ribbon Books.

Susman, Warren I. (1984) *Culture As History*. New York: Pantheon Books.

Sutherland, Edwin Hardin. (1937) *The Professional Thief: By a Professional Thief*. Chicago: The University of Chicago Press.

Tambini, Michael. (1996) *The Look of the Century*. New York: Cooper Hewitt, National Design Museum.

Tarde, Gabriel De. (1969) *On Communication and Social Influence*. Selected Papers, edited by Terry N. Clark. Chicago: University of Chicago Press.

Trask, David F. (1973) "The Imperial Republic: America in World War Politics, 1945 To Present," in William E. Leuchtenburg, ed., *The Unfinished Century: America Since 1900*. Boston: Little Brown.

Trueblood, Elton D. (1966) *The People Called Quakers*. New York: Harper and Row.

Vanderbilt, Tom. (1998) *The Sneaker Book: Anatomy of an Industry and an Icon*. New York: The New Press.

Veblen, Thorstein. (1899/1957) *The Theory of the Leisure Class*. New York: Mentor Books.

Victoria, Queen. (1926) *The Letters of Queen Victoria. Second Series. A Selection From Her Majesty's Correspondence and Journal Between the Years 1862–1878.* Ed. George Earle Buckle. New York: Longman Green.

Villas, James. (1974) "A Short History of the Jockstrap." *Esquire,* 82 (4) Oct.

Vincent, John Martin. (1935/1969) *Costume and Conduct in the Laws of Basel, Bern, and Zurich.* New York: Greenwood Press.

Watson, John B. (1928) *Psychological Care of Infant and Child.* New York: W. W. Norton.

Waugh, Norah. (1954) *Corsets and Crinolines.* Boston : Boston Book and Art Shop.

Webster Noah. (1870) *Webster Reciter; or Elocution Made Easy.* New York, Robert M. De Witt Publisher.

Weitz, John. (1968) "Fashion Through the Designer," *Earnshaw's,* May.

Westoff, Charles F. (1986) "Fertility in the United States." *Science* 234.

Westphal, Uwe. (1991) *The Bauhaus.* New York: Gallery Books.

Whiteford, Frank. (1991) *Bauhaus.* New York: Thames and Hudson.

Whyte, William F. (1956) *The Organization Man.* New York: Simon and Schuster.

Wiebe, Robert H. (1967) *The Search For Order 1877–1920.* New York: Hill and Wang.

Wilson, Elizabeth. (1985) *Adorned in Dreams.* Berkeley: University of California Press.

Williams, Rosalind H. (1982) *Dream Worlds: Mass Consumption in Late Nineteenth-Century France.* Berkeley: The University of California Press.

Wilson, Kax. (1979) *A History of Textiles.* Boulder, Colo.: Westview Press.

Winn, Marie. (1983) *Children Without Childhood.* New York: Pantheon.

Wishy, Bernard. (1968) *The Child and the Republic: The Dawn of Modern American Child Nurture.* Philadelphia: University of Pennsylvania Press.

Wister, Owen. (1902) *The Virginian: A Horseman of the Plains.* New York: Macmillan Company.

Wolfenstein, Martha. (1953) "Trends in Infant Care." *American Journal of Orthopsychiatry* 23.

Worrell, Estelle A. (1980) *Children's Costume in America 1607–1910.* New York: Charles Scribner and Sons.

Worth, Sol. (1981) *Studying Visual Communication.* Philadelphia: University of Pennsylvania Press.

Zeldin, Theodore. (1979) *France 1848–1945: Ambition and Love.* New York: Oxford University Press.

Zelizer, Viviana A. (1985) *Pricing the Priceless Child: The Changing Social Value of Children.* New York: Basic Books.

Zwingmann, Charles A. A. (1959) *"Heimweh" or Nostalgic Reaction: A Conceptual Analysis and Interpretation of A Medico-Psychological Phenomenon.* Dissertation submitted to the School of Education and the Committee on Graduate Study of Stanford University.

Index